KT-469-646

Muslim Women
In America

Muslim Women in America

The Challenge of Islamic Identity Today

YVONNE YAZBECK HADDAD

JANE I. SMITH

KATHLEEN M. MOORE

OXFORD
UNIVERSITY PRESS

2006

OXFORD
UNIVERSITY PRESS

Oxford University Press, Inc., publishes works that further
Oxford University's objective of excellence
in research, scholarship, and education.

Oxford   New York
Auckland   Cape Town   Dar es Salaam   Hong Kong   Karachi
Kuala Lumpur   Madrid   Melbourne   Mexico City   Nairobi
New Delhi   Shanghai   Taipei   Toronto

With offices in
Argentina   Austria   Brazil   Chile   Czech Republic   France   Greece
Guatemala   Hungary   Italy   Japan   Poland   Portugal   Singapore
South Korea   Switzerland   Thailand   Turkey   Ukraine   Vietnam

Copyright © 2006 by Oxford University Press, Inc.

Published by Oxford University Press, Inc.
198 Madison Avenue, New York, New York 10016

www.oup.com

Oxford is a registered trademark of Oxford University Press

All rights reserved. No part of this publication may be reproduced,
stored in a retrieval system, or transmitted, in any form or by any means,
electronic, mechanical, photocopying, recording, or otherwise,
without the prior permission of Oxford University Press.

Library of Congress Cataloging-in-Publication Data

Haddad, Yvonne Yazbeck, 1935–
   Muslim women in America : the challenge of Islamic identity today / Yvonne Yazbeck
Haddad, Jane I. Smith, Kathleen M. Moore.
      p.   cm.
   Includes bibliographical references and index.
   ISBN-13 978-0-19-517783-1
   ISBN 0-19-517783-5
      1. Muslims—United States—Social conditions.   2. Muslim women—United States—Social
conditions.   3. Group identity—United States.   4. Sex role—United States.   5. Islam—
Social aspects—United States.   6. United States—Religious life and customs.
7. United States—Ethnic relations.   I. Smith, Jane I.   II. Moore, Kathleen M., 1959–   III. Title.
E184.M88H34 2006
305.48'697'0973—dc22   2005020204

9 8 7 6 5 4 3 2 1

Printed in the United States of America
on acid-free paper

Preface

In the aftermath of the 9/11 terror strikes on the Twin Towers of New York City and the Pentagon, the presence of Muslims in the United States has increasingly raised apprehensions among the American public. From several vantage points, concerns about the threat of terrorism have overshadowed many other priorities and sometimes caused judgments to be clouded. Tempers have flared, resentments have been aroused, and hate crimes have been perpetrated against individuals suspected of being linked—sometimes in the most tenuous of ways—to terrorism. Often women have been the victims of prejudice and hostility. Some Americans are deeply persuaded that Muslims are guilty not only of violent behavior but also of treating women as inferior to men. For these reasons, we were inspired to write about the circumstances of Muslim women in the United States and Canada, both before and after 9/11, hoping to foster a more accurate understanding of Islam and Muslims in the West.

Tensions between Muslims and American society in general should not be overstated. What follows in this book describes not only the problems Muslims encounter but also the opportunities enjoyed by many American Muslim women to define their own identities and determine their own destinies. Muslim women have been empowered to participate in the public arena to pursue their interests, whether these interests are counteracting prejudice or pursuing professional dreams or serving the common welfare through community service. They have contributed in especially significant ways in the negotiation of what it means to be Muslim in the American context. As such they are deeply implicated in changing the face of Islam as it is seen both within the Muslim communities in the United States, and by non-Muslims who might otherwise continue to rely on conventional assumptions that Muslim women are by definition oppressed and backward. We hope that the pages that follow will illuminate these women's experiences.

Acknowledgments

We, the authors, appreciate the support given by the administration and colleagues at Georgetown University, Hartford Seminary, and the University of California at Santa Barbara as we have pursued this project over the last year and a half. We are also grateful to all the friends and associates who have helped provide the source material for this study. Professors Zahid H. Bukhari and Osman Bakar of Georgetown University read and commented on early versions of the manuscript, and Professor Amira Sonbol, also of Georgetown, provided important assistance and information for the completed volume. Special thanks are due to Georgetown students, for their hard work on various aspects of the research, including Shereen Abdel-Nabi, Mary Arutyunyan, Alexander Philip Owings, Ahmed H. Humayun, Nora Fatima Achrati, and Jennifer Lynn Hill, and to University of California at Santa Barbara students Nadia Nader and Ahmed Metwally. Any errors or omissions of critical information are fully the responsibility of the authors.

Contents

Muslim Women
in America

I

Setting the Scene

"We are now engaged in a worldwide effort to focus on the brutality against women and children by the Taliban," declared Laura Bush, First Lady of the United States, two months after September 11, 2001. In this unprecedented radio address to the nation, Mrs. Bush invoked a theme that echoed the Western characterization of Islam and its females. It identified the oppression of women as intimately linked to what is often portrayed as the violent nature of the religion and affirmed that the cause of liberating Muslim women from their bondage is part of the American mission to the Islamic world. Mrs. Bush argued that the cruel oppression of women experienced in Afghanistan is a central goal of the terrorists who would like to impose their will on the rest of the world. Saving the women of Islam became part of the post-9/11 Western agenda.

It is true, of course, that the Bush administration was targeting one of the most extreme interpretations of Islam, dominant in Pakistan and Afghanistan and enforced by the Taliban. At the same time the White House was attempting to assuage criticism from Muslim allies by assuring them and the American public that "moderate" Islam is a respectable faith and that the war on terrorism is not a war against Islam. For many Americans, however, the distinction is not always easy to see. When the U.S. military overthrew Saddam Hussein in Iraq, the administration asserted that women's rights would be one of the most important goals in its effort to mold Iraq into a model of democracy for the other countries of the Arab world to emulate. It is a sad irony that in some cases the war appears to have generated more restrictions. Under Saddam, as elsewhere in the Muslim world, many women pursued careers and other personal goals in spite of the generally oppressive political atmosphere. At least in the short term, they appear to have lost a great deal in the wake of chronic violence and the growth of religious conservative zeal in "postwar" Iraq.

The issue is not whether repression of women has been present in Muslim cultures or whether it is unique to these societies. It has existed and continues to exist in some Islamic countries, as is true of other cultures, and some American Muslim women have been working in collaboration with their counterparts in various parts of the world to help institute the parity between men and women that they believe to be a fundamental tenet of Islam as revealed in the Qur'an. A recent Internet article written by a woman who emigrated from Lebanon in the mid-1960s advises Americans to beware of making too-easy assumptions about Arab and Muslim women that have little to do with their realities, asserting that most women in the Middle East would find Western stereotypes of Muslim women simply alien to their own experiences. What Americans should do, she proposes, is to think of Arab and Muslim women not in terms of a bin Laden model but rather of a Betty Crocker model, with women choosing to attend to their family responsibilities rather than to their personal freedoms. The various stereotypes of Muslim women that have held sway in the Western imagination are detailed in chapter 2, "Persistent Stereotypes."

Western association of the religion of Islam with the violent oppression of women has been used by more than one American administration to engender emotional support for American adventures overseas. The by-product has been misunderstanding and prejudice, making life more difficult—not easier—for Muslim women living in the United States and Canada. They must contend not only with the rising level of anti-Islamic sentiment but also with the increasingly popular belief that Islam treats women, at best, as second-class citizens. The appeal for a better understanding of the true relationship of women and men in Islam, and the acknowledgment that many of the traditional roles and expectations for Muslim women are changing, often most notably in the West, are high on the agenda of many American Muslims who are trying to determine how they will define themselves in the early part of the twenty-first century.

Muslims living in North America today comprise the most diverse population in the history of Islam. They are immigrants and native-born Americans representing most of the races and cultural groupings of the world. They speak a wide variety of languages and represent a range of cultural, economic, educational, sectarian, and ideological positions. Muslim women in America may or may not choose to publicly identify themselves with Islam as a religion and a way of life. Yet all of them, in one way or another, are facing the compelling questions of how to understand themselves as Americans and how to define themselves so as to be understood by their fellow citizens.

Where Did They Come From?

The first Muslims to begin the process of becoming American, aside from a very few African Muslim slaves who managed to retain their faith, were those who arrived in the West in the late nineteenth and early twentieth century. They came from the rural areas of what was known as Greater Syria, which included the current states of Jordan, Lebanon, Palestine, and Syria, then part of the Ottoman Empire. They were part of a group of migrant laborers, mostly Christian men with a smattering of Sunni, Shi'ite, 'Alawi and Druze Muslims. They worked as peddlers, laborers, and merchants, intending to stay only long enough to save enough money to return to their villages and build homes or establish businesses. Men first earned their livelihood by establishing small ethnic businesses such as restaurants, coffeehouses, bakeries, and grocery stores.

As Muslims realized that the option to return home was no longer viable, they began to settle down on the East Coast, in the Midwest, and as far as the Pacific coast. The early Muslims who settled in the United States often suffered from loneliness, poverty, lack of language skill, and the absence of extended family and co-religionists. Sometimes they imported Muslim brides from the home country, and sometimes they married outside the faith. By the early 1900s more women arrived to constitute Muslim families in America. As women began to join their men, many were forced for economic reasons to find employment in mills and factories, where they worked long hours under very difficult conditions. Seldom did they find life in America to be easy. Despite the rhetoric of a country founded on the backs of immigrants and serving as a "melting pot" for all races and ethnic identities, they often en-countered anti-Muslim and anti-Arab prejudice, complicated by the fact that their sometimes darker skin subjected them to various forms of racial preju-dice. In many cases such designators as "sand nigger" or "rag-head" were used as epithets.

Immigration of Muslims was curtailed with the passage of U.S. immi-gration laws in 1921 and 1924 that imposed quotas on certain nations, re-stricting the number from the Middle East to 100 per year. During the 1930s, the movement of Muslims to America slowed to a dribble, limited specifically to relatives of persons already resident in the United States. After the end of World War II a new kind of immigrant began to come from the Muslim Middle East, often one who had been educated in European and American schools estab-lished by colonial rulers and Christian missionaries. A few emigrated for po-litical, economic, or religious reasons, and some joined relatives who had arrived earlier and were already established in the United States.

Between 1947 and 1960, a small number of Muslims arrived from countries well beyond the Middle East, including Eastern Europe and the

Soviet Union, and a smattering came from India and Pakistan, fleeing turmoil after the 1947 partition of the subcontinent. While many of the earlier immigrants had moved into rural as well as urban areas of the United States, the new immigrants tended to be urban in background and made their homes almost exclusively in major cities such as New York, Chicago, and Los Angeles. Some were members of former ruling elite families. They were generally more Westernized than their predecessors and better educated, and many came with the hope of completing their education and technical training in America.

The majority of Muslim immigrants came after 1965, when President Lyndon Johnson sponsored a bill that repealed the long-standing "national origins" quota system that heavily favored European immigration. Instead of basing immigration quotas on countries of origin, the new policy established preferences for family reunification, occupational preferences in fields for which the native-born workforce was low, and the granting of asylum to refugees. This new immigration policy meant that waves of immigrants began to come from nations that had not previously been the main countries of emigration. Many Muslim professionals, most notably from Iran, Pakistan, and India, first came to the United States between 1950 and 1980 as university students. Many stayed under the provisions of the Immigration Act of 1965, finding employment in fields for which there was a shortage of professionals. The networks they formed served as the basis for future immigration of more Muslims in the 1980s and 1990s under the preference system for family unification.

A number of events in other parts of the Islamic world in recent years have created powerful incentives for those who were either affluent enough or were sponsored by relief agencies to seek haven in the West. The 1967 Israeli preemptive attack on Egypt, Syria, and the West Bank began an exodus of Palestinians to Western Europe and the Americas (particularly Brazil, Argentina, and Venezuela) that still continues. It also opened up Egyptian immigration, until that time restricted by Egyptian President Gamal Abdul Nasser. The Lebanese civil war and the Israeli invasions of Lebanon in 1978 and 1982 precipitated the emigration of significant numbers of Shi'ite Muslims from South Lebanon to the United States. After the Iranian Revolution that brought Imam Khomeini to power in 1979, those who were committed to the regime of the Shah, or did not agree with the Islamic Republic under Ayatollah Khomeini, were prompted to seek a better and safer life elsewhere. Until 1980, the American government granted refugee status to those Iranians seeking to emigrate to the United States. Many relocated in California, where today Los Angeles has the largest expatriate Iranian community in the nation.

While immigration from South Asia (Pakistanis, Indians, and Bangladeshis) was severely restricted from 1882 until after World War II, in the last several decades many more immigrants from that area have arrived on the

American scene for education, work, and family unification. Today they constitute the largest immigrant group, and many of them, including women, are skilled professionals. Despite the fact that the United States government enacted a special restriction on immigration from Muslim nations in the 1980s, political strife and civil war in various nations have brought refugees from Somalia, Sudan and other African countries, Afghanistan, and victims of ethnic cleansing in the former Yugoslavia. Lately, many North Africans have arrived under provisions of the 1980 refugee law or the 1990 immigration law. The latter created a "diversity" visa, granted by lottery, for people from nations that have had low immigration rates to the United States since 1965. Initially established in 1990 to encourage newcomers from former communist nations in Eastern Europe, the diversity law has allowed visas to be awarded to several thousand individuals from predominantly Muslim countries, such as Bangladesh, Egypt, Algeria, Sudan, Somalia, and Morocco.

A major segment of the Muslim population in the United States is neither immigrant nor of immigrant parentage but is part of the indigenous population. The majority are African Americans (perhaps a third of the Muslim population), with much smaller numbers of Latino/Latinas (some of whom themselves are recently arrived or from immigrant families), Native Americans, and Caucasian citizens who have chosen to adopt Islam. In the first three quarters of the twentieth century, most African-American Muslims were either members of the Nation of Islam (NOI), formed in the 1930s, or of much smaller movements such as the Moorish American Temple, formed by Noble Drew Ali in the early twentieth century. The death in 1975 of Elijah Muhammad, founder of the NOI, precipitated a leadership struggle. The two contenders were Louis Farrakhan and Elijah's son Wallace Muhammad. The latter, who took the name Warith Deen Mohammed, formally succeeded his father. Many African Americans have followed his subsequent leadership out of the Nation and into mainline Sunni Islam, while others have joined other Sunni mosques and communities. Some African American Muslims are part of the many sectarian or heterodox movements within Islam, and others continue to be affiliated with Farrakhan's Nation of Islam. A few African Americans affiliate with Shi'ism. Conversion to Islam of women—African American, Caucasian, Latina, Native American, and other—is the subject of chapter 3, "Embracing Islam."

Religious Identities

Reflecting the affiliation of the Muslim population of the world, most American Muslims of all racial-ethnic identities are Sunni. While only an estimated 10 percent of the world's Muslims are Shi'ites, however, in the United States they may constitute about 20 percent. Most are Ithna 'Ashari or

Twelver Shi'ites, with smaller numbers from the Isma'ili or Sevener and the Zaidi branches. Both Sunni and Shi'ite communities are to be found in all of the major cities of North America. Many American Muslim women do not actively practice their faith. While those who do share many commonalities, certain religious practices serve to distinguish them. Conservative Sunnis are increasingly looking to the wives of the Prophet, designated as the "Mothers of the Believers," as role models or guides providing images of strength, learning, professionalism, and piety worthy of emulation. These models are especially important to American women who are eager to find validation for the full participation of women in the public arena and particularly in leadership positions. Chapter 7, "Claiming Public Space," explores some of these new leadership roles. Many Shi'ite women look to the Prophet's daughter Fatima, mother of Muhammad's martyred grandson Husayn, as a model for spiritual guidance, and participate in ritual activities remembering the suffering of Fatima and the family of the Prophet.

A small but important number of Muslims, cutting across sectarian and racial/ethnic lines, are part of Sufi or so-called mystical movements of Islam. Along with a few traditional orders existing in America in the middle of the twentieth century, Sufi groups often reflected aspects of the New Age movement. More recently there has been a growth in adherence to more traditional Sufi orders in the United States, with leaders trained in the classical disciplines. The music, the dance, the ritual, and the fellowship make Sufism an engaging practice for some American women. A few Sufi orders in the West allow women to take part in ceremonies that formerly were available only to men. Others find in Sufism the opportunity to combine the mystical and spiritual (often very emotional) aspects of faith with the intellectual rigor required of the serious student of Sufism. Many women see Sufi Islam as liberating all Muslims from legal restrictions and freeing women from many of the customs that suggest men have more rights and responsibilities in Islam. Increasingly Sufism is being cast by some as the valid expression of Islam compatible with American policies, a counter to the more legalistic expressions propagated by conservative movements such as the Salafis and Wahhabis.

Some women express their allegiance to Islam in very public ways. Rejecting the social norms of Western culture, they try to dress, speak, and live in as close adherence as possible to what they understand to be the dictates of the Qur'an and the traditions of the Prophet. Others may practice Islam in private and with their families but do not choose to show publicly that they are Muslim. Only a fairly small percent actually participate in the life of a mosque, however, or attend services, except perhaps for the major festivals. For the majority, being Muslim may not be their most important focus of identity, and they seldom if ever frequent the mosque, even for Islamic holidays, and would never consider wearing conservative Islamic dress. See chapter 4, "Practices of the Faith," for a fuller examination of the religious activities of both Sunni and Shi'ite women and some of the new ways in which women are challenging what they see as outdated and patriarchal traditions.

Islamic Dress

Among the most visible ways a woman can affirm her identity with Islam is by wearing Islamic dress. The majority of Muslim women in America choose not to wear garb that would distinguish them from the rest of society for a variety of reasons: they never did so before coming to America; they were born in America and have no desire to wear distinguishing garb; they do not want to be pushed into such a choice by friends or family; they do not want to draw attention to themselves or to have other Americans know they are Muslims because it may cause discomfort or discrimination; they believe that in time they may decide to dress more modestly but are not ready to "take the step"; they do not like the look of most Islamically-fashioned outfits; or they refuse to wear anything that will make them uncomfortable ("Summers in Houston are bad enough without all that extra material wrapped around me. . . ."). Many simply have never given serious consideration to wearing so-called modest dress. "I'm a very modest person and I hope my dealings with others reflect that," says a young university student in the Midwest. "Why do I have to prove it by what I choose to wear?"

Various terms are used to describe the clothing that is loosely referred to as Islamic dress. *Hijab*, veil, and scarf refer to a head cover, which is worn either with conservative clothing such as a long skirt and long sleeves or with some kind of robe which may have different names determined by regional or cultural association. Only a portion of the female Muslim population in America wears the *hijab* or other Islamic dress, and not all religiously observant women feel that it is required. What most Muslim women do agree on, whatever they choose to wear, is that conservative dress does *not* represent constriction, repression, or any of the other terms by which Westerners have generally understood the Muslim woman's "condition." Women who dress Islamically insist that their choice affords them freedom, liberation, relief, and even great joy.

It is no secret to anyone who travels, watches the news on television, or reads even popular journals that Muslims overseas have moved steadily toward the adoption of Islamic dress for a great many personal, religious, social, and political reasons. In the late 1980s, at an international women's gathering at Harvard's Center for the Study of World Religions, two of the doyennes of women's rights in Islam were discussing the apparently growing adoption of the veil in Cairo. Fellow Cairene Nawal Sa'dawi, famous for her work in opposing female circumcision practices in Egypt, argued that the veil was a passing fad that the great majority of Egyptian women would never tolerate.

Her Moroccan colleague Fatima Mernissi, best known for her expose of the traditional treatment of women titled *Beyond the Veil*, agreed entirely, and the two laughed merrily at the images on a new video showing Cairene women in various stages of "Islamic cover." They both felt that the filmmaker was distorting reality and presenting a false image of the situation in Egypt. They regarded veiling as a very limited phenomenon connected to the pressures of urbanization as more rural peasants moved to the city centers for jobs and education. They also questioned the filmmaker's motives and wondered whether she was a CIA agent who was propagating the veil! At the time, they were not ready to concede that the re-Islamization movement was underway in Egypt. To some real extent it must be acknowledged that the appropriation of Islamic garb by Muslim women in the United States is part of an international movement whose complex causes have been analyzed in a range of contemporary literature.

For many American Muslim women, dressing Islamically—which in its most common form means covering the hair, arms, and legs—is not about coercion but about making choices, about "choosing" an identity and expressing a religiosity through their mode of dress. Some women say that by veiling they are making a statement against Western imperialism, which sees Muslim piety as a sign of terrorism, and against conservative Islam, which seeks to impose a traditionalist understanding of Islam that oppresses women. Others consider it a signal of purity, and say that it curbs their sexuality and/or their sex appeal. Paradoxically, some have noted that they had expected that wearing the headscarf would end the objectification of their bodies but instead have found that they became more frequent "objects" of Western gaze. Many young Muslim women are wearing the headscarf as a means of expressing identity and spirituality as well as modesty. One group of college women raised money selling T-shirts with the logo, "We cover our hair, not our brains."

Most immigrants continue to wear the Western dress they were wearing before coming to the United States. Others who had turned to Islamic garb before they moved continue to wear it in the new environment. Many convert women, though far from all, decide to wear a form of Islamic dress. In general, Muslim women do cover themselves in one way or another when they attend the mosque. Within the Islamic community itself the issue can be divisive. Those who choose to wear the *hijab* are sometimes sharply critical of other Muslims who are not comfortable with it or do not feel that it is appropriate for them. Those who leave their heads uncovered may consider some of their sisters a bit overzealous in the degree of their insistence on Islamic dress.

A few families allow daughters to begin dressing Islamically at a very young age, perhaps pressured by Islamic schools or other groups to do so. At the Shi'ite Islamic House of Wisdom meeting of the Muslim Scouts of Michigan in May of 2004, a play titled "The Path" portrayed the struggle of prepubescent girls (ages eight through eleven) about whether or not to veil.

Devils were represented as tempting the young girls at the time of the Taklif festival, which marks their entry into adulthood, telling them it was too early to hide their cuteness. Angels then appeared, reminding them that their real beauty is in their faith. Some parents agree that the age of puberty is the right time for girls to adopt the veil, while others encourage them to postpone such a decision until they are older. Many Muslim families strongly disapprove of a daughter's desire to veil, no matter what her age, while a few may force their daughters to veil as early as kindergarten.

Wearing Islamic dress is growing in popularity among Muslim youth, both in high schools and on college campuses. Some Muslim Student Association members report that girls need to wear *hijab* to be considered "cool" in the MSA, although they may remove it when not at association meetings. Dressing Islamically sometimes presents practical problems on college campuses. Andrea Armstrong, University of South Florida women's basketball star who was seeking NCAA approval to wear religious clothing during practices and games, quit her team in September 2004 on the grounds that she did not want her religion to be a distraction to the team. Friends say that the real reason was the hate e-mails she was receiving. Another basketball player who wanted to wear long pants, a long-sleeved shirt, and a headscarf with her uniform during games was approved by the NCAA, only to be told by her coach that such dress would make her teammates uncomfortable and thus was not allowed. Young women in sports such as volleyball, track and field, and even kick-boxing may get official approval for special dress by school boards and athletic associations, but experience significant disapproval at the local level.

Islamic dress, along with being religiously mandated for some, is also big business. Women can find all manner of dress available, from head coverings of many different kinds to long robes and pantsuits. Some outfits are ready-made while others can be fitted to the individual customer. Production houses with names like "The Hijab Boutique" or "Islamic House of Beauty," for example, offer ready-made or styled-to-order clothing for women, men, and children, and many items are available from online catalogs. Women running such establishments are generally able and willing to create any special fashions that their customers would like. Some Islamic boutiques offer a wide variety of Islamic wedding gowns "for your special day." Or for those who need individualized styling, "full figure designs" are readily available. Many stores feature imported Islamic wear such as the *hijab*, *niqab* (full-face veil), and long dresses or robes called *jilbaab*, *burqa*, or other names depending on the style and country from which it comes. Some companies offer dress tailored in the style of the Indian subcontinent, featuring loose trousers and tunics known as *shalwar khameez*. Tailors report a steady flow of orders for various kinds of Islamic dress, while stores and retail houses specializing in assorted styles are burgeoning. Many accessories are available, including matching shoes, gloves, and jewelry. Pendants, earrings, pins, and other gold and silver jewelry often contain words or brief passages from the Qur'an. Opportunities to dress both Islamically and stylishly are seemingly endless. General Network Limited, for example, advertises conservative but stylish clothing for the modern Muslima with the tagline: "Modesty is her way . . . elegance is her style."

African Americans have been particularly creative in developing fashions that fulfill the requirement of modesty but add a particular flair. *Azizah Magazine* recently featured a series of outfits produced by different clothing companies using African American models. The titles suggest the innovative design: *Urban Verve*—black gauze peasant top with a tangerine A-line skirt; kimono-styled wrap with vicuña-brown sash of crushed silk over slim harem pants; *City Style*—T-shirt with denim lettering over a long denim skirt with leather pockets, celery-green asymmetrical peasant top in crushed silk with boat neck and bell sleeves over flared denim skirt with floral silk paneling; *Urban Chic*—moss-green A-line dress with embroidered sleeves; green army fatigue A-line dress in comfortable rayon; *Modern Vintage*—A-line dress made from three pairs of denim pants; multicolored floral print cotton skirt with black diamond-shaped shirt; *After Five*—paisley and sequined wide-leg jumpsuit; rayon wrap dress in two tones of burnt orange. All models for Islamic dress wear some kind of head cover, from more traditional *hijab* to turbans or large beret-style hats. Designing and making these styles, referred to as "fiber arts," is the province of women in the United States, as opposed to most other countries where men are the stylists and tailors.

It is becoming very popular in various parts of the country to feature Islamic dress at specially designed fashion shows. The Council for American Islamic Relations in Dallas/Fort Worth, for example, hosted a show in April 2004 in which a variety of clothing stores participated. Attendees were offered a special discount on the clothing, with the option of donating the savings to the work of CAIR in that area. In the Silicon Valley of California in September 2003 a company called Flippant, headed by three Muslim women, featured its line of clothing at the Santa Clara Marriott Hotel. Its pitch was to "second-generation Muslim hipsters hungry to dress in something more than floor-length robes." Denying that their outfits were sexy, as that would be forbidden by Qur'anic injunction, they featured "beautiful fashions" such as splashy tie-dyed sari skirts, silky beaded formal wear and '60s-style flared jeans with embroidery. Some dresses had thigh-high slits, with modest leggings to be worn underneath.

What to wear, and how to wear it, is an important issue for many Muslim women in America, and non-Muslims are watching with interest as fashion, as well as modesty, plays a role in their choices. Chapter 2, "Persistent Stereotypes," discusses the veil as the most stereotypical symbol of what it means to be a Muslim woman in the eye of the average American.

Woman as Participants in American Society

Muslim women increasingly are full and active participants in American society and play major roles in virtually all aspects of professional life. Many immigrant men and women who arrived after 1965 on preference visas were highly educated professionals, including physicians, engineers, pharmacists, and similar professionals, coming from societies in which education is highly valued. For other Muslim women, however, education was not easily accessible in the countries from which they came, and life in the United States provides access to new freedoms and opportunities. Since primary and secondary education is mandated by law, all girls and women are guaranteed to receive an education in the American public school system. Muslim leaders are vocal in their insistence that education for all Muslims was part of the platform of the Prophet Muhammad, and that a viable American Muslim community must consist of well-educated females as well as males.

Increasingly, especially in the last several years, women have become more aware of the importance of being educated and well-versed in religious traditions and policies so that they can help spread accurate information about the religion of Islam to an often skeptical American public and can participate in the general movement of *da'wah* or calling to Islam. More conservative families, most notably first-generation South Asians and Yemenis and some of the refugees from South Lebanon, Iraq, and Afghanistan, may prefer not to have daughters or wives continue with higher education, fearing that it will discourage them from fulfilling responsibilities at home or expose them to currents and trends contrary to traditional Muslim structures. In general, however, support for women's education in the American Muslim community is high.

While family support for the idea of Muslim women from immigrant families working outside the home is not always enthusiastic, many women are employed either by choice or because additional income is needed to meet family expenses. Most American Muslim women can and do drive or use other means of public transport, do the shopping for themselves and their families, and are able to access health care. Their particular needs can often be met by local social service centers offering assistance and counseling. Women increasingly are encouraged to vote and to participate in political processes by local and national Muslim organizations.

It is also true, however, that not all American Muslims feel that the growing rights and opportunities available to Muslim women are appropriate within the traditional understanding of Islam. As women differ in terms of place of origin, racial-ethnic affiliation, education and professional involvement, and observance of Islamic practice, they also differ in the degree to which they choose to identify with mainstream American life and culture.

Like other recently arrived immigrants, some who come from more conservative Islamic cultures believe that their children should keep as separate as possible from the prevailing culture. They worry that too much exposure to Western ways of doing things may lead Muslims away from their faith and diminish the importance of Islam as the basis for daily decision-making. Those who share this concern sometimes believe that women should be discouraged from engaging in activities outside the home. Some immigrant Muslim leaders in America have encouraged their co-religionists to keep as isolated as possible from public life.

Subject to pressures from within and without the Muslim community, women struggle to determine what is possible, acceptable, and workable. Some might wish that they could be more open about their criticisms of certain elements of Islamic tradition but do not wish to be seen as participating in American prejudice against Islam. Others regret that they are not able to be more public about their affiliation with Islam, or to wear Islamic dress, but know that such a choice may have serious professional and social ramifications that they are not able or willing to assume.

Among the many challenges faced by Muslim women and their families in the American context is that of raising children in Western society. Parents struggle with such issues as:

- Keeping their children insulated from what the parents perceive to be dangerous Western secular values at the same time that they acknowledge their children's citizenship in the West and want to prepare them to be able to live their lives in a Western culture. Mothers are working with public schools to share elements of faith and practice with teachers and non-Muslim children, and are cooperating with other interested citizens to see that school curricula are free of demeaning stereotypes and inaccurate information about Islam.
- Educating children in the elements of the faith, if they so desire, at the same time that parents provide their children with an academically sound education. A few Muslim families are opting for home schooling as an alternative to public education. Others work together to establish Islamic schools, besieged by concerns for finances and quality education. Some Muslim homes are the venue for after-school or weekend classes in Islamic subjects, especially if mosques or Islamic centers are not available for such purposes. Educational materials produced in great quantity and with technical sophistication by many Islamic groups and organizations often reinforce the ideal of a family that serves to protect its children from the temptations of a basically secular Western society.
- Keeping children aware and appreciative of the values of the "home culture," wherever that may be, while supporting the efforts of young

people to work toward an indigenous form of Islam. While some young Muslims slide almost effortlessly from their public "American Muslim" personas to their familial cultural identities at home, others resent the degree to which their families seem to cling to the "old cultural ways."

Chapter 5, "Gender and Family," expands on the concerns faced by American Muslims in terms of women's education and employment and relationships among husband, wife, and children.

Anti-Muslim Prejudice

Immigrants who have come to the United States since 9/11 looking to share in the promise of America and seeking religious and political freedom have arrived at a difficult moment. "I used to think that this was the best place in the world to be safe and protected," said one, "but it is impossible to feel that way now that the government is cracking down so severely on Muslim immigrants." In some cases, males who have done nothing wrong other than be born in a Muslim country such as Pakistan, Bangladesh, or Yemen have been detained and deported, while the women of their families remain in the United States often without the resources to cope. Other women have returned to their countries of origin because of the loss of income when their husbands— the breadwinners—were detained. Although the restrictive immigration and counterterrorism laws enacted by the Clinton administration in the mid-1990s served as a first platform for these tough measures, laws authorizing such deportations have been enacted and strengthened significantly since 9/11.

Immigrants and women of color, recent arrivals or American born, are all finding that the level of prejudice against Islam is on the rise in the United States, validated by recent surveys of the American population. Many hundreds of incidents have been recorded over the past four years of Muslim women being subjected to offensive and even physically harmful abuse by those who find their Islamic dress objectionable or think that wearing such clothing somehow identifies them as being terrorist. Specific cases illustrating such incidents are described in chapter 6, "Muslim Women in the Crucible." Immediately after 9/11 a few non-Muslim women expressed their solidarity with Muslim sisters by themselves wearing headscarves, though that response has faded in the succeeding years. Paranoia appears to have prevailed in some quarters. Some incidents are simply ridiculous. In June 2004, for example, the Council on American Islamic Relations (CAIR) reported that law enforcement officers were called to investigate the accusation of a Virginia man that a group of Muslim Girl Scouts was waging "violent jihad." The six Scouts were selling cookies outside of a grocery store, but happened to be wearing Islamic headscarves over their Scout uniforms. National Muslim organizations like the many branches of CAIR are vigilant in identifying harassment of Muslim women in the workplace, in schools, and in other public venues and often are successful in providing public exposure as well as justice for the abused women.

Issues of Identity

The roles that women play in Islamic culture(s) are generally related to factors such as age, family relationships and responsibilities, and status in the community. In traditional societies it is very clear that expectations for females are specifically related to their movement from childhood through puberty, marriage, and aging. A growing number of American Muslim women are actively engaged in the effort to identify which elements of Islam are essential, mandated by Qur'an and Sunnah (the way of life exemplified by the Prophet Muhammad), and which are culturally determined rather than religiously prescribed. Definitions of women's roles are clearly subject to cultural and ethnic variations that come into play as Muslims try to determine how closely they want to or are able to adhere to traditional ways and what kinds of adaptations or changes are desirable or necessary in a new context.

Increasingly, Muslims who serve as spokespersons for Islam in America, often self-appointed but also representing some of the political, intellectual, and religious groups formed in the United States, are eager to stress that such diversity is to be celebrated. Tolerance for other Muslims is a by-product of American pluralism and has been learned by those who have been resident in the West for a period of time. However, they also understand that particularly in today's political climate it is urgent for Muslims to try to fashion a common identity whenever possible and to stress those things that do unite them in the bonds of Islam rather than separate them religiously, culturally, ideologically, or in any other way. Young people, sometimes influenced by associations such as the Muslim Youth of North America (MYNA), may be eager to tell their parents that while following a particular custom is historically and culturally interesting, the most important thing is to understand their commonalities with others as Muslim Americans. The beauty of Islam, as Malcolm X claims to have discovered in 1964 in his first pilgrimage to Mecca, is said to be that it does not distinguish on the basis of race, ethnicity, color, or national origin. Many Muslims today are urging that this list of "no distinctions" also includes the lack of discrimination on the basis of gender.

An emphasis on commonality is also extremely appealing to Muslims who may be part of the more disadvantaged sectors of American society. Immigrant Muslim women are often forced to think through and perhaps negotiate their personal, sometimes called "hyphenated," identities—is one a Muslim-American-Pakistani, for example, or a Pakistani-Muslim-American? While emotional ties to ethnic and cultural identities are generally respected, many affirm that their dual orientation is to be both Muslim and American, with the understanding that these identities are mutually supportive rather than exclusive.

The rhetoric of commonality may represent an important development in American Islam, and certainly has its advocates in many corners of American Muslim society. Still, such identification is easier said than done for many women who reasonably think of themselves first as Arab or Indonesian or Nigerian, with Islam simply an understood ingredient in that identity. What it really means to be American, for them, may be somewhat more difficult to figure out, and some immigrant Muslim women simply do not have the educational or emotional resources to deal with it. Their concern is rather with their children and making sure that somehow cultural particularities are not completely lost in the search for new identities. "I don't care what you call yourself," said a Muslim mother from Bangladesh to her teenage daughter, "but in my house you can behave properly and that means doing things as we have always done them."

For those who are immigrants or come from immigrant families, it is crucial to come to terms with one's identity, although often that process may take place more on a subconscious than a conscious level. On the one hand, women who come from Islamic countries, or who are from families who immigrated in earlier generations, must find a balance among the various commitments that claim them: to the particularities of the cultures to which they are related, to Islam as the common bond among all American Muslims, and, given their current residence or citizenship, to the reality of living in the United States. They must determine whether one or another of these options claims priority or whether it is possible to try to balance them altogether. Different kinds of occasions tend to bring out unconscious allegiances that may affirm the sense of community of American Muslims or may serve to emphasize the differences and distinctions. Attending a national meeting of an Islamic organization may engender strong feelings of pan-Islamic association, while celebration of an 'Eid, or ceremony ending one of the major Islamic holidays, in a culture-oriented mosque such as Pakistani or Turkish may solidify one's identification with the country of origin. Many local and national organizations are formed around particular ethnic activities and relationships that are not concerned with religion per se. Muslims from Bangladesh, for example, may enjoy Bengali music and literature, while those from Pakistan may enjoy Urdu poetry. These activities may be seen by conservative Muslims as distracting from Islamic solidarity or even may be deemed as the allurement of Satan.

That Muslim women have the freedom to think about identity questions is an opportunity that forces some into a process of redefinition. In most Islamic societies one's identity is given according to the culture of the society as well as by ideologies fostered by the state itself, or adopted as women join organizations that foster modern options. In America more options are at least theoretically possible, although it is obvious that the opportunities for any given woman to consider them vary according to her personal situation. Among the variables are the opinions and pressures of her individual family and of her community (if she has been able to find or establish one in this country), the particular religious leadership she and her family may subscribe to, and the exercise of free choice and decision that increasingly characterizes many Muslim women in the United States. Who should be involved in the adoption of identity and the selection of personal choices is being debated in a range of public and private forums today. The range of alternatives adopted by Muslims themselves will determine the future of American Islam; there seems little question that the door will continue to open and horizons to expand for women.

Growing numbers of American Muslim women see themselves not so much as Muslims who also hold other identities but as Americans who are part of an Islamic heritage. They understand that almost everyone chooses to make certain compromises in order to be successful, to be happy, or perhaps simply to survive. Unwilling to abide by the detailed prescriptions either of cultural expectations or of the foreign or American leaders of Islamic movements and groups, they are searching for appropriate guidelines as to their own identity and place in their families, their communities, and American society as a whole. Some are convinced that Muslims not only can find a way to live "Islamically" in Western culture but that those efforts are legitimate and important. Practicing their religion or not, Muslims know that if they are to have a significant voice in helping shape American attitudes and policies, they must not isolate themselves but become more publicly active. This mandate, in general, is understood to include Muslim women. Muslims hope that with increased representation in local and national governing structures they may become empowered to better control their lives. Chapter 7, "Claiming Public Space," suggests some of the many ways in which women are seeking and achieving empowerment through public participation.

Feminism

The discourse about Muslim women's participation in American society inevitably is influenced, positively or negatively, by the claims of Western feminism. Some Muslim women choose to call themselves feminists. Others qualify its meaning by placing feminism within the parameters of what they define as an Islamic understanding. They may adopt certain of the feminist assumptions about freedom of access and opportunity for men and women.

They reject, however, the common assumption that Western feminist formulations of equality are necessarily appropriate in the Islamic context and struggle to determine which ideas are most effective and consonant with Muslim values as they try to define their identity within their own family and communal settings. Muslim women's participation in and support for Islamic organizations both in North America and abroad has often provoked a strong response from Western feminists across a broad range of perspectives. A common reaction on the part of non-Muslims who are feminists is that Muslim women are mere pawns in an intrinsically patriarchal system. If liberated from their religious ties, they would be able to see the fundamental contradiction in the term "Muslim feminist" and how inimical Islam is toward women's rights. Despite these presumptions, however, the groundswell of Muslim women studying and teaching each other Islamic scriptures, doctrines, and social practices (see chapter 4, "Practices of the Faith") and the growing number of Muslim women in academia (see chapter 8, "Competing Discourses") have forced feminist scholars to reconfigure some of their beliefs about women's subordination within Islam.

The right of both men and women to exercise *ijtihad*, individual interpretation of Islamic law, is being invoked as some Muslim women and men struggle to argue on the basis of texts and traditions that Islam does not discriminate between men and women. They reason that while roles and opportunities may differ between the sexes, the overall Islamic prescription for gender relationships is fair and equitable. Some converts to Islam who are attracted by the modern interpretations of women's role in Islam, in particular, may be troubled by what they experience as sexism on the part of some immigrant communities and turn to serious study of the Qur'an in the effort to find gender equity. Nonetheless, the specter of Western feminism in its many permutations looms over these discussions, with the result that most Muslims insist vigorously that whatever new interpretations they try to coax from Islamic tradition are categorically different from the assertions of non-Muslim feminist activists in the West.

Since the 1970s, African American women in particular, including those who were part of the earlier Nation of Islam movement and more recent converts, have favored arguments for women's equality with men and their full participation in American society. By and large, however, they do not embrace the Western feminists' critique of the nuclear family as a source of women's oppression. Instead, they have argued that freedom, for them, has entailed the ability to form families, since the long history of slavery and racism in the United States has served to break up their families, communities, and social networks. For the most part these women do not believe that men and women should perform the same societal or even familial roles and look for alternative ways in which to support the parity of women. Although most of them need to work outside the home, they take very seriously the role of women as nurturers and maintainers of the family and the faith. Being a good mother and wife is ordained by God, they believe, and is a role that involves a greater degree of responsibility than working in the public sphere.

A few African American women are writing about the sexism they experienced as members of the Nation of Islam in its early days. They argue that true Islam supports complementary relationships between men and women, not ones of inferiority and superiority. Both as Muslims and as African Americans they reject the term "feminist" as white and elitist, abstract and alienating, and often turn to the interpretations of African American "womanists" for an understanding of how to effect their own empowerment. The term "womanist" has been adopted by African Americans as an alternative to "feminist," which they believe contains assumptions of race and class that do not include their experiences as black women. Often working from narrative rather than theory, they tell stories and share their life experiences in the struggle to create a harmonious family life based on Islamic values of reciprocity and respect. See chapter 8, "Competing Discourses," for a detailed discussion of "Islamic feminism" and new models of Qur'anic interpretation.

Muslim women who are working for a contemporary reinterpretation of Islam in the West are struggling to determine a viable alternative to traditional structures that have served to repress women on the one hand and to the influences of Western secularism (and sometimes feminism) on the other. Many call for women to exercise their right of individual interpretation of the Qur'an and traditions of Islam. They see Islam as a dynamic and flexible system, rather than a static and rigid set of rules and regulations, and want to open up avenues of participation in which women as well as men are the public faces of Islam. In the process they will be important contributors to the definition of an American Islam that flows directly out of its many contributing streams but that will have its own structures, definitions, and contributions to make to the complex picture of religious society in the United States and Canada.

Many women in America for whom Islam is a cultural identifier are professionals, homemakers, and others who have no particular interest in religion or in being recognized as Muslim. We, the authors of this volume, acknowledge that the material we are presenting concentrates primarily on Muslim women who are actively affirming Islam as a religious and/or a cultural association and are living their lives in ways that make that affirmation clear. The many different ways in which they publicly and visibly identify with Islam, and the consequences of their choices as they struggle to be both Muslim and American, are described in the succeeding chapters.

2

Persistent Stereotypes

The caption alongside a *National Geographic* magazine photo of a fully veiled Muslim woman reads, "A designer veil sports the logo of Yves St. Laurent. Most accept the veil for privacy and protection from male harassment, not as a symbol of oppression, and cling to a tradition that defies Western understanding." The woman in this photo remains a mystery, an object wrapped in secrecy not penetrated by the camera's lens, and the caption gives no detail about when or where the photo was taken. But the irony captured on film is what Westerners find to be not only surprising but incongruous—a combination of the Islamic veil with a French designer emblem. Can East really meet West in such a way? By showing this union of cultural symbols, the photo hints at the specter of the global spread of Islam, and the continued salience of a tradition that "defies Western understanding."

A book that has shed light on this issue is Linda Steet's *Veils and Daggers: A Century of National Geographic's Representation of the Arab World*. The volume looks at *National Geographic's* photo coverage of Muslim areas of the world for over a century. Steet, who is of Arab American heritage, suggests that *National Geographic* deliberately constructs images such as the designer veil—images that reflect less the realistic portrayals the journal claims to provide than the prevailing idealized images of Arab women already existing in the American imagination. Tracing images of Arab (and Muslim) females from 1888 to 1988, she identifies several consistent themes, from the dancing girl or prostitute to the anonymous, veiled, and "primitive" woman. These representations differentiate

oticized Eastern" female, marking her as essentially "other" than the
the women in the world. Such photographs have the effect of fostering
suppositions about Islam that denote it as a faith and cultural system that is basically inferior to that of the West.

Many times women have been the focal point of Western efforts to understand the Islamic faith, and yet Western images of Muslim women all too
often have been distorted or incomplete. In popular Western media, such as
movies and television, Muslim women are depicted as passive victims of mas-
culine dominance, either fully shrouded and demeaned or seminaked and
kept in harems for the fulfillment of male sexual fantasies. Thus representations of Eastern women become objects of the West's "Orientalizing gaze,"
as scholar Edward Said puts it. Western perspectives on Muslim women historically have been based on portrayals ranging from sexualized women with
bared breasts but cloaked faces, or wearing scanty harem pajamas and di-
aphanous scarves, to silent images of oppressed victims of male brutality.
These accounts of the Muslim female have as much to do with defining the
West through its opposition to the Orient—the West is democratic, modern,
and a place where women are liberated—as it does with describing the Orient,
which is defined as primitive, barbaric, and despotic.

Oversimplified Western conceptions of women have been used throughout the long history of relations between the Christian West and the Islamic
world, and are evident in representations from paintings and photographs of
the eighteenth century to contemporary film and TV images. Their persistence is a result of a complex of factors, including both the credibility of the
images themselves, based on the authority of the media in which they are
found, and the ascendance of European and American global power. Some of
these images were generated by propaganda bureaucracies of imperial governments to justify the control of the populations of occupied lands in the
interests of colonialism. They tend to cloak their real motives with altruistic
intent to make the colonies appear to be subject to (and weaker than) the
power of the imperial center and to justify to their own populations that
brutalizing and subjugating these territories was necessary because it was for
a noble cause. When naked force was not enough to sustain colonial domination, they had to convince everyone concerned of the superiority of European values with the certitude that Western standards of knowledge and
technology are far higher than those of the Orient. Most importantly, the
depiction of Muslim women as primitive, unenlightened, and subjugated
served to reinforce and justify the colonizing mission of the West coming to
rescue oppressed and vulnerable women. This chapter will consider the heritage of these various kinds of Western imperialism and the concomitant ways
of fostering popular stereotypes that Muslim women must deal with as they
come to terms with their own identity in the context of twenty-first century
America.

Western Colonialism

The immigrant Muslim women of America have brought with them a range of cultural, social, ideological, and religious expectations, formed and influenced by the variety of societies from which they have come. Women who lived under Western hegemonic powers share a consciousness forged during colonial rule and the burdens of that oppression, as well as the ideological consequences of having been subject to such domination. It is a history that reflects not only the impact of the Western incursion itself, but also the defensive mechanisms and apologetics developed over two centuries of the most intimate of encounters. Thus, they come not only with varying conceptions of national and ethnic identity but also with a clear awareness that the West has subjugated Muslims in the process and depicted them as the "other."

The elaboration of the difference between Islam and the West has often centered on the status of women in the Muslim world. The likeness of a veiled Muslim woman appears to many Americans to be in stark contrast to the freedoms of Western democracy. This image, reinforced constantly by the media, inevitably links what is seen as the oppression of women to the religion of Islam. For many Americans, for example, the prevailing symbol of Western victory in Afghanistan was the expected image of Afghan women throwing off their enveloping *burqas*. In a political environment of increasing hostility toward Islam, the manipulation of gender to reinforce the so-called "clash of civilizations"—portraying Islam as oppressive of women and the West as liberated—has placed Muslim women in Western societies in an extremely difficult position.

This juxtaposition of Islamic and Western models of womanhood goes back to the early foundations of the American Republic. For Americans who could read, the written word was their only point of contact with the Muslim world. Thus they relied heavily on European texts in order to familiarize themselves with Islam. At first, early America simply appropriated European images and caricatures of Islam and Muslims. This was a natural process, since the earlier colonists were European, mostly British, and continued to identify themselves as such for some time. But it was not long before they began to produce images of their own in literature and the arts. A recent study by Jalaluddien Khuda Bakhsh shows that such American Romantics as Emerson, Hawthorne, and Thoreau used Islamic imagery in their writings in such a way that a new form of Orientalism became a major theme in American literature. Washington Irving wrote a series of novels with Islamic motifs, including *The Alhambra* (1832). Edgar Allan Poe made use of the "Arabesque" style in his Gothic literature. Some of these authors, including Herman Melville and Mark Twain, actually traveled to the region, albeit as Christian pilgrims. As a result, their work shows more subtlety and accuracy with regard to the Muslim world than that of many of their contemporaries. Unfortunately, most of these American authors lacked immediate contact with the Muslim world and thus had little accurate knowledge of it, with the result that their writings often present inaccurate and distorted images, especially of women.

By the nineteenth century, colonialism and the Victorian era of European and American Christian missionary activities in the Middle East, Africa, and Asia came to provide the lens through which Muslim women were seen in the West. The image of women in need of assistance and "liberation" was one of the justifications for Western imperialism, especially in Muslim regions of the world. Studies of Western imperialism and Christian missions in Islamic countries have shown how colonial officials and missionaries themselves actively enforced stereotypic categories of gender roles and femininity, which reflected and reinforced the social institutions found in the major cities of Europe and North America. While a man, according to Victorian doctrine, was expected to be active in the public realm, functioning as the public representative and head of the household in the workforce and the political world, a woman was identified with domestic life and defined by her role as wife and mother. The cultural systems of the day gave authority and value to the activities of men; the woman's place was in the home. These categories stemmed from Victorian tenets that provided ideological support not only for imperial ventures—the civilizing mission of bringing Enlightenment to colonized peoples—but also, specifically, for the model of womanhood imposed during the late nineteenth century and most of the twentieth century.

Christian Missionary Crusades

American Muslim women in many cases are the products, directly or indirectly, of many years of Western missionary attempts to convert them to Christianity. With the best of intentions, these missionaries generally saw themselves as releasing Muslims from the oppression of their Islamic environment in the process of bringing "enlightenment" to Islamic cultures. Muslims coming to, and making their home in, the West in the latter part of the twentieth and now in the twenty-first century immediately encounter the residue of these long-propagated stereotypes. They also carry with them the defensive polemic and ideological responses to those stereotypes generated in Muslim nation-states for over a century.

Protestant missionaries established schools designed to train "heathen" Arab girls and young women (both Muslims and Greek Orthodox Christians) how to be model wives and mothers. Some accounts in missionary magazines at the turn of the nineteenth to the twentieth century tell of Arab women in desperate need of domestication. A young mother is portrayed in the pages of one such magazine as "a fierce, wild animal," and a young girl who tried to resist the imposition of Western-style practices of hygiene was described as untruthful, wily, and manipulative. The status of married life in Muslim countries often has evoked the consternation of missionaries, whose literature contrasts Muslim women treated by their husbands as "chattel" with Christian treatment of wives as their helpmeets and companions. This perceived difference in the treatment of women has served as a polarization between East and West, reinforcing the contempt of many missionaries for social arrangements in the Muslim world. The result has been that most Westerners believe that what they have seen and still see as "the backwardness" of Muslim cultures is due to Islamic customs, traditions, and beliefs, particularly in relation to women, rather than to socioeconomic or political factors that have created poverty and substandard living conditions.

For women missionaries from Europe and the United States, evangelizing Muslims, especially women, offered an important opportunity to express their religious piety. Muslim women, as shapers of the future generation, became desired targets for conversion. If conditioned properly, such missionaries assumed, women would become the agents of the creation of a new society patterned after the Christian West. The ministry of Christian missionary women, who devoted their lives to service with the best of intentions, in some senses depended on their "heathen" sisters being *in need of* salvation. This means that the lowly state of women had to be understood in terms of a lack of moral virtue. Despite the reality that entrenched disparities in wealth and income were instrumental in creating and sustaining conditions of poverty, the missionaries believed it necessary that their sisters' lot be improved primarily through religious conversion and training in the Western virtues of cleanliness, honor, and education rather than through changing political and economic arrangements. The attitudes that Christian missionary women held toward the women they sought to convert reflected their determination that reaching women was the best means to opening the door for more widespread evangelism. To convert young women, who would be the society's childbearers, was to reach the greatest source of influence in forming the next generation and to have a direct impact on the morals of the local population.

Nineteenth-century travelogues and personal accounts by Westerners who were neither missionaries nor functionaries of colonial governments provide further insights into the ways Muslim women were commonly viewed. Historical accounts provided by the likes of such explorers as Sir Richard Burton and Edward Lane captured notions of European superiority. These texts represented Islam and the Orient as bizarre and sexually deviant and so formed Western opinion about its nature. Descriptions of women focused on their alleged promiscuity, devilishness, and voracious sexual appetites and reduced women to objects of sexual desire. Writers such as Gustave Flaubert and painters like Eugène Delacroix frequently portrayed Muslim women as naked or scantily clad, lounging in harems guarded by slaves and eunuchs. Often vulnerable, naked women were represented as symbols of captive beauty and, at the same time, victims of barbaric Middle Eastern men, in need of rescue at the hands of Westerners.

Contemporary Efforts at Evangelism

Much, of course, has changed in the former colonies of European empires. With the advent of independence for many nation-states in Africa, Asia, and the Middle East in the twentieth century, Christian missionary activities were strictly regulated or stopped altogether. Yet there is still resonance today between past missionary work and the present efforts at Christian evangelism on the part of theologically conservative denominations and groups. Western missionary strategists, who have always reasoned that "oppressed" women would be the weakest point at which they could penetrate and convert Islamic societies, continue today to identify the release of Muslim women from the yoke of male domination as one of their primary goals.

As mainline denominations that used to proselytize—such as the Presbyterians, United Church of Christ, and Episcopalians—have altered their mission activities from efforts at conversion to service, Christian evangelization of Muslims has been assumed by the conservative and evangelical branches of the church. Muslims perceive many, though not all, missionaries as having served as agents for the subjugation of Islamic society precisely by undermining the role of women in the process of trying to present to them a better—that is, Christian—way of life. In the attempt to record and disseminate to the West their observations about Islamic life, and the role of women in it, both male and female missionaries have shared in producing the stereotypes of "repressed and downtrodden females."

The timelessness of the stereotype of the Muslim woman persists. Contemporary Christian evangelicals see it as their calling to convert Muslims to Christianity. Since the national tragedy of 9/11 in particular, there has been a concerted effort to publish testimonials in this area. Titles such as *Daughters of Islam: Building Bridges with Muslim Women* (2002) and *Ministry to Muslim Women: Longing to Call Them Sisters* (2003) present compilations of Christian evangelical women's experiences actively proselytizing Muslim women. Unlike the writings of the early twentieth century, the contemporary missionaries do not paint all Muslims with the same brush. In an attempt to be more effective, they contextualize the message, tailoring it for their specific audience. Occasionally such works try to acknowledge the heterogeneity of Islam and the Muslim world, noting the varied ethnic, sectarian, and linguistic groups included in the region and populations they cover. While the pitch may be contextualized, the message is the same: The Muslim woman is the "other" in need of salvation. The ideological effect is the legitimization of the religious imperative to convert and thereby counteract the forces of darkness (read: Islamic fundamentalism) that are coded as Muslim or Middle Eastern in these texts.

Many of these writings on contextualization as a strategy for conversion do provide a more balanced picture of Muslim women than is reflected in traditional stereotypes. Miriam Adeny, for example, in her book *Daughters of Islam*, attempts to clear away prevailing stereotypes by portraying the range of possible forms of religious expression by Muslim women, from the folk level to a more educated or secularized version. While some women, she says, know a good deal about the religion, others do not know much and therefore resort to saint worship and magical practices and still others are members of fundamentalist sisterhoods. Despite the attempts to differentiate, however, the net effect is to lump all of these variations into one category, Muslim Woman. Women are thus represented in an essentialist way: They are tied either to folk traditions or to politicized waves of radicalism. In either case they appear to resist modernization. This description helps frame the readers' expectations about Muslim women, in order to help them understand why Muslim women might "come to" Jesus Christ—for example, because something is missing—from the core of their religious experience. Muslim women, who provide the window into an alien and foreboding culture, are the perceived vulnerable point of access that will help bring down the edifice of Muslim intransigence.

The mission field for conservatives and evangelicals has also expanded to include the West. Muslim women in the United States today are faced with persistent missionary efforts to convert them. Conservative Christian denominations produce instructional information teaching Christian women the best methods for getting Muslim women in the United States to feel comfortable with them before trying to persuade them that only Christianity is the way to salvation. "Who will reach our dear friends in Islam?" they ask. "Who will join us in our pursuit of a holy fellowship of believing women from Muslim backgrounds?" One Muslim student on the campus of San Diego State University reported being befriended by two Christian women who took turns urging her to convert. Feeling quite vulnerable because she was not deeply conversant with Islam, she decided to cover and join the Muslim Student Association on campus in order get support.

Such efforts have impeded the integration of Muslim women in America, and often thwarted Muslim participation in interfaith dialogue, as Muslim women suspect any act of friendship to be a means of seduction in an effort to have them relinquish their faith.

Stereotypes in Popular Culture

Studies of identity politics have tended to focus on differences among people that come to appear self-evident. For instance, individual characteristics such as skin color or cultural heritage become prevalent markers and thus descriptive of an entire group. Supposedly inborn qualities (for instance sex or race) are both defined and experienced as inherent and immutable, in contrast to other kinds of denominators such as class, income, or educational level, which at least in recent times are perceived as structured by social processes and access to opportunity. In popular discourse, identity seems to be constructed—and understood—through variations, but it implies sameness in two ways: First, all humans are the same in having identities, and second, those sharing an identity are considered as essentially the same. Although identities have many sources and the historical roots of any particular identity are complex, Western politics and societies provide an increasingly productive forum for eliciting, contesting, and negotiating expressions of identity.

Cinema is one of the most powerful tools of popular culture, and images of Arab women in motion pictures have an enormous impact on the public mind. Popular movies and television fare have portrayed Muslims as religious fanatics and terrorists. From its very beginning, the motion-picture industry has featured fictional images of Muslim women as submissive and exotic objects of men's desire. Silent movie shorts at the turn of the nineteenth into the twentieth century introduced Fatima, the star of the 1896 World's Fair in Chicago, as a buxom belly dancer swathed in opaque scarves. In the "Arabian Nights" fantasy films, such as *The Sheikh* (1921) and its sequel, *Return of the Sheikh* (1926), both of which starred the swarthy Rudolph Valentino as a hot-blooded Arab abducting an Englishwoman, Arab women appear as disposable ornaments with bare midriffs, closeted in private women's quarters in the prince's palaces or displayed for sale in slave markets. The trope of the harem still exists in today's motion picture industry. Disney's 2004 remake of the film *Around the World in 80 Days*, for example, featured Arnold Schwarzenegger in the role of Prince Hapi, a sheikh with "100 or so wives."

Children in America have never been exempt from the constant stereotyping of Arabs and Muslims in cartoons, shown first in local theaters and now on television. As early as 1938 an episode of *Porky Pig* in Egypt shows Muslims first praying and then turning into gamblers shooting craps, while a lady of the harem—looking sexy in her seductive clothing—drops her veil to reveal a particularly ugly visage. Studies have shown what a deleterious effect such programming has on the ways in which children view members of other ethnic traditions. Unfortunately while strong sanctions have been put in place outlawing crude characterization of members of most racial/ethnic and religious groupings, thus far that has not been the case for Muslim and Arabs except in a few situations as a response to the efforts of Muslim organizations.

Still other films show Arab women in less seductive poses. In earlier productions, such as Alfred Hitchcock's *The Man Who Knew Too Much* (1956) and the Bob Hope comedy *My Favorite Spy* (1951), Arab women lurk in the background, perhaps as destabilizing props and certainly as unattractive beasts of burden, carrying jugs on their heads. Jack Shaheen, who has studied stereotypes of Arabs and Muslims in films and television for a number of years (his *Reel Bad Arabs: How Hollywood Vilifies People* serves as a guide to nearly 1,000 films), notes that popular imagery has long cast women as bumbling servants of men, voluptuous belly dancers, temptresses hanging around the edges of slave markets, and, more recently, violent actors in terrorist schemes. They are either exotic and darkly tempting; unattractive, uneducated, and enslaved behind black coverings; or evil participants in anti-West terrorist activities.

Even recent films such as *Protocol* (1984), *The Sheltering Sky* (1990), and *Deception* (1993) feature Muslim women as cackling hordes of crows and shapeless mounds of black, ululating and trailing at a distance behind their unkempt (and presumably radical) male relatives. It is primarily in the last decade, and especially since 9/11, that we see them as perpetrators of violence. In an especially vicious anti-Arab and Islam-bashing film, *Rules of Engagement* (2000), co-starring Tommy Lee Jones and Samuel Jackson, an attorney represents an American military officer facing a court martial for ordering his soldiers to fire on Yemeni civilians—opening frames of the film show the slaughter of eighty-three men, women, and children. Yet at its conclusion the film reveals the motive for the officer's decision to order the massacre. A flashback shows Muslim men, women, and children carrying concealed guns, shooting at Marines.

Even films designed as comedies yield to the temptation to caricature Muslim women. As Shaheen observes, since 1992 the Walt Disney company has released a number of films in which Arabs and Muslims are portrayed in a demeaning light. The remake of *Father of the Bride, Part II* shows a happy American couple (Steve Martin and Diane Keaton) who feel that they need to sell their house when a crass Muslim family, the Habibs, moves next door. Mrs. Habib is shown as cowering before her mean and ill-mannered husband, who shouts at her in a mixture of Arabic and Farsi, perpetuating the image of a submissive woman with no personality of her own.

Stereotypes of Arabs and Muslims thus have been conflated to the point where the public does not distinguish between the two sets of images. Films that feature Arabs are understood to be telling stories about Muslim religious and cultural values and practices. In popular culture, Arab and Muslim women have long been associated with demeaning fantasies of violence, sex, and oppression. Women from other Muslim cultures fare no better.

The story of Betty Mahmoody, the American wife of an Iranian man, is told in the book and popular 1991 movie, *Not Without my Daughter*. Initially on a short family vacation to Iran, Mahmoody begins to see her husband "revert" to cruel and patriarchal norms once in the company of his relatives. When her husband decides not to return to the United States, Mahmoody attempts to leave Iran but is told that she can not take her young daughter with her because, in Iran, the father has custody of his children. Refusing to leave Iran without her daughter, Mahmoody is subjected to a secluded life filled with abuse. Her story relates the dangers she faces as she plots to smuggle herself and her daughter out of Iran. The power of this book, and subsequent movie, depends largely on Western assumptions about the misogynistic nature of Islam and the disproportionate power of men over women in conservative Muslim countries. The Iranian father, after abusing his wife, boasts that Islam is the greatest gift that he could give his daughter. The film not so subtly suggests the connection between the behavior of the husband/ father and the model set by Iranian Ayatollah Khomeini. While moderately successful in the United States, both the book and the movie were enormously popular in western Europe. Muslims have vigorously protested the film as promoting the stereotypical impression that all Muslims treat their wives in this fashion. It is as accurate, they say, as a film suggesting that an abused battered Christian or Jewish woman abandoned with her children and living in a shelter is the Christian or Jewish way of treating women.

Muslims in the entertainment media are generally described by buzz words such as fundamentalist, terrorist, and insurgent that become symbols projecting a deviance from what should be seen as "normal." If the storyline involves a Muslim who apparently hates the West, the producers portray him or her as a totally irrational person or one who can barely speak English. American television stations repeatedly offer up the standard stereotypes of Arabs and Muslims as terrorists in their "fictional" programs. In one of two segments of the 1998 *Soldiers of Fortune*, entitled "Top Event" (contrived well before 9/11), Arab terrorists are portrayed releasing truckloads of poison gas in Los Angeles. The female Muslim participant in this grim maneuver, when asked to whom she is responsible, shouts that she works only for Allah. More recently, Fox TV's program 24 raised the ire of the Council on Arab-Islamic Relations for its depiction of an Iranian-American Muslim family—wife, husband, and teenage son—as a "sleeper cell" at the heart of a terrorist plot against the United States (ratings of 24 went up a whopping 36 percent after they took on the theme of terrorism.) CAIR was so insistent in its protests that on February 7, 2005, Kiefer Sutherland (who plays the role of a counterterrorism agent) gave a disclaimer acknowledging that "the American Muslim community stands firmly beside their fellow Americans in denouncing and resisting all forms of terrorism." In watching the program, said Sutherland, one should bear that in mind! Meanwhile Kiefer's character Jack Bauer has killed some 100 Muslim American "fanatics."

The popular NBC crime series *Law & Order* kicked off a new series on February 27, 2005, with an episode featuring an American Muslim woman of Iraqi origin. While it included some strong indictment of the American invasion of Iraq, the program wound up by proving the Iraqi woman guilty of the murder of a female American soldier whom she considered partly responsible for the torture and death of her brother at Abu Ghraib prison. The victim was dressed in a white shirt with a cross smeared on it in pig's blood, symbolizing a fallen Christian Crusader. The crime was portrayed as having been committed not only as an act of *jihad*, reinforcing the image of Muslim violence, but also as an act of Arab vengeance, calling on another common stereotype of Arabs and Muslims. On both counts the Muslim woman was culpable.

News Media

Television news, of course, has found the images of Muslim women in Afghanistan, Iraq, Saudi Arabia, and other countries irresistible, and photographers delight in showering the American public with shots of women in all-enveloping *burqas*. Such pictures are even more appealing, it seems, if Islamically-clad women are seen dropping votes in a ballot box, fostering the kind of apparent ambiguity that is conveyed in the image of the Yves St. Laurent face veil described above. Can such shrouded women actually vote?

If images of Muslim women proliferate today, however, such was not the case until fairly recently. A study, done in the mid-1990s by Karin Gwinn Wilkins, of American press photo coverage of the Middle East reveals the extent to which women have been significantly underrepresented. The *New York Times*, for example, virtually always has featured male images associated with "hard" news about conflict and politics, while women, if covered at all, have been photographed in connection with stories about social issues, such as education, children, family, and religion. Moreover, in almost two-thirds of the *NYT* photos of Middle Eastern women published in the 1990s, the women are wearing the veil, perpetuating a stereotype instead of representing the majority of women. Veiled women are much less likely to be named and identified in the photos than nonveiled women, reinforcing the anonymity (and invisibility) attributed by the veil. Wilkins notes that Middle Eastern women constitute a kind of cultural landscape: They are seen in the distance, suggesting their passivity as nonactors, impersonal and unworthy of being identified as people in themselves.

At the beginning of the twenty-first century, many news articles about Muslim women in American newspapers and popular magazines portrayed them as the oppressed victims of a conservative brand of Islam. With the fundamentalist "Islamic threat" positioned as the new global enemy in the post–Cold War era, and Muslim populations increasing in many Western metropolitan centers, long-held anxieties about the intent of Islam to destroy the values and lifestyles of Western-style democracies have come to the fore. Both before and after 9/11, consumers of Western-based media outlets were supplied with various analyses of Islam, many of which featured the powerlessness of Muslim women. Many accounts have portrayed women as passive victims of oppressive and harsh laws. The *Time* cover story of December 3, 2001, titled "About Face for Afghan Women," describes the *burqa* in Afghanistan as "a body bag for the living," the symbol of the Taliban's oppression of women. According to *Time*, Afghan women are said to be "silent, shapeless figures encased in shrouds," a potent symbol of the suffocating force of a fundamentalist regime.

Conditions for women in Afghanistan became a *cause célèbre* in the United States and Britain when public figures there criticized the practices of the Taliban military regime. For instance, in 1997, less than one year after the Taliban came to power, Mavis Leno, the wife of American television host Jay Leno, made her own fame as an outspoken critic of the harsh treatment of women in Afghanistan. She testified at a March 1998 U.S. Senate hearing, chaired by Dianne Feinstein, pointing to the Taliban's violation of women's human rights: Women and girls were no longer permitted to attend school; women were no longer allowed to work or to leave their homes except in the company of their husbands or other male relatives; and women were not allowed to be treated by male doctors. After the terrorist attacks the critique became more sharp.

First Lady Laura Bush's radio speech citing the brutal oppression of women under the Taliban, referred to in the first chapter, was echoed in an address by the wife of the Prime Minister of Britain. Cherie Blair publicly condemned the oppression of women in Afghanistan, stating that "The women here today [visiting her at the Prime Minister's Downing Street residence] prove that the women of Afghanistan still have a spirit that belies their unfair, downtrodden image. . . . We need to help them free that spirit and give them their voice back, so they can create the better Afghanistan we all want to see." To the ears of Muslims all over the world, echoes of the Victorian legacy can be heard in these proclamations, which cast women in dichotomous terms, comprehending Afghan women's conditions primarily vis-à-vis the liberating project of Western ideology. "We" women in the West are defined in contrast to the oppression that Afghan women suffer, and the justification for the American-led war in Afghanistan is to liberate the demeaned female Other. According to this logic the Taliban are to be opposed not only because they represent a credible threat to global security but specifically because there are women in need of emancipation. The relation in this twenty-first-century entreaty to "fight for the rights and dignity of women" and the nineteenth-century Christian women missionaries' dependence on their "heathen" sisters' need of salvation to give expression to the missionary women's religious piety is clear.

President Bush and other top officials characterized the war in Afghanistan, and more generally the war on terrorism, as a battle for "civilization" and a "crusade." However, this argument obscures two important features to which Muslims call attention. First, long before Western advocates began campaigning on behalf of Afghan women, many women in Afghanistan were starving and facing violence, not only because of the Taliban but due to a long history of conflict in which the United States had been deeply implicated; whether the women in Afghanistan would have been subjected to such extreme forms of Islamic conservatism without American material support for the *mujahideen* remains an open question. Secondly, while there is no doubt that the laws imposed by the Taliban were draconian and conditions in Afghanistan were deplorable, the Western focus on the need to rescue Afghani women papered over a diverse range of women's engagement and activism in Afghanistan and elsewhere. Scant media coverage of democratic organizations on behalf of Afghans, such as the Revolutionary Association of Women of Afghanistan (RAWA), began to appear on networks such as CNN in late 2001 as spokespersons for this women's humanitarian and political organization sought to educate Americans and raise money for their cause. Similarly, dozens of women's solidarity networks and organizations have begun to post Web sites and host chat rooms for Muslim women who are activists, educators, and professionals. Such activities, except in very rare instances, escape the attention of the American news media and thus never become part of the consciousness of the American reading and listening public.

Escalating political tensions in many parts of the world make the task of interpreting Islam increasingly difficult for American Muslim women. The press revels in portraying what it sees as violence associated with Islamic movements, resulting not only in rising American fears but also more stereotypical responses to what is depicted as the oppression of Muslim women in Iran, Saudi Arabia, Pakistan, and elsewhere. Israel's erection of its long wall separating itself from Palestinian territories, called "Defensive Shield," has led to new modes of resistance by Palestinians. In some cases these have involved women, either the few who themselves have perpetrated acts of violence or Muslim mothers who have been portrayed in the American press as proud supporters of their sons' participation in suicide attacks against Israeli citizens. Press coverage of these events fosters and strengthens stereotypes of Muslim women as fanatics and willing participants in violent struggle. American Muslim women are being called on to explain and somehow take responsibility for the actions of their sisters overseas, while the press continues to fail to fully represent the political and emotional reasons why a few women believe such violence is their last desperate resort.

Muslim Media

Images of Muslim women and stereotypes of Islamic culture are among the first things that Muslim immigrants encounter when they come to the United States. While the immigrants are confident that they do not conform to the images depicted of them by the American media, and that their sense of self and dignity is not contingent on what the other says about them, the constant barrage of demeaning and gratuitous portrayals that they experience daily begins to grind them down. One response is to assign this deliberate obfuscation to ill intent, while another is to believe that it is due to ignorance and seek to find ways to combat the distortion.

Some Arab and Muslim Americans thus have taken it on themselves to address the stereotypes. They question, for example, why Americans believe that Islam forbids women to drive, since Saudi Arabia is the only nation whose traditions and culture insists on such restrictions. Saddam Hussein, on the other hand, is never given credit for the fact that he encouraged women to drive buses and trucks. For their part, some Muslims have developed counterstereotypes of Western women based on what is depicted in B-rated movies and popular television such as *Dynasty* and *Desperate Housewives*. In their sermons and writings, traditional Muslims tend to depict Western women as leading empty lives, morally bankrupt, loose, addicted to drugs, and abandoned by their boyfriends and husbands. Emulation of such "typical" Western behavior, they warn, will lead to the debasement and ruin of Muslim women. A handful of Muslim media production companies also have been established to produce alternative "Islamic" media. Ranging from newsletters and magazines to audiotapes, videos, CDs and DVDs, Muslim productions are creating a special niche in print, television, and electronic media.

If Western media are fascinated with the stereotypical "veiled" Muslim woman, many journals designed for an American Muslim audience seem to project the same image, if for a quite different reason. In such periodicals as *The Muslim Magazine*, *The American Journal*, *al-Jumuah*, and *Islamic Horizons*, for example, Muslim authors defend the position of women in Islam and specifically address the question of women's roles in articles dealing with education, parenting, and marriage. Like their non-Muslim counterparts, however, many of these magazines underrepresent Muslim women in subjects outside of the domestic sphere. In depictions not dissimilar to the stereotypes of Muslim women perpetuated in the non-Muslim media and press, Muslim journals portray women largely functionally, seen in relation to men within the context of the family, as sisters, daughters, wives, and mothers. Women not choosing to wear some form of Islamic dress generally are not pictured.

Particularly in the more conservative Muslim magazines, women are frequently advised about appropriate feminine behavior. Obedience, sacrifice, and being unobtrusive by keeping one's voice soft and low are typical virtues extolled in these articles. A woman's primary responsibility, according to the conservative publications, is as a wife and mother. A good Muslim woman is expected to set aside any personal aspirations until her husband's and children's needs are met. Further, mothers are to be exemplary in their piety and a foundation of Islamic education for their children. *Al-Jumuah* maintains that it is best if married Muslim women do not work at all. In *The Muslim Magazine*, the publication of the women's network KAMILAT (www.kamilat .org), the tagline is, "Helping Americans to better understand traditional Islam, while building integrity among women of diverse cultures"; the mission is to promote the empowerment of women from within a specifically Islamic context. This magazine presents Islam as the "historic champion of women" and argues that Islam liberates rather than oppresses women through, for instance, the rights and protections offered under Islamic family law. According to this magazine, women's rights extend to contraception, the right to initiate a divorce, and pursuit of career options. Activism and compassion are seen as two important virtues of Muslim femininity.

The underlying assumption of many of these journals is that there are significant biological and psychological differences between women and men and that these differences make women uniquely suited to being wives and mothers. Men are presented as physically and emotionally stronger than women, and it is suggested that the world is best organized hierarchically, based on the hierarchy of the family. *Azizah*, a magazine written by and for Muslim women and inaugurated in 2002, presents a broader set of images of Muslim women than do many of the other Islamic journals; *Azizah* will be discussed in more detail in chapter 7, "Claiming Public Space."

Not only magazines, but also CDs, DVDs, videos, and television shows have been produced and distributed by Muslim individuals and organizations in an effort to counteract the negative stereotypes and perceptions westerners have of Islam. Such visual materials—used in the education of adults, children, and non-Muslims alike—convey the message that Muslims would like to present to insure that future generations of Muslims have a positive context for group identity. Production of positive images for children's consumption is a growing industry. These productions, which include children's television shows, present an idealized version of the way Muslims in the West, and in the United States in particular, see themselves and would like to be seen by others. They consciously try to build a particular vision of Islam and an Islamic identity by repeating dominant themes like Muslim diversity, featuring child actors who look South Asian, Arab, East Asian, and African American, but noticeably *not* European American; Muslim unity, stressing that despite diversity in culture, history, and language, all Muslims are one in their faith; and the glorious past of Islamic civilization. Many of these children's programs and animated films are aired on Islamic cable-TV channels, offering an alternative to mainstream children's programming which portray negative images of the Muslim world as violent, alien, and threatening.

In several of these productions, women either play no role at all or play a secondary and supporting role to their male companions. In one series, *Adam's World*, only one episode speaks explicitly about women and then only in the context of a Prophetic saying that "Paradise lies at the mother's feet." By featuring women exclusively in their function as mothers, this program in effect marginalizes the presence of women and provides only one very limited role model for Muslim girls. In much of these media, the image of women is compatible with a patriarchal understanding of family structures insofar as women are depicted as secondary vis-à-vis men. Again, only women covered in Islamic dress are presented as part of an idealized Islamic identity.

Some new productions, however, are designed to deal directly with post 9/11 realities and with new images of American Muslim women, particularly young women. *Born in the U.S.A.*, for example, a film by Soliman Productions, features two American-born, second-generation Muslims, a young man and a young woman. It depicts the conflict they face as members of a minority group. Dina, a person who clearly chooses to make her own decisions, elected to continue to wear the *hijab* despite cautions from other Muslims that she should remove it because of the rise in hate crimes after 9/11. The film includes a discussion among American-born Muslim youth who are struggling to define their place in America as Americans and Muslims.

To a large degree the process of claiming an Islamic identity in America, perhaps especially for African Americans, has involved challenging prevailing stereotypes, embraced by non-Muslims, of Islam and Muslims as inferior. However, there has also been another deep, if not contradictory, influence exerted on the invention and expression of modern identities. That is the adoption and appropriation by some in the Muslim community of "inverted stereotypes," using them to celebrate the uniqueness of the identity group and its perceived distance from the mainstream. It makes the substance of the stereotype its possible opposite—no longer a reason for subordination but a reason for group pride in the innate.

The rap music scene provides many examples of Muslim cultural pride, especially but not exclusively among African-American Muslims. The popular artists Native Deen, for example, have produced many best-selling recordings that reflect their version of identity politics. Take, for example, the following lyric from "M-U-S-L-I-M" (on *For the Cause of Allah*, release date 2002):

> *Don't know about you, I know about me,*
> *I'm proud because I'm rolling Islamically*
> *Everywhere I see, even on TV,*
> *People talking trash about the way I be.*
> *But what they all hate, is if we get great*
> *Cause we're the only ones with our heads on straight*
> *Don't ever frown, or your head looking down,*
> *If you read the Qur'an you're the best in the town.*
> *Y'all have doubt say- we have no clout*
> *But-within-a-few years see how we've come about.*

We're back on the scene, The number-one deen,
I'm proud to be down with the Muslimeen!

Chorus: *M-U-S-L-I-M*
I'm so blessed to be with them....
M-U-S-L-I-M
I'm so blessed to be with them....

In another song, called "Busy Bees," Native Deen speaks directly to Muslim women:

You just came back from a cool MYNA conference,
Islamical atmosphere, was there and had its influence on you,
   to do, A very pious rule,
You said you wanna cover wear Hijab (Islamic head covering) its cool.
You thought how happy Allah was gonna be for you!
You said you'd don it for your life not just a week or two,
So Tuesday morning you got up and read your fajr prayer.
And after breakfast you put on the clothes you plan to wear,
You went to school with baggy clothes and everything,
But all your friend they be thinkin' your an alien!
What's with the scarf girl, wrapped up like a mummy.
They all made jokes and they said that you look funny.
You ran into the bathroom and your friends began to scoff,
After that encounter you had planned to take it off,
But then you thought how much Allah likes how your dressin'.
Pleasin' him was top priority to you no question.
You walk right out of the bathroom with a super-strong conviction.
You realized in this world we Muslims have a mission!

Now we're buzzy bees.
We're not at all at ease.
We have a mission to complete Allah we want to please.
We know we are the best and we never ever rest.
We understand that this life was only but a test!

These lyrics illustrate particular dimensions of the identity construction process: the appropriation of contested images, and the subsequent redefinition of personal identity through the recombination of these images. White society has tended to characterize African Americans in terms of group stereotypes rather than the individual identities of its members. This rap shows how members of such a subordinated and racialized group have responded by seizing an alternative identity (Islam) that flies in the face of the negative suppositions of mainstream stereotypes (ghetto gangs, drugs, and crime), at the same time embracing the alternative means of encountering resistance and pressures to conform. Part of the reconstruction of the image of American blacks here involves the adoption of another identity, Islam, which is reviled in conventional public understanding. The convergence of the two identities— black and Muslim—authenticates the experiences that Native Deen talks about. Islam is used as the compass point to navigate out of the subordinated and demeaned conditions of the American ghetto. For much of the American public, the nation's inner cities have represented places where one's worst fears are realized: drugs, prostitution, street crime, and gang violence. Native Deen's appropriation of Islam as a means to combat the oversimplified reduction of inner city life to these categories serves to reinvent Islam as a means of liberation and a paragon of moral virtue in the midst of moral breakdown.

The Image of the Headscarf

There is little question that the *hijab* has become the most stereotypical symbol of Muslim womanhood for most Americans. The majority of media presentations feature women in headscarves as if it were given that all Muslim women choose to wear this headgear. A number of articles in Muslim journals and recent videos take the *hijab* as a central theme. Sometimes they try to argue for the "correctness" of women covering in Islamic dress and often outline the reasons for wearing the *hijab*. A primary consideration, apart from modesty, is the shielding of women from sexual objectification and supposedly "Western" standards of attractiveness. Women who wear the *hijab* are praised for their modesty in the face of immodesty and for their resolve in the midst of an immodest and amoral or immoral society. Many times the depiction of a covered Muslim woman is juxtaposed to a half-naked Western woman; for some in the American Islamic community the women of the immoral West have become a measure of societal corruption and a peril to Muslim youth.

February 27, 2005, *Daily News Herald* (Arlington Heights, Illinois) staff writer Nadia Malik took the occasion of an exhibit of clothing and photographs in Palatine, Illinois, taken by journalism students in Tehran, to share her personal thoughts about how difficult it is for her to see the veil through the stereotypical lens generally applied by the American public. Malik, raised in America in a devout Pakistani immigrant family, recently chose to wear Islamic dress over the objections of her unveiled mother. Asked by a local rabbi for her opinion of the exhibit as a person who is herself now veiled, Malik mused, "How can I explain to people who see *hijab* as a tool of oppression that [deciding to wear it] was one of the most liberating experiences of my life?"

The range of opinions within the Muslim community as to whether wearing the veil is an Islamic requirement or not is wide, and it is generally a woman's choice as to whether she does or not. There is no question, however, that as a symbol the veil or scarf or head cover symbolizes to most Americans anything from repression to backwardness. Because of the fostering of this stereotype for all of the reasons suggested above, Muslim women who do choose to veil experience prejudicial treatment in many walks of American life.

Feminists in both the United States and Canada have been articulate in describing the *hijab* as a symbol of subordination and oppression of women. Such arguments affect Muslim women in several ways. While some adopt certain elements of the critique and are themselves articulate in opposing Islamic dress, albeit in their own terms, others deeply resent such "interference" on the part of those who are not Muslim. Oppression comes in many forms, they argue, not least from those feminists who want to save Muslims from what many believe to be a commandment from God. On the whole, American Muslims themselves try to respect the right of a woman to make her own decision about dress as about other things, and wish that the rest of the American public would do the same.

Women often believe that if they dress modestly they are free to enter any profession because there is no danger that the men with whom they work will make unwanted advances. Unfortunately the very garb that in her own understanding, or that of her family, allows a woman to work unharassed by male colleagues may, in the American context, mitigate against her professional advancement or even getting a job in the first place. Employers often look askance at a woman wearing *hijab*, fearing that customers or other employees will think it strange or that it may indicate some kind of religious fanaticism on the part of the wearer. The headscarf is sometimes prohibited in the workplace as part of general regulations against clothing that attracts too much attention. Ironically, regulations that may have originated in response to clothing considered too skimpy, such as miniskirts, now may function to prohibit clothing that serves the opposite purpose.

The fact that some women do face discrimination for wearing *hijab* puts women who are attentive to Qur'anic injunctions between a rock and a hard place. However the *hijab* is viewed by Americans—as a symbol of cultural difference (and thus inferiority), a threat to secularity, or simply as a personal expression of religiosity—it frames the female body as an icon of the "clash of civilizations" and has far-reaching political and social implications. The importance attached to the *hijab*, by Muslims and non-Muslims alike, has led many to take a one-dimensional view of what it means to be Muslim. Muslim feminist organizations such as the Muslim Women's League and KARAMAH have courageously addressed the contentious question of what the *hijab* means. Drawing on a Qur'anic framework to explain the significance of the attire, they insist that the overriding motivation in covering is modesty. What is unfortunate, these groups say, is that the headscarf has become the litmus test of a Muslim woman's piety, and even those who dress conservatively but do not cover their hair and throat are judged as women who have "not quite arrived" at the ideal level of devotion to God. Among practicing Muslims and leaders of some Muslim organizations such as CAIR (Council on American-Islamic Relations), the issue of *hijab* has risen to such heights as to be called, sarcastically, the "Sixth Pillar" of Islam, alongside prayer, fasting, alms-giving, pilgrimage, and witnessing to Muhammad as the "seal" of the Prophets and to the oneness of God.

In recent years CAIR, in its effort to mitigate the backlash against the *hijab*, has been working hard to expose cases of prejudicial treatment in the workplace. Instances where women are not hired because of the scarf, or where it can be proven that they are not allowed professional advancement because of their dress, are immediately reported and publicized in the Islamic press and over the Internet. Companies who practice such discrimination may be forced to apologize, to reinstate or promote a female worker, or even to undergo special kinds of antidiscrimination training. In some cases compensation is made to the Muslim employee.

Whether cradling her baby, aiming an assault rifle, or walking ten steps behind her oppressor husband, the stereotypical images of a usually fully veiled Muslim woman are burned deep into Western consciousness. Muslims making their home in the West in the latter part of the twentieth century, and now in the twenty-first century, immediately encounter the persistence of these long-propagated stereotypes, just as they also carry the defensive polemic and ideological responses to them generated in Muslim nation states for over a century. Western imperial history and theological dispositions have served to reinforce these images, as our entertainment industry and our governmentally have encouraged justifications for international political involvements. Muslims themselves, struggling both to free themselves from such stereotypes and to establish their own multivalent identities, often in contrast to prevailing Western secular values, sometimes act in ways that reinforce such images. The authors intend for the chapters that follow in this volume to illustrate that Muslim women in the West should not be subsumed under any such stereotypes and that in a great variety of ways they are members of American society who act in conformity neither with Western assumptions nor, necessarily, with the dictates of Islamic traditionalism.

3

Embracing Islam

Why any Western woman would choose to become a Muslim is quite beyond the comprehension of most Americans. Prevailing stereotypes of Muslim women draped in heavy clothes and oppressed by their men make it extremely difficult for the average non-Muslim to imagine such a voluntary choice. The fact remains, however, that for what is probably a growing number of women, Islam holds a genuine appeal both as a religion and as a way of life. It offers a range of possibilities that are far more attractive to them than those they have experienced in Western society. "I have weighed the alternatives seriously and after considerable study and prayer," said one middle-aged American woman, "I have come to the clear conclusion that I will be happier, freer, and more enriched as a Muslim."

A range of recent studies on the phenomenon of conversion among American as well as European women points to the variety of reasons that have compelled Anglos, African Americans, Latinas, Native Americans, and others to adopt Islam as a faith and a source of identification. Much of the testimony of new converts, as well as the questions of those who are weighing such a decision, is available in Muslim missionary tracts, journal literature, and on the Internet. Testimony, of course, is intended to be persuasive, both to engage the interest of those wanting to know more about Islam and to justify to the convert and her family the wisdom and security of her choice. "Islam is the answer," say Muslim missionaries, a claim that converts find satisfying and reassuring. Women who have chosen to become Muslim point to many causes for their decision and often talk in detail about what they are consciously getting out of as well as what they are getting into. Not every decision to become Muslima (a female Muslim), of course, is without repercussions and occasional disappointments, and the testimonials from, as well as the scholarly literature about, these converts is both interesting and compelling.

Since the events of September 11, 2001, the issue of conversion to Islam has emerged on the American public agenda. Surveys conducted through the Council on American Islamic Relations conclude that some 20,000 people convert each year, with women outnumbering men approximately four to one. The United States appears to have become more vigilant in trying to restrict the activities of Muslims that are seen as attempts to propagate the faith, linking Islam to militancy and terrorism in ways that are considered unfortunate and unfair by Muslims. Many Americans fear that Muslims in the United States have a master plan to convert the country to Islam and to impose Islamic law on Americans. That fifteen of the terrorists who perpetrated the World Trade Center attacks were Saudi is offered as proof. The fear of conversion is fueled by the fact that such notorious figures as "American Taliban," John Walker Lindh, and Richard Reid, the Shoe Bomber, are converts.

At the same time it is apparent that the fact of Americans converting to Islam, particularly if they are Anglo or happen to occupy positions of high visibility, has been an important element in the public defense that immigrant Muslims have put forward against American anti-Islamic prejudice. High-visibility Muslim converts such as Cat Stevens (a.k.a. Yusuf Islam) are increasingly referred to as the "rock stars" of the faith, and are often "showcased" at Muslim gatherings and on occasions when it is hoped that their adherence to Islam will be a motivating factor in the decision of others to consider joining the community. They are also useful in persuading Muslim youth that Islam is an attractive, viable alternative to the temptations of American secular life.

The First Women Converts to Islam

From the earliest days of Islam the phenomenon of women converting to the faith has been of significance in the life of the community. The prophet's earliest converts included many women whose adoption of the new faith is part of the Islamic historical record. Indeed, much has been made of the fact that the first person to have believed in the revealed message of Prophet Muhammad was his first wife Khadija, a successful merchant whose adoption of Islam demonstrated that she was a free and independent spirit. Some historians claim that her trust in the prophetic mission of her husband may have been influential in the conversion of other members of his tribe. Several other women of the Prophet's family also publicly acknowledged their adherence to the new religion. Women were prominent among the converts from other tribes from Mecca and surrounding areas who became allied with the Prophet's cause, and when he moved his community to Medina, women were apparently among the first to pledge their allegiance to Islam and its Prophet.

In the United States the first converts were not *to* Islam, but *from* it, in the context of forced conversion. Slave owners insisted that their new acquisitions, a substantial number of whom were from East and West African Muslim tribes, adopt the beliefs and practices of Christianity. (While most of them did in fact become Christian, recent research has revealed that a few were able to retain their Islamic faith.)

In the early days of the twentieth century, the first Americans to be attracted to what they believed to be Islam were blacks who were seeking a new identity in the wake of continuing post-emancipation racism. Groups such as the Moorish American Science Temple, founded by Noble Drew Ali, sought kinship with "Asiatics," or so-called Moors, with whom they felt that they shared a bond of color and of faith. They sought to complete the journey from bondage to freedom by affirming their identity not with racist white Americans but with Asians, people of color, whose religion was Islam. Little in the Moorish American ideology—including its Qur'an—bears much resemblance to the orthodox movements of Sunni or Shi'i Islam, although the group continues in small pockets today as an interesting example of the varieties of heterodox Islam that have developed in America over the past 100 years. Most of these groups appeal especially to African Americans, many of them young. The most prominent example is the Nation of Islam that developed in the 1940s and continued as a powerful voice for black independence, pride, and ethical responsibility for many decades. It is still present on the American scene under the leadership of, among others, the voluble Louis Farrakhan.

Much of the initial discussion within the immigrant Muslim community has been focused on the issue of whether or not it is legitimate for Muslims to actually live in countries that are not Islamic in orientation. The consensus of legal scholars is that its legitimacy lies in the opportunity it affords for Muslims to be propagators of the faith. Commitment to *da'wah*, propagation, for many has meant the acknowledgement that new conditions bring new specifications, and that Muslims are an integral part of Western society. Thus *da'wah* is not simply an activity of certain Muslim missionaries, though missionary groups have been and continue to be active, but the expectation is that all believers are under an obligation to share their commitment to Islam with their new fellow-citizens.

Beginning in the 1920s the most significant and sustained efforts by Muslim missionaries to convert Americans were those of the Ahmadiyya movement, from what was then northern India. The Ahmadis were particularly successful among African Americans, and Ahmadi women in full Islamic dress were among the most visible in the fledgling American Muslim community. Neither the Ahmadis nor members of the Nation of Islam are recognized by mainline Muslims today as "true Muslims," primarily because of claims made by their leadership of bringing a message from God, a claim seen as impugning the uniqueness of the status of Muhammad as the last Prophet. Likewise other sectarian movements that have developed over the last century—some still in existence and others having petered out—are judged by orthodox Muslims to be beyond the pale of Islam.

Da'wah activity has been adopted as an important responsibility by many of the Muslims who emigrated to America after the repeal of the Asia Exclusion Acts in 1943. It has also been a major commitment of Muslim foreign students on American campuses, with the Muslim Student Association functioning as the most effective instrument of propagation of the faith in the United States. That responsibility has been taken up by a number of Muslim organizations, most specifically the Islamic Society of North America (ISNA), the Islamic Circle of North America (ICNA), and the Tableeghi Jamaat, the last group primarily Indian and Pakistani and especially devoted to da'wah among the believers. Propagation of the faith has had the triple effect of maintaining the religion of the immigrants and their children, protecting them from the American environment, and providing a witness to the citizens of America. A number of foreign organizations that came into existence in the latter decades of the twentieth century have focused on da'wah activity in the United States. African Americans have concentrated their conversion work in the inner cities and particularly among prison populations.

For African Americans, and now perhaps it can also be said about Latino/Latinas, Native Americans, and other minority groups, one of the initially compelling attractions of Islam has been the challenge it seems to provide to the continuing reality of white racism and economic exploitation, and to the exclusion of people of color from the upper strata of American society. Gwendolyn Zohara-Simmons has written compellingly about her own earlier identification as an American black nationalist who found in the Nation of Islam a way of framing a response to racism and injustice at the same time that she and other black women and men were addressing their need for spirituality and religious faith. She identifies the Nation and other heterodox Muslim movements as venues for the expression of different forms of black nationalism on the part of converts. The movement itself addressed social, racial, and economic issues while its linkage with Islam provided the much-needed structure within the African American community for ethical and moral discipline, group identification (including a strong emphasis on family), and satisfying symbols and rituals. Black women could experience pride and confidence in their new identity and hope for an antidote to the increasingly shaky structures of black family life. That such sectarian movements as the Nation of Islam were not always successful in meeting those needs will be addressed next page.

With the transition of most of the members of the Nation to the leadership of Warith Deen Mohammed, many African American women either found themselves part of his evolving group or decided to join other branches of orthodox Islam. Their experiences have been detailed in the writings of Aminah Beverly McCloud and the recent study of Carolyn Moxley Rouse called *Engaged Surrender*. McCloud, one of the first scholars to examine African American women converts, talks of the tremendous appeal of Islam for African Americans who yearned to be acknowledged as fully human in light of the burning of crosses by the Christian Ku Klux Klan. Even the African American Christian church has been viewed as being complicit in the racist history of the United States. Islam provided a new kind of hope, one that allowed for a spiritual separation at the same time that it validated African Americans as a legitimate part of American society. McCloud says that Islam offered "the ultimate protest"—the shedding of the Christianity that had been forced on them but never helped them.

African American women have been important contributors to public efforts to formulate Islamic identity in the Western context, and they are increasingly vocal when they experience what they see as familiar forms of racial or gender oppression by their husbands or men of their community or by some Muslim immigrants, especially male leaders. For many black women, Islam truly has provided a vehicle for self-affirmation, participation in a welcoming community, and the practice of faith within a reasonable and manageable structure. They find the Islamic emphasis on the direct responsibility of the individual to God to be clear and refreshing. Some African American Muslim women are from very poor social and economic circumstances, are accustomed to being on welfare, and hope that Islam will offer them a better life. Others come to Islam from the context of black power groups, seeing in the religion a way of political participation as well as philosophical and spiritual satisfaction. Most Muslim women who are black choose to adopt Islamic dress and Islamic names and to participate as much as possible in Friday prayers and other mosque activities.

The later decades of the twentieth century saw increasing numbers of Anglo women finding that Islam provides an appealing, challenging, and viable way to meet their personal needs. Some women, of course, choose to adopt Islam because they want to marry Muslim men, despite the fact that Islamic law does not require a Christian or Jewish wife to convert. Conventional (and uninformed) American wisdom assumes that the only reason an American woman would want to become Muslim is to attract a husband or make herself acceptable to his family. The personal testimonies of convert women, however, indicate that many accept Islam out of conviction of the rightness of the faith rather than because of any factors relating to marriage, though such an assumption is difficult to prove.

Some have argued that Sufi Islam has served to attract the most Anglo women converts, although numbers are difficult to estimate and there are some indications that the appeal of Sufism is proportionately less than it was several decades ago. Marcia Hermansen reports from her studies of American Sufis that the spiritual seekers of the "flower children" days, who were drawn to elements of mystical Islam as well as of other religions, have declined in number and that membership in many of the spiritual movements that emerged in the so-called counterculture is graying and not being replaced. However, our research has found that American-born Muslims are increasingly interested in Sufism. Particularly attractive to American women are Sufi groups such as the Bawa Muhaiyadeen Fellowship in Philadelphia, established in the 1960s by a Sri Lankan Sufi. The Fellowship continues to thrive and attract converts, of whom a majority are women. Some converts confess that without Sufism, they would probably not have accepted Islam.

The first American Hispanics to convert to Islam were located in the barrios of the Northeast in the early 1970s. Primarily first-generation Puerto Ricans, they generally affiliated first with African American mosques. Organized Muslim missionary efforts since then have concentrated on Latino/Latina populations in various parts of the country, including the West Coast, as well as in prisons. Many are arguing for increased efforts at providing basic Islamic instruction in Spanish and for translating the Qur'an and other works into the Spanish language. Typical of the growing number of Muslim organizations devoted to *da'wah* in the Hispanic community are PIEDAD (Propagacion Islamica para la Educación y Devoción de Ala'el Divino), Alianza Islamica in New York, and ALMA (the Asociación Latina de Musulmanes en las Americas) in California.

Latinas and Native American women often see in Islam elements that resonate with their own cultures, such as respect for family and elders, appreciation of the rhythms of nature, and the integration of religious and spiritual beliefs with the whole of life. Numbers of Latino/Latina converts are rising to some extent due to intermarriage. Many Latinas find that Islam provides more effective resources than Christianity for dealing with urban problems such as gang wars, economic disadvantage, and various forms of ethnic strife. While Latinas may miss certain elements of their culture frowned on in Islam, such as music and dancing, drinking, and general effusive socialization (no one, of course, can monitor such activities as merengue and salsa music played softly within one's home), they affirm that the rewards are worth the sacrifice. Latina converts report that their new identity has given them strength, security, and confidence. For some, Muslim moral codes provide a relief from the harsh realities of racial identity in America such as the disproportionate number of people of color imprisoned for possession of drugs. Both African American and Latina women have found themselves incarcerated because of their connections with men involved in the trafficking of drugs. Islam, they believe, can provide a way to escape from that unhappy circumstance and restore the moral compass of their partners.

The Process of Conversion

Islam is available to potential converts in a variety of ways, including personal contact with Muslims, information supplied by Muslim organizations and Islamic centers, listening to taped lectures by Muslim luminaries, and investigating some of the many ways in which Islam is discussed on the Internet. Crucial for many new Muslims have been their initial encounters with Muslims—friends, boyfriends, spouses, and neighbors—who were willing to spend time sharing their own experiences and explaining various points in question. From beginning to end on the route to conversion, which many have described as a process rather than an event, such companions have served as mentors and guides. Converts often write that they were impressed by the inner peace, serenity, and strength of belief they witnessed in these Muslims.

Many women interested in Islam began researching the topic through reading and studying the Qur'an, learning about the cultural and political history of Islam, studying a variety of Islamic texts including philosophy and Sufism, and becoming familiar with the guides for Islamic living available everywhere from libraries to mosques to ethnic grocery stores. Sometimes as students in college or university classes they encountered information about Islam through class assignments or by hearing special lecturers. Many converts report that it was during this research that they first learned about the equal treatment of men and women in the Qur'an and the special rights afforded to women in Islamic law.

The Internet has become increasingly influential in helping potential converts understand the faith due to the plethora of information available online, in chat rooms, and through testimonials provided by those who want to share their pleasure at having joined the community of Islam. Literally hundreds of sites are ready for the viewing, and the opportunity to exchange questions, opinions, and even reservations with others who have gone through the process of contemplating conversion seems to be invaluable. In some cases converts initiate the search with the hope of finding material that will allow them to prove the falseness of Islam. Internet sites such as www.sistersinislam.net are designed specifically to assist Muslim women in understanding what is involved in adopting the new faith. A female-engendered site called AMILA (American Muslims Intent on Learning and Activism) purports to help its readers find freedom from emotional conflict and to encourage a sense of spirituality; the sponsor hopes that a progressive Islam may emerge. Sites intended for specific target audiences, such as Jews-for-allah.org, encourage readers to personally identify with the arguments being presented.

Often mosque communities are active in personal ways in helping new converts make the transition into sisterhood. Seminars especially for women are offered on the basics of Islam, how to perform the prayer, raising an Islamic family, reading and interpreting the Qur'an, and many other relevant topics. Occasionally, as in the All Dulles Area Muslim Society in Sterling, Virginia, converts are paired with other Muslims to serve as mentors. The emphasis is always on a combination of personal growth and knowledge and finding the support of a community ready to help at whatever point in the conversion process such assistance might be required.

The actual ceremony at which a new Muslima formally attests to her acceptance of Islam as her faith and community is quite simple. Technically consisting only of her declaration that she affirms the oneness of Allah and the prophethood of Muhammad (called the *shahadah*), the testimonial normally takes place in a communal context such as a mosque service. The convert may say something about herself and her experience before and during her adoption of Islam and then say what the new faith means to her. Two witnesses affirm that she has said the two parts of the *shahadah*. After this formal declaration the new Muslima is welcomed by members of the community with great enthusiasm, surrounded by her sisters who smile and hug her in affirmation of her new identity. This process of acclamation may take some time if the congregation is sizable. The new convert is made to understand that making the *shahadah* is in one sense the end of a journey and in another is the beginning of the process of learning how to assume her new identity as a Muslim.

It is clear that adopting Islam means more than simply "adding a religion" to one's curriculum vitae. For most new converts, being Muslim is a full time endeavor, involving them and their families in both private and public ways. A new Muslima may engage in the various duties and responsibilities of Islam privately, but she also must decide to what extent she wants to publicly identify herself with Islam in terms of dress, prayer in the workplace, adopting a new name, and generally being recognized as having undergone a transformation. Many converts acknowledge that this rethinking of public identity, of helping present the public face of Islam, is one of the most challenging aspects of the process of becoming Muslim. What, then, are some of the reasons why American women decide to take the important, and perhaps irreversible, step of becoming Muslim?

Islam Is Personally Compelling

Generally speaking, women tend to express their responses to Islam in several ways: personal, social, spiritual, and intellectual. Often individuals will cite all of these elements as reasons for their choice of a new religion. Many say that they have spent long periods of time studying the new faith and its texts, especially the Holy Qur'an. (The Yusuf Ali translation seems to be one that women find especially beautiful and inspirational. It provides a commentary with carefully selected interpretations that smooth over potentially controversial passages, especially those having to do with women.) For a number of women, study of the Qur'an appears to be the single most important element in their decision to adopt Islam. Many profess their amazement at its straightforwardness and logic: "It just makes sense! No matter how I try I can't argue with it." Many women find in Islam intellectually gratifying answers to their religious and philosophical questions. A number of female converts say that they have spent major portions of their lives in a long spiritual search, looking into many different religious traditions to try to fill what they describe as a kind of spiritual void. "Until I found Islam, with its beauty and its mixture of praising God and serving one another, I was desperately afraid I would always feel spiritually bereft."

In theological terms, converts report that the image of God in the Qur'an is clear and expresses the basic monotheism that they cherish: "What the Qur'an says about one God is what I have always known to be true." Some converts go so far as to affirm that the religion of Islam was chosen for them by God in such a clear and specific way that it was beyond their own volition. Others, in some sense echoing the classical Islamic tension between affirming God's absolute authority and also affirming human free will and responsibility, counter that the beauty of Islam lies in the ability and necessity of one's exercise of personal choice. The sense of being chosen for Islam comes from the frequently-cited Qur'anic verse 7:172 which states that when all humans were latent in the loins of Adam—that is, before creation itself—God appeared to all humanity and asked, "Am I not your Lord?" To that question all humanity said, "Yes," fostering the Islamic understanding that everyone in her or his basic core is essentially monotheist (or in the common Muslim understanding, really Muslim). Therefore, to many converts the act of conversion symbolizes the powerful feeling of "coming home."

Most women who are engaged by the teachings of Islam find the importance of community, especially the urgency of maintaining strong family units, to be one of its most attractive elements. Islam, they are taught, always situates the individual solidly within the context of the larger social unit, providing protection, communal identification, and support. "I will never have to think of myself as alone again—I am part of the wonderful large family of Islam." The very fact that fellow Muslims in America are greeted as sisters and brothers reinforces the familial image. All of this companionship and solidarity, of course, is seen to contrast vividly with the individuality of American society, which had often been experienced by converts as cold and impersonal. Such feelings are reinforced by the persuasive rhetoric of Muslims about the superiority of Islam.

Those who want to emphasize the familial and communal aspects of Islam, of course, may do so at the neglect of what many converts immediately recognize, namely, that unity is often challenged by the reality of competing ethnic and national identities. Converts are especially active in fostering the notion that what unites Muslims in one cooperative whole is far more important than the separateness of other competing identities. New Muslims may tend to romanticize the multiethnic and multiracial nature of Islam, glossing over its difficulties in the effort to promote the ideal of cultures and races in one harmonious mélange.

Women converts to Islam cite their concern not only for the isolating individualism of Western culture but also for what they see as the disintegration of the ethical and moral fabric of American life. Islam, by contrast, seems to offer a way of life whose structure and clear set of personal responsibilities serve both individually and corporately as a positive and constructive alternative: "I no longer have to worry that my daughter will become pregnant or involved with drugs. Islam provides a guide for my life and my family's life." Based on traditional values, Islam is seen by these women as an authentic and viable way to counter the problematic secular humanism that has come to characterize the American society that in earlier days had seemed to be so safe. Far from rejecting their identity as Americans, they find in Islam a more valid way of expressing the values that they believe to be consonant with the America they love.

While it may be an exaggeration to say that many women have converted to Islam explicitly because of the events of September 11, it is nonetheless true that the several intervening years have seen a marked growth of interest in Islam, at the same time that anti-Islamic sentiment seems also to be on the rise. Some women confess that they came to a deep appreciation of the faith precisely because it became obvious to them that this religion is the opposite of a terrorist-supporting, violent way of life. Joining the cause of countering such accusations led, in some cases, to the acceptance of Islam as a personal faith.

Islam Makes More Sense than Christianity

One of the most commonly cited reasons for the conversion of American women to Islam is their having seen the light, so to speak, about their discomfort with Christianity. Many women profess to having long struggled to understand Christian doctrines and to be greatly relieved to find what they consider to be the more straightforward tenets of the Islamic faith. Most of the women who cite religion per se as the reason for their conversion believe firmly in the theological superiority of Islam over Christianity. They reject the doctrine of original sin along with the Trinity and the divinity of Jesus.

The most common response of these women is to confess that they have come to believe that there are deep contradictions in Christianity. In contrast to the unity they hear stressed in Islam, or at least the ideal of a community committed to the worship of God, they wonder why there are so many different Christian sects, denominations, and churches. Who is going to be saved and who not, they ask, when Christians themselves have no commonly agreed-on answer? Former Roman Catholics in particular, but Protestants as well, report that as children they never received good answers to the questions they raised: "I have read the New Testament many times and found it full of ambiguities. Nobody has ever helped me sort it out." Potential converts in the process of learning about Islam sometimes report that they are encouraged to raise as many questions as possible, and those who are schooling them in the faith are rigorous in their attempts to provide answers. Often, however, these answers are ones that have been carefully developed over several centuries of encounter between Muslims and Christian missionaries to Islamic countries.

Roman Catholics seem to have particular questions about their (former) faith, such as what really happens to children who die before they are baptized, what it really means to say one is partaking of the body and blood of Christ at Communion, why there seems to be such inequity between priests and nuns, and why the "special status" of ordination is necessary. Many say that they find the seeming simplicity of Islamic doctrine and ethics to be both an intellectual and an emotional relief. Others critique the fact that certain branches of the Christian church seem to redefine their understanding of God simply to fit current trends or new scientific discoveries. "Give me a God who doesn't change according to fashion or political correctness, and who isn't male one day and female the next," these critics say. They stress the Islamic understanding of Allah, who is never defined according to gender. They find the Christian notion of the Trinity simply baffling in its complexity and the assertion that God is a male father and Jesus a male son to be sexist. Some have noted that they always found it hard to see the Old Testament and the New Testament as part of the same scripture; "Not only are they different in style, but the Old Testament clearly says that there is only one God while the New Testament, well especially Paul I guess, really seems to say that there are three despite the claim that these are simply aspects of one unity. I don't think God would have changed his mind!"

The Christian assertion that Jesus the man died on the cross and was resurrected, with the implication that this event serves as a means of salvation for all believers, is specifically denied in Islam. Among the many things converts have said they find unpalatable in the Christian faith is the idea that one is not personally accountable for his or her actions on the day of judgment and that Jesus has, in effect, already taken care of it for us. "Where is moral responsibility?" they ask. "Why should I take the hard road of trying to be good when I can do what I want and still be absolved?" Converts appreciate the action-consequence formula of Islam, whereby each person, male and female, is directly accountable for everything said and done during a lifetime.

Converts to any different way of thought and action are notoriously zealous in their critique of the old and defense of the new. Women who choose to adopt Islam are no different, and one can sense in their stories an eagerness to convince themselves that Islam is truly superior to Christianity in many important ways. Those who may miss the direct "love language" of the New Testament find consolation in the often-mentioned Qur'anic affirmation that God is merciful and compassionate and that implicit in the human response to God's oneness is the responsibility to always act towards others with integrity, love, and compassion.

While African American women cite many of the same reasons for their decision to embrace Islam, their critique of Christianity often includes bitterness and resentment towards the church. Christianity in general is criticized as supporting racism and sexism, and the African American church in particular is viewed as being complicit in the racist history of the United States. By contrast, black Islamic movements, especially the Nation of Islam (NOI), are seen as always having tried to reach poor blacks, as well as those who have broken the law. The NOI is often portrayed as fostering the idea of a classless brotherhood that welcomes the repentant into its fold, even by Muslims who may reject some of NOI doctrines. In its day the NOI was very effective in helping counter the accumulated psychological effects of slavery and racism on blacks, a task that African Americans assert that the black Christian church has failed to tackle effectively. More black men than black women convert from Christianity to Islam, a fact clearly related to a new sense of empowerment that they did not feel in their former religion.

Islam Is the Best Religion for Women

In direct contrast to what most Americans believe, female converts are persuaded that Islam is not only theologically and socially superior to Christianity, but is also the most supportive of women in a variety of ways. "I can understand why Christian missionaries have had so little success," says one. They love the idea of the bonds of female companionship that they are promised, above and beyond the emphasis on family stability. A few admit frankly to being tempted by Islam because they hope it will help them find a husband, and many say that they have more confidence that the marriage process will be facilitated by their Muslim sisters than by their preconversion friends. Most converts insist that they would never be part of a polygamous marriage, though they sometimes try to defend the system in theory because it is Qur'anically acceptable. A few insist that if circumstances permitted they would be amenable to the companionship and (perhaps) the economic advantages of having a co-wife.

While Western society delights in featuring images of oppressed Muslim women, converts are vocal in turning the tables and insisting that it is the West that exploits women because it does not know how to deal with sexuality. Rather than providing modest alternatives for dress and behavior such as are found in the Islamic system, the West with its emphasis on exposing the female body dressed as scantily as possible leaves women feeling exposed, vulnerable, and therefore powerless. The Muslim woman, on the contrary, especially one who chooses to dress Islamically (which a large number of converts do), is freed from having to portray herself as a desirable sex object and can follow her pursuits without being under the wandering gaze of men. "Thank goodness I don't have to struggle into a size six dress anymore, or pay a fortune to have my hair done every week." Female allure—never undervalued in Islam—is reserved for one's husband.

Modest behavior as well as modest dress, argues the convert, fosters an atmosphere in which male respect replaces male lust, providing for a much more truly equitable public relationship between men and women than is normally possible in Western society. (Such a relationship does not necessarily pertain in the context of marriage.) Converts are taught early, and find it easy to accept, that Islam was one of the first of the great religions to treat women fairly. They recognize, of course, that such parity has not always been reached in Muslim societies and certainly has not been achieved in most parts of the world today. Part of their defense of "true Islam" is a serious critique of cultures in which women are isolated, debased, and forced into circumstances that support only male egos and opinions. Muslims understand that while Islam, according to the Qur'an (5:3), is perfect, they must constantly struggle to concretize this idealized society.

One of the areas in which converts sometimes find themselves in disagreement with their sisters, both new and born to the faith, is the extent to which relations between men and women (especially in the home) are idealized as truly equal. Many prefer the term equitable (more or less equal but different). They argue that a woman's primary vocation is in the home as wife and that only secondarily, or if necessary financially, should she enter the public domain for employment. They feel quite comfortable with the assurance that raising children is their main responsibility and that they will be provided for financially and otherwise by the males of the family. This argument is particularly potent in the face of what they see as disintegrating family values and relationships in the United States. Others, particularly if they have been raised during the decades of burgeoning Western feminist movements, argue that the beauty of Islam is that it allows for cooperation in all things between men and women, both in determining the affairs of the household and in holding their own in the workplace.

Those women who are looking into Islam for the first time are always impressed by the religious and spiritual equality afforded to men and women in the Qur'an. Both genders are accorded equal rights and responsibilities and an equal measure of accountability in the hereafter. They also affirm their appreciation for the emphasis that most moderate Muslims today, certainly those in leadership positions in America, put on the importance of fully educating females as well as males. A major part of the Islam's appeal to potential converts is the Islamic emphasis on the positive value of being a woman, both a wife and a mother, and also a partner in all dimensions of married and social life.

Despite all these affirmations and positive experiences, however, things are not always as rosy as converts may have expected or hoped for. The realities of being a new member of an established community, or one in the process of negotiating its identity, soon impinge, and converts recognize that their problems are not all solved simply by the act of becoming Muslim.

Contending with Reality

Religiously or spiritually speaking, most converts believe that the advantages of being Muslim far outweigh whatever one might lose by leaving their former religious affiliations, or feel glad simply to have found a viable religion at all. Most of them understand, at the same time, that leaving patterns of belief and response that have fashioned them since childhood is not an easy process. "I have always been so close to Jesus," said one, "that it is like deserting my best friend as well as losing the person whom I have known as my savior." Another says that the whole process of making such a decision was so painful she felt like the devil was taking her on one wrong turn after another: "How do I know what I really believe? Why are my sister Muslims so sure about this decision and I am torn one way and another?" Most converts affirm that once the decision is made the torment and confusion cease and they are at peace and sure that they belong to Islam.

Fear of conversion manifests itself in ways other than strictly religious. Many are deeply concerned that making such a life-changing decision, particularly given the negative depiction of Islam in the press, will lead to deep division in their own families and even outright rejection. Carol Anway's popular book, *Daughters of Another Path*, details the agonies she and her family underwent when her daughter dated and married a Muslim, then became Muslim herself, and finally adopted Islamic dress. While Anway's situation improved greatly because of her own perseverance in understanding Islam, the fear of family tension is undoubtedly real and a major factor in the decision of any potential woman convert. Some parents have frankly told their daughters who have become Muslim that they have betrayed them, their relatives, and the ethics and values of their upbringing. It is particularly disturbing for some mothers and fathers when their daughters choose to wear clothing that they as parents believe to be confining, unattractive, and even embarrassing.

Some converts, of course, say that their families are fully accepting of their choice, even expressing relief that the woman in question has finally settled into a reliable way of life. "I thought my daughter would never settle down," said one mother. "I'm delighted that she has found religion, and it hardly matters which one!" "Thank goodness my daughter will not have to go to work every day now, and can count on the support of a reliable husband," said another. Even families who are overtly accepting of the new reality, however, often lack the resources, or the knowledge, to make their homes comfortable for a Muslim daughter or sister. For women who want to follow the rules of diet and purity there may be problems with food, cooking utensils, and, especially if dogs are present, with finding clean and appropriate space for prayer. Families of converts sometimes feel that they are the ones to make all the compromises while new Muslims appear rigid and uncooperative. "I really can't understand why she has to be so insistent about everything," said one mother. "I'm doing my best but when I have to buy new pots and pans because I may have cooked bacon in them I think that's too much!"

Few women considering conversion are willing to discuss their reservations, especially in light of the enthusiasm of their sisters at their new status. But some confide that little things seemed very big, at least in the beginning. "I'm really not a racist, or at least I hope not," said one, "but the fact is that people of color are still discriminated against and that's what Muslims are considered to be—not white!" "I'm not really sure Muslims have much fun. I love to have boyfriends, date, and go to parties. I'm afraid my old friends will think I have become boring and strange." "Would I have to leave my husband if I converted? Because I know that he isn't going to want to be a Muslim. What if he wants to divorce me and tries to take the children?" "My job is really important to me and I don't want to lose it. What will my boss think if I suddenly show up with a scarf covering my hair? Should I just not wear one to work even though I think as a Muslima I ought to? Will my colleagues want to eat lunch with me?" "So many people now think Muslims are terrorists, and I guess some of them in some countries really are. How will I handle it if people think I am joining a scary religion like that?"

When a woman actually decides to convert, some of the fears are naturally realized. Few new Muslims would say that the decision was not worth it and that the liabilities outweigh the benefits. Nonetheless, life in the new fold clearly is not without its painful moments. The sisterhood for which many of these women longed may be present to a greater or lesser extent, but it is also often hard to achieve when one has to cross ethnic and cultural barriers. Immigrant women may be quite bossy in their attempts to insist that Islam must be practiced according to certain cultural variations. A new Muslim may have difficulty determining what is Islamic and what is cultural and may not be easily accepted by the established female community if she is unwilling to accept their "suggestions" as to what is appropriate behavior. This may be a special problem for an American woman who marries into a Muslim family of immigrant origin. Immigrant sisters, on the other hand, sometimes feel that convert women are a bit "pushy" and too eager to make them participate publicly in the presentation of Islam in ways that make them feel uncomfortable.

For new Muslims of any ethnic group, being a single woman in a community that puts extremely high value on the family can be very difficult. Muslim sisters sometimes complain that new converts are depleting the limited supply of Muslim men, given the fact that women, as prescribed by Islamic law, cannot marry outside of the faith and the pool is therefore limited. Muslim women may find it hard to include single women in their activities, which are generally either family-oriented or are women's groups in which talk about husbands and children dominates. In some cases the pressure to marry may lead to a new Muslima committing to a relationship or marriage with a Muslim man before she is ready or really wants to. If the union is actualized in too great a hurry, however, the couple may well find that they are incompatible and unable to live together.

Many converts are often quite well informed about Islam, usually having given considerable time to its study before making the decision to convert. Often they are leaders in mosque organization, planning social events, religious instruction, scout troops, and Qur'an study groups. Because indigenous American women may be more comfortable making public presentations than their immigrant sisters, they are often called on to "represent Islam" by giving talks or participating in interfaith dialogue sessions. However, some find that because they may not be familiar with the many cultural and even theological variations of Islam as it has developed historically and geographically, their apparent ignorance is easily revealed in public presentations. This then may cause their Muslim sisters to criticize them for misrepresentation of the faith. A convert also may be put in an uncomfortable position if she is expected to espouse publicly a certain political position in regard to events in Muslim countries about which she may not know much or even be in agreement with her immigrant sisters.

While some women have in fact realized their dreams of finding community with Muslim sisters, despite differences in their ethnic identities, others have expressed their disappointment at the difficulty they have experienced "breaking in." In general both black and Caucasian converts feel welcome at African American mosques, although joining in black community life may not be easy for white converts. Converts may find themselves more comfortable in small, interethnic communities than trying to affiliate with groups that have a distinct cultural and ethnic identity that they do not share.

In some cases, converts admit that after the excitement of the conversion ceremony itself they have never been contacted by the sisters whose companionship they wanted. Sometimes the Muslim women who are most active in da'wah are actually not regular mosque attenders and fail to be in touch with new converts after they make the shahadah.

This experience of loneliness is also true of some, though certainly not all, young women who have experienced their conversion in the context of college or university life. While most profess themselves very happy with their new status as Muslims and feel part of Muslim community life on campus, a few are disappointed at the lack of social cohesion. "Once I actually became Muslim the girls who had helped me learn about Islam seemed to disappear. I can't relate easily to my non-Muslim friends anymore, and I feel more lonely than I had imagined." Da'wah activity is an important ingredient of some Muslim Student Association groups, but the socializing often seems to be determined along different lines. "The Egyptian girls I know from the MSA were very happy when I joined, but I am never invited to their rooms or even out for coffee."

Accommodations for women in mosques are troublesome for some converts who may have been raised in churches or synagogues where men and women sit together. While they agree that mixing is not the best way to worship, they question why separation need be hierarchical. "I'm OK with not sitting in front of or next to a man when we worship, even my husband. But I don't see why women need to be in a completely different place, especially when it is a closed room apart from the men. There is no other word for it but segregation." Having difficulty with new languages may present a real problem for converts, including not knowing enough Arabic to understand a sermon or the details of the prayer ritual. When one is not familiar with the spoken dialect of whatever immigrant group one may be most naturally drawn to, it is very hard to establish the much-cherished communication and fellowship with its members, both female and male.

Despite their assertions about gender balance in Islam, the reality of expressions of patriarchy has been a bit disillusioning for some converts. In the 1950s and 1960s, many African American women became part of the Nation of Islam precisely because they had had enough of sexism in the black community. Several women who have since left the movement decry the secondary status of women in the NOI and are active in campaigning in their Sunni or Shi'ite communities for the kind of equality between the sexes that they believe is at the heart of Islam. Gwendolyn Zohara-Simmons describes the propaganda projected by Elijah Muhammad, who said that women are less intellectually capable than men and more susceptible to the whisperings of Satan. Simmons worries that some of this attitude has carried over into African American Sunni groups today.

Also problematic for some women raised to question patriarchy wherever it is found is the near-absolute authority granted to the imam in many mosques or Islamic centers. They generally do not object to male leadership in worship but question why other women look to the imam to make decisions about virtually all community matters. As is becoming clear to most Muslims in America, imams may or may not have adequate credentials in terms of Qur'an and Islamic law, but in most cases they certainly are not trained to understand the vicissitudes of American culture or the subtleties of human relationships needed for personal counseling. In a range of ways they find that the very patriarchy they believe is absent in the Islam to which they are now devoting themselves is often alive and well in the real-life functioning of the community.

Likewise, in the case of some converted women, the hopes for assistance in finding an appropriate husband may be subtly thwarted. African American and Anglo Muslims are no more likely to marry one another than non-Muslim blacks and whites in American society. Blacks generally marry into the black community or sometimes marry Latino/Latinas and Bangladeshis. White converts sometimes encounter greater difficulty getting married, because the numbers of Anglo male converts are still relatively low, and young men from immigrant backgrounds often succumb to family pressures to marry "within the group." Women who have struggled and sacrificed to assume a Muslim identity may find these efforts at exclusion to be both frustrating and painful. Many marriages between convert American women and Muslim men are highly successful and satisfying and serve to justify the woman's confidence in the Islamic family structure. At other times pressures from the adopted family may be both irritating and highly stressful: "I love my mother-in-law a lot and I try to respect her wishes. But she thinks she can stick her nose into all of our private affairs, and I find that really unacceptable. My husband, to make matters worse, doesn't see why I get so annoyed!"

African American women who convert to Islam may also set themselves up for some amount of disillusion. The social justice they expected in Islam may not include the active support of immigrant Muslims for the problems that plague the black community, and blacks themselves may not want to espouse the various international causes so close to the hearts of their co-religionists. The ethnocentricity of some immigrant communities may mean there is little tolerance for African Americans who are newly come to the faith. Certain Islamic restrictions, such as a general ban on most kinds of music, can be difficult to accept. Many blacks experience difficulties in keeping their jobs when they appear in Islamic dress. Those who continue in the welfare system find that the already-humiliating experience of being "on the dole" is made even more difficult if social workers respond in prejudicial ways to their being Muslim.

Sexism and racism, both of which African Americans believe to be absent in Islam in its ideal form, continues to surface, and black women are beginning to actively identify what they often experience as the triple whammy of being black, female, and Muslim. Robert Dannin, in his ethnographic research on African American converts, cites examples to illustrate that sexual politics and gender stereotyping continue to be problematic for Muslim converts in the United States. He relates the story of a young female activist who converted because of her fiancé but faced suspicious women in the mosque for reasons of her status as a single women, her lack of desire to be a mother, and her light complexion. As a result she spent more time with her fiancé and his male friends, which increased the hostility of the other Muslim women. She ended up canceling the engagement and not returning to the mosque.

African American converts may also feel excluded from the larger community of immigrant Islam. Sometimes the alternative for such women, as Aminah McCloud observes in her fictional sketches of three African American convert women, is to adopt a less rigorous and less visible version of Islam that allows them to escape prejudice in the workplace and maintain connections with the black non-Muslim community. African American converts also complain that immigrants tend to be more enthusiastic about new Anglo members of the community than they are about blacks. African Americans thus experience racism again, this time in the very religion they believed could offer an alternative. This concern is only heightened when they observe that immigrants sometimes hope that their children will marry white converts so as to produce lighter-skinned offspring. McCloud is articulate about her experiences with women in other Muslim communities who are very ethnocentric and states that this is one reason why African American women are generally not introduced to Islam by other Muslim women but by their husbands. McCloud argues that African American women wearing the *hijab* are treated with more hostility than immigrant women. Americans seem to accept that women from other parts of the Muslim world may look different, while not accepting such difference on the part of African Americans.

Still, almost all black women who adopt Islam believe that, despite the difficulties, it is far preferable to the racism and sexism of general American culture. As numbers grow and communities solidify, women are finding in their sisters a positive sense of support and solidarity. The strong affirmation of the family generated by Elijah Muhammad in the old Nation of Islam has been continued by Imam Warith Deen Mohammed, and provides a welcome change from the broken families and fatherless homes which many have experienced.

Converts of whatever race or ethnic group face the critique of other American women for the choices they have made. In general, American society finds it difficult to accept such a choice. Not surprisingly, clothing is probably the subject of the most criticism; most non-Muslims just cannot understand why covering is necessary. "I heard a young Muslim convert say that clothing can give you peace. It sounds more like a security blanket to me. She thinks that by dressing Islamically she can protect herself. She must be suffering from some kind of paranoia!" American women are also very skeptical about the claims that women are granted more rights in Islam than in other religions; "I have heard too many stories about how Muslim husbands treat their wives, so I wonder if converts won't let themselves see the truth, or if they are not free to tell the real story."

Conservative Christians are often the most concerned about new converts to Islam. If a convert was not involved in a Christian church before, many Christians tend to say that "this would never have happened to her" if she had been raised in a strong Christian family. Muslims find it ironic that these may be the same Christians who belong to churches and denominations that are eagerly seeking to convert Muslims to Islam both in America and abroad.

The reasons for women's conversion to Islam range over many different kinds of needs and opportunities and are only beginning to be explored and discussed. For some American women, Islam has a spiritual, intellectual, or emotional appeal apart from social concerns, while for others it is a choice precipitated by frustration with Western norms and/or the desire to become part of a larger social unit. Some converts are engaged or married to Muslim men. There is no doubt that female converts play a major role in the constitution of American Islam. As Karin Van Nieuwkerk observes, a major reason why Islam has become one of the major players in the Western "religious market" is because its message makes sense to individual converts. Caucasian, African American, Latina, and women of other ethnic groups in the United States and Canada are finding in Islam answers to some of their most pressing personal and social concerns.

The degree of convert women's active participation in American culture varies widely. Some women choose to identify as closely as possible with the Islamic culture of their husbands, comporting themselves in ways often seen as more traditional than contemporary, more private than public. Sometimes conversion is initiated and encouraged by Muslim religious organizations or collectivities and fostered in an atmosphere of close religious and communal support. In such cases women generally articulate clearly their affirmation of the tenets of the Islamic faith as well as its particular obligations and rituals, including dress and other external modes of recognition. Still others may consider themselves Muslim in a private and personal way, eschewing either public identification with the faith by wearing Islamic dress or even a headscarf, and rarely if ever participating in a mosque or Islamic organization. In any case, it is apparent that a number of the women who decide to convert are contributing significantly to the current discourse about Islam and its changing role in Western society in general and American culture in particular.

4

Practices of the Faith

Muslim women who choose to actively practice their faith may do so in a variety of ways, reflecting factors such as sectarian affiliation, personal piety, family conditioning, individual preference, and changing social and political circumstances. There are many ways in which to describe the variety of activities through which a woman might put into practice her devotion to God. We have chosen here to group these practices into three main categories: mosque attendance and participation in mosque-related activities, observance of the five "pillars" or duties expected of all Muslims, and the involvement of increasing numbers of women in learning and teaching the traditional religious sciences of Islam.

Women's Changing Roles in the Mosque

On the eve of Ramadan, 2003, a young Muslim woman walked through the main door of a mosque in Morgantown, West Virginia, and sat down to attend Friday prayers. Many Americans might not find this surprising and would perhaps have difficulty understanding why it has stirred the imagination of some young Muslim women. The concern at this mosque was her audacity in breaking tradition. The main entrance of the mosque had been designated specifically for men, and the prayers were taking place on the main floor of the mosque, which is where men traditionally assemble. When asked to leave, Asra Nomani refused.

While many, perhaps most, Muslim women might not agree with the challenge posed by this act and see it as unnecessarily confrontational, others are finding it engaging. One person compared it to the statement made by Rosa Parks in her celebrated refusal to sit in the back of the bus. The young journalist who defied tradition by daring to occupy the male section of the mosque won no popularity contest with the mosque leadership, although her father has supported her from the beginning. She and her colleagues, however, see themselves as working to foster equality for women in the house of worship, as well as fair representation on mosque governing boards. If Islam is truly democratic and the greater *ummah* or community is truly Islamic, she has argued—echoing the affirmations of many Muslim leaders in response to Western critique—women must be treated as full and equal participants. She asked for the support of the Islamic Society of North America in the battle for women's rights. Although insisting that such issues must be addressed at the local level, ISNA leaders said that they were supportive of this struggle and mediated the issue.

Both ISNA and CAIR (Council for American-Islamic Relations) have indicated that better preparation of mosque leadership—including that of women—is high on their agenda and are working to provide educational programs to help achieve this end. In June of 2005 ISNA published a pamphlet entitled "Toward Women Friendly Mosques." Nomani addressed the 2004 ISNA national convention on women's rights in mosques. Since her initial act of protest, more women have joined in the effort to empower Muslim women in the mosque. Nomani herself has written a book, titled *Standing Alone in Mecca: An American Woman's Struggle for the Soul of Islam* (2005), describing her experiences on the pilgrimage to Mecca before 9/11 and her subsequent efforts to fight for the rights of Muslim women.

Many immigrant women come from cultures in which women seldom if ever attend the mosque. While few scholars disagree that the Prophet Muhammad not only allowed but even encouraged the participation of both women and men in communal worship, this has not been the general practice in Islamic societies. Muslim women in the United States for generations have been able to attend the mosque if they want to. They also have been significant players in the efforts to actually establish mosques, as in the case of several Lebanese mosques of the early twentieth century. They have supported the activities of the institution by participating in numerous fund-raising ventures, such as selling baked goods, collecting for rummage sales, and soliciting funds door to door. Except in houses of worship established by South Asians and a few Salafis who adhere to traditional customs, women have played, and continue to play, key roles in mosque social activities as well as in various forms of education. They often help the mosque to serve as a point of community cohesion. Princeton University Professor Amany Jamal, working with the Columbia University study on Muslims in New York City, emphasizes the civic roles played by many mosques in comparison to their exclusive function overseas as prayer halls.

There is no question that many immigrants, both men and women, are finding it difficult to break with traditional customs of role separation in mosques, even if they support the equal participation of men and women in most other public arenas. Increasing numbers of American women who identify religiously with Islam do attend the mosque for various kinds of prayers, including the communal prayers of Friday afternoon (the traditional time for congregational worship). For some of the immigrants attendance is required only of men, a fact increasingly challenged by women who insist that the Prophet's wives attended the prayers. Sunday morning prayers, an American innovation both to accommodate the realities of the work week and to provide a time for children's education, are held at most mosques. A national survey reports that some 15 percent of mosque attendees at Friday prayer observances are women. More women prefer Sunday to Friday prayers, seeing them as more family-oriented.

Mosques and Islamic centers in America, some 1500 in number, vary greatly in terms of both size and construction. Less affluent groups may worship in converted houses or storefronts, or even in churches that they rent or have bought and refurbished. Communities with more resources may decide to construct large and well-equipped mosques, often as part of larger Islamic centers. During the 1970s and 1980s such construction was often financed, or supplemented, by oil-rich Islamic countries, although this support mostly ceased after 1991. Many of these purpose-built houses of worship constructed after the 1960s have allowed for separate entrances and facilities for women. In Dearborn, Michigan, a mosque built by early Lebanese immigrants, in which women were very active, was taken over by the growing community of Yemeni immigrants; women now worship in the basement.

American mosques in earlier generations were often the locus of social occasions such as wedding celebrations (including folk dancing) and other "seasonal" activities. Immigrants coming afterwards in the 1960s looked with disdain at such activities, which they considered to be much too Americanized. Although conservative leadership has tried to eliminate such practices from the house of worship, coming together for different kinds of social activities is an important feature of mosque life. Many mosques in the United States function in ways that are more like churches and synagogues than mosques abroad. Today in America mosques serve as community centers, welfare organizations, and sites for voter registration drives and political campaigns, as well as offering classroom instruction and facilities for social gatherings. In most cases women are active in all of these new mosque functions.

Very few Muslim women say that they want to worship side by side with men. At issue is the physical nature of the prayer in which worshippers stand shoulder to shoulder, foot to foot, and which requires the position of prostration. "I don't want men to look at me like that and be distracted from their attention to God," goes the argument, "nor do I wish to look directly at the rear parts of men during the prayer." Separation of the sexes is handled in a variety of ways in different mosques. In fairly rare circumstances men pray on one side of the hall and women on the other, with a small barrier separating them, as is the case in Toledo, Ohio. The most common style in African American as well as most immigrant mosques is to have men pray at the front part of the hall and women at the rear. Other arrangements have men worshiping on the main floor of the prayer hall with women praying behind some kind of curtain or barrier, in a balcony from which they can look down and observe the imam, or in a completely separate room where they participate in the prayer service via loudspeaker or on closed-circuit television. When space is severely limited women may find themselves worshiping in less desirable areas such as hallways or basements. Despite the fact that the Fiqh (legal ruling) Council of North America has determined that according to the Islamic law it is not necessary that any kind of partition separate men and women during worship, national figures suggest that approximately two-thirds of Muslim women who attend the mosque pray separately. It is this separation that a few younger women are now actively challenging.

Despite the historical interest of women in seeing their local mosques succeed in their various tasks, until recently women have seldom played institutional leadership roles in their places of worship. In most branches of American Islam, imams, or prayer leaders who in the U.S. function much like priests and rabbis, are always men when the congregation is of mixed gender. In the penal system and in the military women serve as imams for women, but not for men. A few lone voices are occasionally raised in America, sometimes by South African or African American scholars, calling for the institution of women as imams. So far such appeals have not elicited much attention or support, although the Agha Khan, leader of the Ismai'ili Shi'ite community, has given approval for a few women imams to lead the prayer for both men and women, as has Louis Farrakhan, leader of the Nation of Islam.

On March 18, 2005, an event occurred that has been interpreted by some, but certainly not all, Muslims as a courageous first attempt to prove that women have every Islamic right to lead both men and women in prayer. It was picked up by American, British, and Arab TV, discussed at great length by legal scholars, and debated in internet chat rooms. At the Synod House of the Cathedral of St. John the Divine in New York City (several mosques and Muslim Student Associations refused to host the event) African American Muslim scholar-activist Amina Wadud of Virginia Commonwealth University became the first Muslim woman on public record to lead a mixed-gender jum'ah or Friday prayer. Professor Wadud, whose contribution to the interpretation of the Qur'an is noted in chapter 8 ("Competing Discourses"), not only led the prayer but also gave the sermon, or khutbah, to some 80 worshippers and a large number of journalists. Some observers accused the group who staged the event of pulling a publicity stunt to promote the latest book of supporter Asra Nomani, titled *Standing Alone in Mecca*. Adding to the controversial nature of the occasion was the fact that some of the women, rather than occupying traditional prayer space either behind the men or in a separate balcony, sat to pray with men in the front rows of the gallery. The effort was sponsored by the organization called Muslim Wake-Up! as part of its effort to reclaim the right of women to be the spiritual equals of men and to assume leadership roles that reflect the Islamic values of tolerance, justice, equality, and compassion.

While virtually all Muslim jurisprudents agreed that Wadud had gone "too far" and that nothing in the law or Sunnah allows for this kind of worship, some observers believe that Nomani, Wadud, and their colleagues may have nudged the lid off Pandora's box and that more such efforts will follow. Even before the Wadud event, in November of 2004, a second-year female student at York University in Toronto also broke with tradition when she became what at that time was generally acknowledged to be the first woman to give a *khutbah* to a congregation of mixed gender in America (Wadud herself gave a *khutbah* in South Africa a decade ago). At the United Muslim Association near Toronto Maryam Mirza delivered the second part of the sermon at the *al-fitr* service celebrating the end of Ramadan, following the message delivered by Imam Ali Jabar. "Women have the ability to be leaders—why not in prayer, why not in religion?" asked Imam Jabar in justification of this tradition-breaking move. While the congregation of the mosque, mainly from Guyana and the Caribbean, supports Mirza, others in the Islamic Council of Imams of Canada clearly do not. A female may preach to other females, said one, but never since the time of the Prophet has a woman given a sermon in the mosque. (More historical research is needed to discover whether this claim is really true.) Acknowledging that most Muslims are going to object, Mirza's father says that they are just trying to break the ice. They know, he admits, that it will not be easy.

Less controversial, perhaps, but apparently the first event of its kind, a Muslim woman recently officiated at a Muslim marriage. "While, in theory, there was nothing to prohibit it," says Brandeis University postdoctoral fellow Kecia Ali, an expert in Islamic marriage law, "no one wanted to be the one to actually break the unspoken barrier." But early in 2004 Ali did break it, and, in the front of a ballroom filled with immigrant Muslims, mainly Pakistanis dressed in wedding finery, she gave a brief sermon in Arabic and a longer talk in English on marriage and officiated as the bride and groom exchanged their vows. Ali checked with fellow legal authorities, and concluded that there is no legal obstacle to a woman performing a Muslim wedding, although surely it is a remarkable break with tradition. The wedding went off with no hitch, and Ali reports that almost everyone was quite positive about her new role. People seem to recognize that times are changing, she concludes, and that it is good that Muslims are changing along with them just so long as the basic laws of Islam are not contravened. Ali has since discovered that a few Sufi women also have performed Islamic marriages.

In most Islamic centers and mosques in the United States, major operational decisions often are made not by the imams but by lay leadership in the form of governing boards and committees. These boards have generally been made up of men, although that reality is slowly changing. The small but growing group of young Muslim women who are arguing for what they see as their Islamically guaranteed rights in the mosque want greater and more direct role in governance. Many mosques and Islamic centers are taking steps to ensure that women are actively represented on their executive committees, especially since 9/11. Surveys indicate that about half of the immigrant mosques in America do allow women to serve on their governing boards. While perhaps only a quarter or so actually fulfill that promise, such changes must be seen as revolutionary, because having a woman in a comparable leadership position in virtually any Muslim country is still unheard of. Generally speaking, African American mosques today have the highest number of women leaders—over 80 percent allow women on their boards—and profess themselves to be quite open to female participation. South Asians have the fewest female board participants, and Arab mosques are somewhere in the middle. Some mosques have elected women to their governing boards because of their particular legal and/or financial expertise. The fact still remains, however, that in most mosques men dominate the decision-making activity, while women end up doing the hands-on work.

In both northern and southern California women have been pushing for greater inclusion and do enjoy a higher level of participation. They are encouraged by many among the Arab male leadership there, although Salafis are against it, as are many in the traditional Indian subcontinent leadership. The Islamic Center of Southern California has had several women board members over the years and is receptive to the efforts of women to enjoy full and active participation in most aspects of its work. In Winnipeg, Manitoba, modest but important measures are being taken, such as including women in prayer space and providing child care to allow women to participate more fully in mosque activities. Until recently, the president of the congregation at the Islamic Center of Greater Toledo, one of the largest and most beautiful mosques in America, was a female attorney. A mosque in Long Island had a woman as chairperson of the board in the 1990s. Many Muslim women serve their mosques as fund-raisers and primary spokespersons for Islam in community presentations, interfaith dialogues, and efforts for da'wah.

What do Muslim women themselves think about the incipient changes, if in fact they come about, in traditional mosque life? Given the huge diversity of the community, it is no surprise that responses differ. Nothing resembling a nationally organized movement has been established, and women working in one area may not be aware of the activities of those operating elsewhere. Some women, as we have seen, not only welcome change but are actively trying to make it happen. Others believe firmly that while the very fact of living in a Western environment inevitably means changes in culture and practice, the mosque should remain a symbol of traditional values and a model of a different kind of male-female relationship than that advocated by Western feminists. Thus, many new mosque structures with traditional separate entrances for women and separate places of worship are being built by Muslims who are well educated, professionally successful, and ideologically certain that the preservation of gender distinctions in the place of prayer is essential.

Some women very much enjoy the relative freedom they experience sitting with their children in the company of other women. They are able not only to share a "woman's prayer experience" but also to socialize in a relaxed manner in the company of women to whom they may not be physically related but who function as their "surrogate" sisters, mothers, aunts, and other relatives. Many other women, when asked what they think about new women's roles in the mosque, simply sigh and say that it is extremely difficult for real change to come about, especially since men seem to have such a vested interest in controlling things. "I suppose men just feel afraid that we will give away too much to American culture," said one, "and are threatened that they will no longer be making the decisions." But women also recognize that change is inevitable, and a few even go so far as to say that if men do not loosen things up, so to speak, some mosques may find themselves without the participation, and support, of women at all.

Observance of the Pillars of Islam

As they are traditionally listed, the five pillars or religious responsibilities required of all Muslims are recognition of the oneness of God and the Prophethood of Muhammad, ritual prayer five times each day, fasting during the month of Ramadan, paying zakat (alms-tax), and going on pilgrimage to the holy city of Mecca at least once in a lifetime if one can afford it. Many, if not most, Muslim women in the West choose not to observe all of these specific expectations and remain uninvolved in any religious practices. Some observers, however, feel that the proportion of those who do choose to follow the rules, observe the rituals, and participate in related festivities seems to be growing.

New Muslims acknowledge their affiliation with Islam by publicly taking the *shahadah*, the testimony that there is only one God and that Muhammad is his Prophet. The *shahadah* is part of the call to prayer as well as the ritual prayer itself, and on various special occasions, including the birth of a child,

Muslim women (and men) include the *shahadah* as part of a prayer of celebration. A Muslim testifies to God's oneness by trying to act with mercy and justice in all the affairs of daily life, and to the Prophethood of Muhammad by following his example (called the Sunnah of the Prophet) in as many ways as possible.

Prayer, the second of the stated Muslim required activities, generally is understood in the sense of *salat* or formalized, ritualized prayer. According to Islamic tradition it must be performed at five set times during the day—dawn, noon, midafternoon, dusk, and in the late evening, with the understanding that for the Muslim all of life is a prayer. At the appointed times Muslims who choose to observe the prayer stop what they are doing, perform ablutions and give thanks to God, put down something to serve as a prayer rug, turn their faces toward Mecca, and go through the prostrations.

For women, as for men, performing the *salat* at the prescribed times may raise a number of social and professional issues. A woman who is employed in a public profession may need to negotiate with her employer for an appropriate place to wash in preparation for the prayer, a space either near her working area or somewhere more private for undertaking the prostrations (which generally last about five minutes), and permission to "be away from the desk," so to speak, at regular intervals. In some ways this operation is becoming easier as the American public becomes more aware of how religiously observant Muslims want to practice their faith. In other ways, however, it is perhaps more difficult insofar as what may be perceived by co-workers as "oddities," such as full prostration, have the potential to feed into growing public apprehension about Islam and its observance in America. Women who insist on time and space for *salat*, like those who insist on wearing some kind of head covering, may find that they are overlooked for promotions, or, even more worrying, that their jobs are in jeopardy. Some schools of Islamic law are fairly flexible in providing for the possibility of combining the required *salat*, so a woman who finds it inconvenient to pray at one time may be able to double up her prayers at another time. Some women concentrate their prayer time in the morning, doing so immediately after showering since they have, in effect, already done the requisite washing or ablution. Others find combining several prayers in the evening, or before bedtime, is the best solution for a lifestyle with many demands.

Other forms of prayer besides the ritualized *salat* are encouraged in Islam. Women over the centuries in many countries and contexts have turned to the *du'a*, or private prayer of supplication intended for the ears and heart of God. In the *salat* one does not offer personal petitions; those are reserved for moments in which the believer shares her gratitude, or fears and concerns, with the higher power who alone has the ability to respond. In traditional Islamic cultures especially pious persons, usually deceased, have served in a kind of "intercessory" role for women who find the possibility of speaking directly with God to be too intimidating. This kind of cult of saints generally has not had a chance to take hold in America, although some Sufis, both alive and deceased, play extremely important roles in the lives of some women here.

Participating in the *dhikr*, or ritual ceremony of Sufi orders, in America is particularly appealing to some women. The *dhikr* itself, which may take the form of dance, chanting, or some other physical or vocal repetition in ac- knowledgement of the presence of God, serves as a kind of participatory prayer. In certain cases, as, for example, the American branch of the Turkish Mevlevi Order of Dervishes, a few women are learning traditional practices of movement or so-called "whirling" that have always been reserved for men, which is a matter of some consternation for traditionalist Sufis. While Saudi students in the United States and some Salafi Sunni congregations condemn *dhikr* as un-Islamic, since they consider the songs in praise of the Prophet Muhammad to be excessive, Muslims from the subcontinent generally accept *dhikr* as an Islamic, though not required, activity.

For Shi'ite women, an important part of the experience of prayer and response to God comes in the ways in which they remember, and eulogize, the Prophet's grandson Husayn who was cruelly massacred at Karbala in Iraq in the early days of Islam. An interfaith program held several years ago in Connecticut provided an opportunity for women from the Jewish, Christian, and Muslim traditions to illustrate some of their devotional practices through musical presentation. First came a Jewish folksinger, whose songs about love and God reflected a wide range of Jewish cultural experiences. She was fol- lowed by a black Christian women's gospel choir, whose praises of Jesus made the roof rumble. Then the lights in the hall were extinguished, and as soft illumination gradually came back the audience was able to see two black mounds on the stage, from which mournful, soul-touching sounds were coming. After the lengthy lamentations, whose pathos was palpable even for those who did not understand what was going on, the lights came on fully, and the participants explained that they were both grieving for Husayn and praising God's goodness. Engaging warmly with the audience, they shook rosewater on the viewers and offered them tea and cookies. In such ways Americans are beginning to learn about the complexity and variations of the Islamic prayer experience.

The third ritual requirement of Islam is participation in the month-long fast of Ramadan. One ingests nothing—no food, no drink, no substance of any kind—from the first break of daylight until the onset of darkness in the evening and abstains from any sexual activity and from entertaining sexual thoughts. At the end of each day the fast is broken, traditionally in the context of the family, by sharing a communal meal. The end of the month is cele- brated by the second most important ritual holiday of the Islamic year, the *'eid al-fitr*, literally the holiday of fast-breaking. Often a celebration of several days' duration, this holiday is greatly anticipated both by those who have gone through the rigors of a month's fast and by those who may attend the mosque for only that one occasion in the whole calendar year. Women participate in the Ramadan experience in a variety of different ways.

Some women observe the requirements of the fast every day of the month of Ramadan. Islamic law exempts a woman who is pregnant or undergoing her monthly menstrual period from fasting for health reasons, though she must make up the days at a later time. Many even choose to fast for two additional weeks. Because the months of the Islamic calendar are based on lunar rather than solar celestial movements, Ramadan "rotates around" the normal Western calendar inversely; the fast takes place, in effect, earlier each year. Thus when Ramadan occurs during the winter months the hours of fasting are fewer, and when it occurs during the long summer months a day without drinking or eating can seem very long indeed. In Islamic countries provisions traditionally have been made to adjust working hours somewhat during the fasting period to allow for rest and recuperation. In America, of course, few places of employment are willing to make such adjustments, and working women who are also responsible for raising children may find the requirements of the fast too exacting (and too exhausting) to be carried out to the letter. While studies indicate that only a little over 10 percent of Muslim women in America are actively involved in organized religious activities, some 70 percent do observe elements of the fast in one way or another.

The age at which children are expected to fast differs considerably among Muslims. Most agree that girls and boys should not jeopardize their health by going without food for such a long period until they are at least at the age of puberty. Given the current atmosphere in America, in which many Muslims feel the pressure to affirm their Islamic identity in pious and public ways, some girls as young as nine or ten may want to demonstrate to themselves, their families, and their classmates that they know and participate in the requirements of their religion. One young mother reports that she always sends her daughter to school with her lunchbox full during Ramadan, both because she believes the girl should eat and also to avoid any accusation of child abuse by the school administration. Each day the lunchbox is returned in the late afternoon, still full.

The primary role for women during the month of Ramadan traditionally has been to supply the meals eaten at the end of each day of fasting, and particularly the splendid table-groaning repasts of the 'eid al-fitr. Little has changed on that score in America today, and women still bear and enjoy the responsibility for providing the food that fast-breaking Muslims eat not only because they are hungry but also as a signal of their gratitude for the provisions of God. As Americans learn more about Islam, various elements of the month of fasting have been the subject of journal and television presentations. American Muslims generally pray after breaking the fast with dates and juice and before partaking of the full meal. Despite the fact that the custom is modeled after the practice of the Prophet, it is in effect a new practice for many Arab Muslim immigrants who have learned to incorporate it from their South Asian co-religionists. In the last few years more mosques have been holding community *iftars* (daily fast-breaking occasions) so that Muslims who do not have families nearby can enjoy breaking each day's fast in the company of other Muslims.

Ramadan is also becoming an occasion in which Muslims can educate fellow Americans about their religious practices. Some Muslim women enjoy sharing with Christian and Jewish friends their reasons to undertake such a rigorous discipline and the pleasure of sharing with others in one's family and community the bounty of repast. *Iftar* dinners by and for women are increasingly being seen as a way of reaching out to an often skeptical America. Some seventy Muslim Student Association chapters at American universities for the last three years have held what they call a "fastathon," in which they invite non-Muslims to participate. For each person who fasts, money is donated to a local charity to feed people in need, while all share in an *iftar* dinner. First held at the University of Tennessee at Knoxville, the fastathons sometimes raise large amounts of money. Some high schools are beginning to follow the university model and hold their own fastathons.

One of the expectations for the month of Ramadan is that the Qur'an be recited in its entirety, one-thirtieth recited each night. This practice, called the *tarawih*, has been carried out by men and women, usually in the context of home and extended family. Because the mosque now often serves the purpose of that kind of family group for many Americans, the *tarawih* is now also held in most mosques. Women who would never have gone to the mosque in other cultural contexts now find themselves participating in this important part of the Ramadan ritual.

Many articles have appeared in Muslim publications over the past few years detailing the importance of the fast both as a time for cleansing the body, that is, a kind of health regime, and as a time when Muslims not only passively refrain from ingesting anything but actively involve themselves in various forms of public service. It has become popular practice among Muslim teenage girls to perform various forms of community outreach during the days of Ramadan, sharing in the experience of those who are needy by doing such things as visiting the sick and the elderly. "I would much rather do something helpful for somebody," said a fifteen-year old girl from a Pakistani background, "than sit around feeling grumpy because I am hungry. Besides, I want people to know that Islam is about helping others, not just being pious."

For some Muslim women, observing the fast for one month seems more manageable than trying to pray five times daily throughout the year. Others simply find it too difficult to coordinate with the rest of the demands they face. Although they would like to be able to fast, they just cannot seem to "work it in." A significant number of American Muslim women, of course, do not feel bound by this or by any other of the formal requirements of Islam and resist pressure they may feel from other Muslims to participate. High school girls tend to fast more than boys, perhaps because the fast of the young man is said to be broken if he finds himself sexually aroused, as some claim happens in the absence of dress codes or in light of certain behavior on the part of girls in American public schools.

The payment of zakat, the alms payment or welfare tax on all of one's holdings (2.5 percent for Sunnis and 20 percent for Shi'ites), is the fourth Islamic requirement. The men of the family are more likely than the women to determine how this money is to be distributed, though sometimes the decision is joint. Women, however, often find other ways in which to donate their time and resources. They may help out, for instance, in various charitable organizations such as free medical clinics and soup kitchens or participate in other activities working for the good of the community. In downtown Atlanta, for example, a charity to feed the homeless has existed since 1998. Sister Khayriyyah Hanan Faiz, one of the organization's founders, described in an interview with Saudi Aramco World in September of 2004 how she has combined her philanthropic work with study for a master's degree in social work. "We must be concerned about those who struggle and who have less than we," she said, "if we truly are to be considered believers in God." Recent charges by the U.S. government that certain Muslim charitable organizations are supporting terrorism have raised serious concerns on the part of many Muslims as to where they can safely pay their zakat monies.

The final requirement for those who wish to follow the dictates of God as they understand them is that of the pilgrimage to Mecca and Medina, or hajj, which all Muslim women and men are expected to make once during their lives unless illness or some other circumstance prevents it. While many more men than women historically have made the journey, some women throughout the history of Islam have understood the importance of this requirement and have expended every means possible in order to undertake it. The details of the pilgrimage and the slightly differing requirements for men and women are of less importance here than the fact that small but growing numbers of women are making the journey, sharing in the experience of their sisters across the world and through history. Many Muslim organizations provide special package deals for men and women to go to Mecca. Those who cannot go during the formal hajj month, when several million attend each year, may choose to go on what is called the 'umrah or smaller pilgrimage, visiting the holy sites at whatever time is possible for them. Women occasionally say that they are more comfortable in this more personalized way to visit and worship at the sacred shrines in Mecca and Medina. In the mosque at Mecca, the holiest of all cities and the home of the sacred house of Islam, the Ka'ba, men and women are not separated in prayer as they are in traditional mosques and in most mosques in America.

The pilgrimage, by the very fact of the huge numbers of believers it attracts, can be a frightening as well as an inspirational time for young girls. A Kuwaiti woman sharing her *hajj* experience with a women's interfaith group startled her audience by admitting that while most Muslims affirm that the pilgrimage is the spiritual high point of their lives, as a young girl she also found it a bit frightening. "There I was," she said, "holding on to my father's hand for dear life, when suddenly my grip slipped and I was in the middle of hundreds of thousands of milling and swirling men and women. I was really in a panic!" Fortunately her father quickly retrieved her and she completed the seven-day ceremony without further incident. "But," she insisted, "I want very much to go on the pilgrimage again, as an adult, and knowing what to expect. Then I will be able to talk to you about its deep spiritual significance rather then my experience as a scared girl."

After the conclusion of the month of pilgrimage Muslim journals are full of articles written by women who extol the joy and thrill of having performed this religious duty. "My heart was uplifted and I felt a sense of the immediacy of the divine that I never before imagined," said a middle-aged Arab American having completed her first *hajj*. Traditionally the travel of a woman to the holy cities of Mecca and Medina for the pilgrimage has been possible only if she is accompanied by her husband, a male relative, or a man who serves as a *mahram* (a male protector whom she cannot legally marry). For centuries the trip was usually long, arduous, and sometimes dangerous, requiring that women not go without male companionship. Now that air travel has greatly facilitated transportation, security measures in airports are tighter, and many pilgrimage trips are being specially arranged by mosques and travel agencies, circumstances for many American Muslim women are changing. New *ijtihad*, or individual interpretation of Islamic law, has been put forward allowing women to travel on the *hajj* in groups without male companions.

The five major responsibilities as outlined above frame the religious practices of American Muslims, both Sunni and Shi'ite. It is also the case that Shi'ite women have additional religious practices and celebrations, although a comprehensive study of Shi'ite women in the United States is yet to be done. During the sacred month of Muharram, the first month of the Islamic calendar, some Shi'ite women have special classes and *majalis* (religious gatherings) featuring female teachers and speakers. Fasting during Muharram, especially on the day of 'Ashura, is considered highly meritorious. Women sometimes observe special practices on 'Ashura such as wearing kohl and henna, cooking special grains, and sharing their happiness with other members of the community. Shi'ite women also celebrate the blessed month of Sha'ban (considered a particularly meritorious time). At the Jaafari Islamic Centre in Toronto, for example, women hold *milads* or celebrations in observance of the birthdays of several Islamic saints.

Learning the Islamic Sciences

American Muslims have increasingly come to insist that Islam mandates education for everyone, women as well as men. The Prophet Muhammad's injunction to seek knowledge even if it be in China is understood to apply equally to both genders. In the long historical record of Islamic achievements it is acknowledged that a few women have been religiously well educated and have passed on that education to other women. We know, for example, that two women served as teachers of the great medieval mystic-scholar Ibn 'Arabi. Muslim women scholars are working hard to recover the history of their forebears' contributions to Islamic civilization. Today al-Azhar University in Cairo, the oldest university in the world and a renowned center for religious training, has a program for rearing women missionaries at the high school level. Women are also majoring in Islamic studies at universities throughout the Arab world, as well as academic centers in Europe and North America. Most American Muslims are in general agreement that girls and women should receive the best education possible, and that the injunction of the Prophet makes it the responsibility of all Muslims, men and women, to take advantage of the opportunity to learn. Some women affirm their enthusiasm for Islamic learning by insisting that among the questions put to a woman on the day of resurrection will be to defend the ways in which she did or did not make every attempt to increase her education, both for the enhancement of her children and family and to facilitate her participation in the community.

Muslim women in the United States increasingly are becoming aware of the importance of their own education as a means of contributing to the effort to spread accurate information about the religion of Islam to a perplexed American public. Education of the public is one of the important ways in which da'wah, or calling to Islam, is being carried out in post 9/11 America. Muslim women now find that many opportunities are opening up for them to become more literate in the faith, to learn leadership skills, and to become proficient in certain areas that have traditionally been reserved for men. Receiving particular attention today is the importance of training Muslim women for specialized leadership, such as chaplains in the military, hospitals, universities, and prisons (see chapter 7, "Claiming Public Space").

Many parents believe that their daughter's Islamic education should take place in their countries of origin and, if they can afford it, would like to send them "back home" so that they can reinforce their cultural identity, learn Arabic and Islam, and (in effect) be protected from the dangers of American culture. In the recent past young women have gone to places like Damascus, Syria, and Amman, Jordan, to study the Qur'anic sciences and particularly Islamic law. The Syrian authorities, however, under pressure from the American government, have now restricted such activity. Increased attention is now being given to opportunities for women to find the resources to improve their Islamic education in the United States.

Some women, both young and not so young, are tired of waiting for men to make room for them and are simply appropriating for themselves the opportunity to obtain both knowledge and proficiency in the arts and sciences of Islam. While they often do so with the approval of the men in their families, for a significant number of women male approval may be less important than the chance to "get to the heart of things" in terms of Islamic knowledge. They are interested in reading and knowing personally the contents of the Qur'an, learning the basic elements of worship, and experiencing for themselves the beauty and power of oral performance. It is Muslim women who are now the most important players in the education both of children and of other women. Such education includes the study of Qur'an, Sunnah, Arabic, and the rights and opportunities guaranteed for women under Islamic law. "We cannot expect to be a viable community in America today if our children do not know what it means to be Muslim, and if our women are not fully articulate in understanding our scripture and our texts," says one national Muslim leader.

Women's study groups are springing up in many areas of the country. Sometimes they may have the participation or even leadership of men at the mosques. Increasingly, however, they function as women-only gatherings designed to promote religious knowledge and the general enhancement of the faith. Clearly they also serve as support groups in which women both learn from each other and find care and encouragement. "It is truly wonderful to be with a group of friends who can help me learn, who are not judgmental when I admit that I don't know some pretty basic stuff about Islam, and who are also willing to give me personal advice when I have questions about raising kids or being a good wife." Some Muslims believe that these groups are crucial in current efforts to reinterpret and renegotiate Islam, especially since 9/11 and to ensure that gender issues are addressed creatively at the same time that traditional Islamic knowledge is imparted and shared. Women are discovering that they want to know more about scripture, belief, ritual, and practice and that they can learn in a nonthreatening and supportive environment with the help of someone (now often a woman) who has some particular experience or training. Many are convinced that by closer study of texts and traditions they can have a voice in the reformulation of an Islam that is truly gender-inclusive and appropriate for living as Muslims in twenty-first century America.

The term often used for these meetings is *dars* (plural *durus*) from the Arabic word meaning to take or be given study, or *halaqah*, a study circle. They are occasions for religious lessons, generally with a trained leader, leaving plenty of time for questions, debate, and discussion. According to one participant, however, these sessions can also be deductive, beginning with an explanation and paradigm by the leader and allowing some opportunity for participation or contributions by the other participants. Meetings also provide a warm social climate in which all opinions are honored and discussion is lively and creative. "They are an outstanding demonstration of how the reformulation of questions and methods regarding Islam can yield more acceptable, practical, and positive consequences," says Georgetown University student Shereen Abdel-Nabi of her experience with a *dars* group in the greater Washington, D.C., area. Naturally groups around the country differ according to size, composition, and agenda, but all are dedicated to the promotion of Islamic knowledge among American Muslim women.

Groups normally meet in private homes, either rotating from one member to another or meeting in the home of the woman who serves as coordinator or leader. Meetings are regular—weekly, biweekly, or monthly according to the interests and availability of the participants. Many of the participants have recently come from other countries and can bring with them perspectives shared by women in Asia, the Middle East, or elsewhere. These interventions, along with the availability of instant Internet information, make *dars* circles part of a network of women's groups around the world. Some women choose to attend more than one group in their local contexts, providing other ways for cross-fertilization. Because of the relative newness of this overall movement and the speed with which it is spreading, a comprehensive study of its manifestations in the United States and elsewhere is yet to be done.

Some *dars* and *halaqah* groups may be quite homogeneous, made up entirely of immigrants or women from immigrant families, often representing one area of the Islamic world. Other groups are culturally and ethnically mixed. Some are dominated by women who have converted to Islam and who want both to increase their knowledge and to have interaction with women "who have been Muslim longer than we have!" Aminah McCloud describes an African American study group in Chicago which, although now disbanded, was formed a number of years ago and continued to meet for some twenty-five years. The group discussed such issues as faith in God, personal loss, polygyny, and family concerns. According to McCloud they were often vague about the relationship of Islamic principles of faith to more popular practices that have no basis in Islam.

Garbi Schmidt, for example, who has done extensive studies of young Muslims in Chicago, in her book *Islam in Urban America* describes one group led by a trained religious teacher named Umm Khadija. The group is very heterogeneous, made up of women from the Middle East, South Asia, and other areas. Many of the women are converts and use the occasion of the meeting to affirm the rightness of their choice of Islam as a religion and their pleasure at finding "sisterhood" with the other Muslim women. Umm Khadija's leadership is unquestioned, due both to her role as a *hafizah* (someone who has memorized the Qur'an) with degrees in Islamic studies and because of her personal piety. She says that she not only continues to read a great deal but that she takes advantage of the many audiotaped sermons and lessons now available in the United States. She teaches through telling stories, drawing the women personally into the accounts, who then cheer at tales of success and suffer for those who are in pain. The members of the group also share their own stories and usually find not only "Islamic" answers to their concerns or problems but the strong support of their fellow learners.

Typical of many *dars* groups is one in the greater Washington, D.C., area that has ten to fifteen participants weekly, mostly middle-aged wives, mothers, and working women. Some wear *hijab* and others do not, although they all put on a scarf when they pray, as required. Most participants were raised in the Arab world, where they received very little in the way of religious education. While the *dars* group is important to them for many different reasons, the primary theme is the importance of gaining more religious knowledge. Their leader is a strong and knowledgeable woman who, with her husband, takes a group on the pilgrimage every year. The group, initially very small, first learned by listening to religious lectures on tape. After having found their current leader, whom they call "Abla" (technically meaning older cousin and used generally for the woman who leads the session), they have grown in size and find the learning experience to be richer and more helpful. The meeting begins with refreshments and social time. The group then prays the evening prayer, after which Abla begins the lesson. The women feel free to interrupt her with questions or examples from their own experiences, in an atmosphere of both respect for leadership and relaxed give and take. The meeting from beginning to end may take up to two and a half hours.

Dars and *halaqah* groups around the country differ, but have in common the growing sense of empowerment women feel as they make their own decisions about participation, leadership, location, and the topics about which they wish to learn. While they generally believe that they are "taking Islam into their own hands" in ways that have seldom characterized the experience of Muslim women, recent research is revealing that this is a very old Muslim tradition and that often women had special places in which to study. The subjects American women choose to study range from Qur'an to prayer to jurisprudence to the responsibilities of Muslims for charity and good works. Underlying the study is the need for dialogue with the leader and with each other and for feeling part of a specific group as well as of a network of women who are learning to stand on their own spiritual feet. In some cases groups expand beyond meetings for conversation and learning and become involved in outside projects such as fund-raising campaigns, support of local issues, and community and interfaith events. Members feel that as they are growing in religious understanding they are providing the basis for stronger family and community life. "By improving your family," says one *dars* leader, "you improve your community too, and other Muslims. You can't be selfish and just learn for yourself. If you know something, or you improve yourself, you have to improve others as well."

Some of the most innovative forms of education for women are taking place, not surprisingly, in California. The San Francisco area is home to one of the first American *madrasahs* (religious schools) that is popular among young women and in which one can train to be an *alimah* (a female educated in the Islamic sciences). This school, which is innovative in its attempt to educate women yet conservative in its religious orientation, tries to ignore ethnic identities. The emphasis is on Islam itself as the most important factor of identification.

In Southern California Dr. Maher Hathout holds special classes for women, offering a variety of perspectives from which he urges them to choose. "I have a healthy distrust of anyone who tells you that they know the will of God," insists one of Hathout's women students. In this case, as is true of many other areas of the country, study groups for women are held not in private homes but in the Islamic Center itself. Classes include study of Qur'an passages, the context for their revelation, and the various ways in which they have been interpreted. Hathout insists that women learn Arabic so that they can do their own translation of the Qur'an. That way they need not rely on commonly used translations such as that of Yusuf Ali, which Hathout says can be misleading. At the Orange County mosque, Muzammil Siddiqi, former president of the Islamic Society of North America, offers a somewhat more conservative approach to women's education. He and a group of women listen to sermons and discuss issues of importance in their lives. A growing phenomenon in America is the creation of study groups designed specifically for elderly Muslim women.

Many other resources are available for women who want to study Islam, particularly on the Internet. For example, the Muslim Women Lawyers for Human Rights organization (KARAMAH), in the summer of 2003 put on-line a uniquely designed Islamic studies course, with an emphasis on Islamic law. The four-week intensive course was designed to prepare women for leadership from an Islamic perspective. It provided instruction in Qur'an, hadith, life of the Prophet, and major scholarly writings. KARAMAH plans to expand and continue this kind of on-line instruction. As part of its leadership training program the organization held a special seminar to initiate women into a study of Qur'an interpretation that is more woman-friendly than traditional forms, led by a Syrian woman educated in the Islamic sciences. Professor Mona Abul Fadl at the Graduate School of Islamic and Social Science in Virginia would like to transfer course work in Muslim studies to the Internet. Permitting women to take such courses online, she says, allows the Internet to serve as a new *madrassah*, or Islamic school, in the legacy of Islamic tradition.

One of the particular ways in which Muslim American women, immigrant and indigenous, young and not-so-young, are engaging with the basic traditional Islamic sciences is by study of what is called *tajwid*—oral recitation of the Qur'an. They are learning that by engaging in a mode of performance that has always been the domain of men they are not only bringing the text alive for themselves but are learning how recitation can be a transforming experience. Women are teaching one another, and learning from each other, in the context of informal networks that give new meaning to the relationship of sound, worship, and authority.

The Qur'an has always been understood to be the immutable word of God, communicated through human recitation. The science of *tajwid* involves giving each sound and syllable its proper pronunciation and elocution. In America, learning to recite the Qur'an, for those Muslims who want to be religiously literate, usually begins by listening to the father's recitation at home or with some form of Islamic religious education. While many Muslims achieve rudimentary reading skills, it is usually only later in life that they realize the importance of reading in the "proper way." Until recently this realization has not normally been part of women's experience. Women are now learning that gaining new skills in recitation of the Qur'an can be a way of fulfilling one's religious obligation to oneself. Closely related to reciting the Word of God is learning the *adab al-Qur'an*—having the right intention, being ritually pure, sitting up straight, being silent when others are reading, and facing the direction of Mecca.

American women learning to recite the Qur'an can take advantage of various manuals and audio aids that are now available. While some do self-study, most meet with a teacher or friends. Women instructors provide comfort, access, and companionship. As with Qur'an study groups, women learning *tajwid* sometimes meet in classes in the mosque or Islamic center, and at other times gather in each other's homes. Some scholars have noted that the model of meeting in living rooms reflects the practice of women's gatherings in medieval Mamluk Cairo, where women sought educational forums in private homes. Often babies and small children are present, making the general ambiance informal and comfortable.

The more women learn about recitation the more they seem to feel ownership of the Qur'an. But while some women gain the skills to provide instruction to others, for most women knowing the basics of *tajwid* does not give them the sense of authority to transmit what they have learned. Vocalization of the Qur'an using *tajwid* does not automatically mean that one can understand its meaning, and traditionally the sciences of recitation and interpretation have been seen as two separate processes. For women living in the United States, however, one often leads directly to the other. Many women are finding that in teaching their peers, or sometimes even their elders, they not only gain in confidence but also empower other women through the formation of continuing networks. Young Muslim women, following in the footsteps of a few female scholars who have been struggling to interpret the Qur'an according to principles of revelation and justice, are now beginning to engage in exegesis of the Qur'an and to participate in discussions of religious texts in ways that heretofore have been the prerogative of men.

5

Gender and Family

Sunni Muslim, North Indian parents seek
a matrimonial correspondence for 24-year old
daughter, an electrical engineer working for
a Fortune 100 company. Fair complexion, perfect
blend of East and West, bilingual, good family
values. Seek professional, U.S. citizen, age 25–29.
Please respond w. photo.
                    —*Islamic Horizons* Jan/Feb 2004

Good-looking Sunni Muslim 29, U.S. born MD,
seeks well-educated professional cultured and
sophisticated family-oriented girl from a
respectable family. Resume and photo required.
                    —*Islamic Horizons* March/April 2004

The search for a mate—as exemplified in these typical journal
ads—and the process of starting the building blocks of a family
structure is of great importance to American Muslims, especially
practicing adherents of the faith. The nature and value of the family is
high on the agenda for public reflection and consideration. This is
evident in the emphasis that speakers at most regional and national
meetings of Islamic organizations have placed on the various dimensions of family life and responsibility. The Council on American-
Islamic Relations (CAIR), for example, in the fifth installment of a
major 2003 campaign to foster better understanding of Islam and

counter American Islamophobic rhetoric, focused on family as the keystone of the American Muslim community.

For the religiously observant Muslim, the family is also the place where many of the rituals of daily life are carried out, including celebration of naming ceremonies for children, coming-of-age rituals, study of the Qur'an, and sharing stories from the life of the Prophet. Many Muslim homes prominently display calligraphic or other Islamic symbols and art objects, perhaps a legacy of the "Islamization" project of Temple University professor Ismail Al-Faruqi and his wife who encouraged Muslims to surround themselves with Islamic artifacts as a buffer against the dominant Christian environment. Most religiously observant families pray together at home and celebrate the daily breaking of the fast together at the end of each day of Ramadan.

Muslim organizations and businesses are helping parents with both the entertainment and the instruction of their children in the home context by producing a rapidly growing number of games, videos, and other Islamic products that allow for the family to interact together in an Islamically-oriented atmosphere. Mothers looking for ways to both educate and entertain their children while keeping them away from what are often seen as the harmful effects of American TV can choose from a wide selection of Islamically-sponsored products. Fine Media Group (FMG) introduces movie hits of the year for children and family entertainment. For those who want to engage in family activities, a variety of games and puzzles is available, all with Islamic themes. Families can construct three-dimensional models of the Ka'bah in Mecca (fully assembled models are more than a foot high and two feet wide), quiz each other about Islamic history or facts of the faith, or play Islamic card games. "Mission: Survival" is an educational adventure game designed to preserve Islamic identity, cope with societal challenges, and reinforce Islamic values. And for little girls unable to resist the Barbie-Doll phenomenon, NoorArt says, "Move Over Barbie! Razanne is here." Razanne, according to the ad, means a woman who is beautifully modest and shy in the best Islamic manner, "a doll that is 'just like Mom'—one who could serve as a role model for young Muslims." Razanne is 12 inches tall and wears a solid color *jilbaab* (robe) and a white *hijab*. The scarf is removable so that the child can practice the correct way of putting it on. The doll comes in three skin tones—white, tan, and dark brown—to represent different racial and ethnic groups.

For older children, as well as for Muslim women themselves (and, of course, for men) a number of accessories are provided to allow one to become more religiously literate. Sound Vision, for example, provides ways to help children learn to speak and read Arabic, recite the Qur'an, pray, and generally become more Islamically adept under the rubric "helping tomorrow's Muslims today!" Micro Systems International offers a multimedia presentation of the Qur'an on CD-ROM. A large number of books, videos, CDs, VCRs, software packages, and other kinds of instructional materials are available for use in the home. Many of these products serve both as instructional tools and as entertainment, such as Islamic cartoons or films with Muslim heroes and heroines. Numerous companies put out audiotapes featuring presentations by prominent Muslim speakers.

What Is a Muslim Family?

The notion of family has been shaped both by the prescripts of the Qur'an and by the many cultures to which the religion of Islam spread. The Qur'an portrays nature as operating in pairs, male and female, created as mates for each other and thus sets the scene for the partnering structure of human relationships. Its verses, as well as examples from the Prophet's life, have been used by Islamic jurists to regulate many family concerns, including appropriate partners, marriage, divorce, inheritance, and authority within the family. Muslim literature cites the Prophet Muhammad as having affirmed the importance of the family structure and having said that divorce is the last resort for failed partnerships. In every Muslim society over the centuries the family has been such a basic institution that there has been little place for what we used to call bachelors and spinsters.

"Why are Muslim men allowed to have four wives and a woman only one husband?" is a question often asked by non-Muslims, who generally consider such a possibility highly unfair to women. Polygamy (or, technically, polygyny)—the option stipulated in the Qur'an for a husband to take up to four wives—is one of the most difficult concepts for Muslims to explain to their fellow Americans. It is deemed by some Islamic scholars to be permissible only in unusual cases, when the husband is able to provide equally for all wives. Marriage of a man to more than one women has been interpreted by some modernists to be possible only under the most stringent conditions. American Muslim jurists and counselors, as well as imams of mosques, adhere to American law and do not condone performing marriages of men to second wives. In February 2005 a Kuwaiti family was denied immigrant status in Canada, despite their financial and linguistic qualifications, because it was discovered that the husband was trying to bring in two wives. When non-Muslims criticize the Qur'anic allowance of multiple wives, Muslims often counter by pointing to the fact that American society appears to sanction serial polygamy in its practice of permitting "one wife after another," as well as its apparent condoning of mistresses and other forms of promiscuity.

Throughout the history of Islam many women have suffered under the threat of sharing their husband with another wife. Some women, particularly if they are newly arrived from conservative Muslim countries and are unaware of American civil law, may still feel threatened by such a prospect. However, since monogamy is the only legal choice, what is more threatening is the competition from American females who, operating in a different moral context, may try to take their husbands away from them. Muslim women may fear what they see as the aggressiveness of American females, providing serious temptations for men. It is a common assumption among Muslims that home-wrecking is not a concern to many Americans.

Another threat Muslim men have traditionally held over their wives has been the possibility of divorce. The quick "triple renunciation" divorce has often been employed by men in Islamic cultures, although in some of the modern states such facile triple repudiation of the wife is frowned on and restricted by law. Most Muslims, certainly those in America, consider divorce a last and most undesirable alternative. The Prophet himself is often quoted as having said that of all hateful things in the world, divorce is among the worst. The rate of divorce among Muslims in the United States is somewhat lower than that in American society in general, although it has been rising in recent years and is higher than in Muslim countries.

What constitutes a Muslim family in America depends, basically, on who is around. In some cases so many members of one family may have come to this country—often choosing to live as closely together as possible—that some semblance of extended family is possible. More often, however, a husband and wife with their children are the primary and only unit. This may suit a young American-born wife just fine, but it presents significant problems for women coming with or conditioned by other cultural expectations. Immigrant women are often very lonely without the company of a larger support group. If the couple has children and both spouses are working, the young mother may feel the pressure of having no family members except her husband around to provide child care. Americans who themselves or whose parents have adopted Islam as a way of life may suffer from a rupture in relationship with their non-Muslim families, a problem that seems to affect Anglos more than blacks or Latinos/Latinas. African Americans appear to be somewhat more tolerant than others of multiple religious preferences in the same family.

American Muslims, therefore, often find it necessary to seek companionship to substitute for the loss of the natural extended family. In some cases this reinforces feelings of identification with others who share the same national or cultural background and language but not the same religion. Such ethnic rapport, however, has its costs. Bengali Muslims who socialize with Bengali Hindus or Christians, for example, may find themselves enjoying music that is frowned on by Pakistanis in the mosque. In the long run this may actually contribute to further isolation and make it difficult for their children to break out and participate in American society more broadly. American society also contributes to this problem when it justifies keeping immigrants on the margins by saying "they really like to socialize with each other."

A minority of Muslims opt to find their "family" in the local mosque or Islamic center, where they share overall Islamic values but may find themselves affiliated with "sisters and brothers" whose cultural customs in relation to family and other issues differ. "She seems like a nice enough person," said the Egyptian woman, eyeing the bare midriff of an otherwise well-covered Indian woman, "but she really should dress more appropriately in the mosque." The importance of the mosque as an extended family substitute is underscored at the times of religious holidays, or 'eids, which traditionally have been occasions for the extended family to celebrate and enjoy a meal and companionship together. By sharing holidays with co-religionists in the community as well as with immediate relatives, Muslims find new definitions of family that may help to overcome cultural differences. A new phenomenon in North America is hosting an "open house" on the 'eid or Islamic holiday where friends go from house to house and partake of the food prepared for the occasion.

"Dating" and Courtship

New definitions and interpretations of family are theoretically interesting, but are not much help to the young Muslim woman who wants to begin a family in the American context. She is faced immediately with a number of complicating factors. Islamic law, which guides the actions of some Muslims while others create their own definitions of what is required, says that a Muslim man is allowed to marry any woman who is a member of what the Qur'an calls "People of the Book," meaning Jews and Christians. A Muslim woman, however, may only marry another Muslim. Although the Qur'an technically states that she cannot marry an "unbeliever," this has come to be interpreted to include a Christian or a Jew. This stipulation has been defended as necessary to guarantee that the children are raised as Muslims. It also is based on the understanding on the part of many Muslims that men have authority over their wives and determine the religion of the children.

In America, where Muslims still make up only a very small fraction of the population and interaction between Muslims and non-Muslims is virtually unavoidable, it is not unusual to find Muslim men marrying Christian women, Jewish women, or secular women with no religious affiliation. A Christian woman who marries a Muslim man is not legally obliged to convert, though she may do so out of personal preference or a desire to secure a unified family. The fact that men can marry outside of the faith can result, and has resulted, in problems for young practicing Muslim women who are left with a dwindling pool of available partners. Observing Muslims today face increased pressures to marry within the faith both to solve the problem of finding a marriage partner and to ensure the integrity of the family unit.

For Muslim parents in America who want to ensure that their daughters meet potential marriage partners whom they consider appropriate, the problems are real. Sometimes parents arrange for a husband to be imported from the home culture. At other times they capitulate and allow their daughter to marry a non-Muslim, usually with great reluctance. In rare cases they may disown their daughter in order to save face. Among immigrant Muslim families, "arranging" marriages for their children is of great concern. Often the traditional arrangement is modified to make it more appropriate in the Western context, with parents laying the groundwork and the young people making the final determination. While many Muslim youth abhor the idea of their parents interfering in their choice of a marriage partner, others, looking at the high rate of divorce in the West, are willing to concede that there may be wisdom in parental "participation" in decisions about marriage and family life. One young man said, "My mother knows me best and she will be able to choose the most compatible partner for me." Also of concern to some in the Muslim community is the phenomenon of early marriage in which the bride and groom are teenagers or, in rare cases, even younger. Such marriages, which may not be consummated until the couple is older, are contracted specifically for the purpose of making sure that young people marry within sectarian or ethnic groups.

Many Muslims living in the United States and Canada, especially in schools and on college campuses, interact freely across gender lines as is the general cultural norm. And some simply choose to ignore parental restrictions and marry whomever they choose. Statistics show that in Canada some 40 percent of Muslim women have married non-Muslim men, fewer than half of whom have converted to Islam. While no statistics are available for the United States, such marriages continue to be discouraged. It is frustrating for many children of immigrants that their parents are more interested in ensuring that they marry men from their own country or cultural background to ensure harmony (a reality that often pertains to immigrant Christians as well) than they are with whether or not the man is a good Muslim. "I'm just dying to get married," said a young white male convert to Islam, "but I can't find anyone whose parents will accept me. I'm not Pakistani, or Palestinian, or anything but just American. The fact that I'm a really good Muslim doesn't seem to matter."

The disparity between customs in Muslim countries and the United States puts a great deal of stress on parents of girls. One of their major concerns is finding appropriate ways for their daughters to meet potential partners. Some refuse to let their teenaged daughters date at all, or they allow socializing only with appropriate chaperoning. They are even less enthusiastic about interaction with non-Muslims. For traditional Muslim families, especially—but not limited to—those of Middle Eastern origin, the strong commitment to family honor often seems to find its focus in the behavior of its girls and women. It is difficult to overstate the importance of virginity, especially for girls. Young Muslims in America struggle both to respect the honor of the family and to break free of the kinds of expectations it imposes on them. While "dating" is frowned on by more conservative Muslim families, many girls laugh at what they see as outdated customs and enter the American social scene freely. Much of this kind of interchange between the sexes takes place on college and university campuses.

Muslim girls who do observe the traditional prohibitions against dating are becoming more articulate about how frustrated they are that their families often hold a double standard for boys and girls, with more leeway granted to their brothers: "It's just not fair that my brother gets to do anything he wants—dating, parties, who knows what, while I'm trapped at home or with other girls." An Indonesian man admitted that he really cannot control his seventeen-year-old son, but when asked when he would allow his daughter to date he answered vehemently, "Never!" Both locally and through national organizations efforts are being made to bring young Muslim boys and girls together to work on common projects and "pursue Islamic purposes" in the context of a highly structured set of activities. "At least this way we can supervise them," said one official, "and can make sure that their male as well as female friends are Muslim."

Young Muslim women who are frustrated at the difficulties they are having finding a husband now have many places to which they may turn for help. A range of opportunities is available to aid young Muslims in finding the right marriage partner, from Web sites to "halal" singles evenings in local restaurants to organization-based services to self-styled marriage brokers. Both women and men put ads in national Muslim journals announcing their readiness for marriage. Sometimes their families may provide this service for them. In some cases, as for example the American Pakistani community, matchmaking is still alive and well. In other instances the role traditionally played by matchmakers in Muslim societies is now being appropriated by a range of electronic, social, and professional entrepreneurs. And these new means in many cases seem to be working.

Matrimonial services are provided by many of the major Islamic organizations. Annual national conventions of the Islamic Society of North America, the Islamic Circle of North America, the Muslim Student Association, and various professional associations provide contexts in which young Muslims can get to know each other in structured situations. Dozens of Web sites offer matchmaking services to Muslim women and men, providing chat rooms where singles can get to know each other as well as advice on how to be a good wife and stay married after the wedding has taken place. The ISNA Web site http://www.isna.net, for example, includes a matrimonial service, and a number of other such Web sites (http://matrimony.org/, http://muslimweddings.com/, http://naseeb.com, etc.) are easily available. Shi'ites can look to such places as http://shiamatch.com/. For a monthly fee, zawaj.com (from the Arabic word for marriage), based in Oakland, California, will provide many opportunities for a young woman or man to "check out" a possible partner. Members are asked to put their pictures on-line and to provide biographical profiles as well as indications of what they may be looking for in a spouse. A group called "Muslim Gatherings" (www.muslimgatherings.com) brings together young singles for networking and meeting at contemporary restaurants for dinner events. Female participants are invited to bring their own chaperones if they wish.

Young Muslim women may spend months chatting on-line with men, exchanging comments and information and determining whether or not they might want to change their electronic relationship to a more personal one. There is a consensus among Muslim religious leaders that Western-style dating is forbidden, some even saying that voice contact through telephone conversations is sexually arousing for the man. Matrimonial Web sites are therefore gaining acceptance even among more conservative Muslims. Electronic communication gives single adults some degree of control over their relationships at the same time that they are operating within accepted cultural and religious boundaries and also can allow for the participation of their parents should the relationship flourish.

Many Muslims look to the matrimonials sections of popular monthly and quarterly journals. Young men and women, or often their parents acting on their behalf, can post their own credentials and their hopes for qualities that they would like to see exhibited in their mates, for example, "Young woman of Egyptian heritage, full-time professional, seeking educated man, aged 28–45, who is Islamically observant and enjoys outdoor activities." Once a contact is made, the two parties (or their families) may decide that they would like to carry on a courtship. For those who want to honor traditional cultural practices, Islamically appropriate ways can be set up for potential mates to meet and get acquainted, including the use of chaperones. Other young people may simply arrange to meet and decide in the typical American way whether or not to see each other again.

Marriage

Partly in response to the fact that American Muslims have as part of their heritage a great range of differing marriage customs (and, of course, partly because it is profitable), businesses are growing up to assist brides and their families in all aspects of the planning and carrying out of the wedding itself. Journals, books, and numerous electronic means are available to the prospective bride and groom. "If you are getting married, congratulations! May God bless you and your spouse-to-be," says SoundVision.com. "But on your journey to marriage, there are more than a few details that need to be ironed out." SoundVision advises couples to keep weddings simple and affordable despite the fact that they will experience various cultural and social pressures to the contrary. A comprehensive wedding guide is offered to help couples and their families move smoothly through the process.

While SoundVision recommends a low-budget wedding because Islam is against ostentation, many Muslims splurge on the event, in some cases attempting to replicate typical marriage ceremonies in their home countries. Thus an Egyptian wedding may have a *zaffah* in which the bride is accompanied by a band. The wedding may feature a belly dancer, into whose waistband or shimmering top money is put by appreciative viewers, and the bride and groom are showered with fake coins. In some Pakistani weddings the groom dresses in a "Maharajah" outfit and rides a horse to the wedding to claim his wife. Such ceremonies are more likely to happen in more secular families. Religiously conservative families may favor more pious forms of entertainment such as a chorus of children singing the popular American-created song "*Alahu akbar*" ("God is the greatest!" [literally, "greater"]) with enthusiasm and crescendo:

Leader: *Alahu akbar*
Children's response: God **is** the One!
Leader: *Alahu akbar*
Children: the **only** one!
Leader: *Allahu akbar*
Children: He **has** no son!
All: *Alahu akbar* [repeated more and more softly until it becomes a whisper]

It often comes as a shock to young American women who fall in love with, and marry, Muslim men to find that in traditional Islamic countries marriage involves more than two people. "Can't you ever make a decision without checking with your family?" asked the new American wife of a Kuwaiti graduate student in irritation. "Sometimes I think you must love them much more than me!" Trained counselors working with engaged interfaith couples warn that a woman really is marrying not only a man but an entire family. Traditionally marriage has meant a bonding not just (or even primarily) of individuals but of larger family units, a concept that is often difficult for those raised in the individualist society of the West to understand and accept. Often men who have spent considerable time in America really believe their own promises to their fiancées that they will never succumb to the pressures of family. Such promises work well until the couple visits home, especially if that means to a conservative culture, and the traditional attitudes often slip back into the consciousness, and thus the behavior, of the husband.

Marriage between Muslims and non-Muslims was a common practice when there were only a relatively few Muslims living in America. Now that sizable communities of Muslims have been established in virtually all of the major American cities, most Muslim families strongly encourage their children not to marry outside the faith. In some places in the country Muslim imams are working with Christian clergypersons to counsel young people who want to enter into an interfaith marriage, not always discouraging them but making it clear that there are real problems to be faced. One of the reasons why some Muslim parents refuse to let their youth, especially girls, participate in interfaith activities is concern that they will find young non-Muslim men attractive!

Muslim concerns are now matched by Roman Catholic worries about marriages between Catholic women and Muslim men. In the spring of 2004 the Vatican issued a document discouraging such marriages, citing "profound cultural differences" between the two faiths. Among the reasons for this statement is rising concern on the part of the Church for what it perceives as the unequal treatment of wives by Muslim men, particularly in some immigrant communities, as well as concern for the baptism of the children. The document insists that if such marriages do take place, it must be with the understanding that no agreement will be made that the wife will take the shahadah or Islamic profession of faith and that participants must agree that their children will be baptized in the Catholic faith. The Conference of Catholic Bishops held dialogue sessions with ICNA in the mid-Atlantic region on the subject of marriage and the family, which produced a manual for priests and imams.

A relatively rare form of Islamic marriage, most commonly practiced by Shi'ites, is called mut'ah, referring to a union contracted for a specific period of time. Sunnis frown on the practice, some going so far as to call it legalized prostitution when the contract is for the short period of an hour, a day, or even a specific number of months or years. They also criticize mut'ah marriage when it is done in secret without the appropriate witnesses. Such practice has been relatively unobserved on the American scene until recently, when it has begun to attract some attention. Lori Peek notes that the practice is sufficiently prevalent that the imam of an Islamic Institute in Dearborn—a city with a large Shi'ite population—wrote a booklet explaining its rationale and outlining its proper restrictions. Mut'ah marriage has also been practiced in some parts of the African American Muslim community. In what was in effect a sanctioning of mut'ah, the Mufti of Saudi Arabia, Bin Baz, gave permission for Saudi men to marry American women when they came to the United States and then divorce them before returning home, saying that would help satisfy the sexual desires inevitably evoked by the wanton and seductive American environment.

The vast majority of Muslims living in America, those from immigrant backgrounds, African Americans, or other converts to Islam, come from traditions and personal circumstances in which males are the dominant voices within the family circle. Virtually all traditional Muslim cultures support male authority. The Qur'anic verse 4:34 is usually translated to mean that men are in charge of women when they provide for them (financially) from their means. For many American Muslim women, male authority and control taken at face value, however, tends to run up against the general climate of American discourse about equality and justice between the sexes, and the feminist-initiated but now more generally accepted notion that the family unit is one in which both males and females have an equal share in responsibilities and in decision making. It is obvious that not all American families (or other units of society) approximate or even extol this ideal. Yet for many women, it is still a powerful counterimage to what much of the Muslim community continues to see as the scripture-based and tradition-supported Islamic model of male authority, both in the family and in the larger units of Muslim society.

Responses from within the Islamic community to this kind of challenge are greatly varied. Much of the contemporary discourse, joined by both men and women, portrays the liberal Western model of "equality" between the sexes as unrealistic, unnatural, and leading ultimately to many Western women trying to raise children alone and below the poverty level. The Islamic system, they affirm, will never allow such degradation because it is based on the understanding that male authority over females is always tied to their responsibility to provide financial support for the women and children of their families. Attempts are being made by both women and men to reinterpret Qur'anic texts that seem to support male dominance over women, trying to argue that the justice of God affirmed in the holy text cannot allow women to be subordinated in any way to men.

African American Muslims often experience their understanding of family as either part of, or specifically in opposition to, the position taken by Elijah Muhammad and the Nation of Islam. An emphasis on family has always been an important ingredient of African American Islam, whatever version that Islam takes, and an assumption of certain essential differences between the sexes has informed the Nation's policy of strict gender roles. Men are expected to be strong, self-reliant, and moral. They are responsible for protecting and providing for their wives and children. Women are the caretakers of the home and of their husbands and children, tasks to which their gender is believed to be ideally suited. In the Nation of Islam the woman has always been considered to be of value due to her status as the original woman and the mother of future generations of Muslims.

Although there is considerable discussion about the respective roles of women and men in virtually all African American communities, and while love and affection between the two parties is considered essential, in general the expectation is that the wife's primary role in the marriage relationship is to support her husband. All African American groups put special emphasis on the importance of a happy and peaceful marriage, particularly given the reality of the number of broken homes in the inner cities of this country. American social welfare laws, however, intended to provide financial assistance, actually serve to encourage African American males to leave the family so that the wife and children can collect government support. The effect of these laws may be the undermining of the stability and the authority of males of low-income, often African American, families.

The Nation of Islam under Elijah Muhammad sometimes talked about the value of having multiple wives, although it has been forcefully opposed by Warith Deen Mohammed and other African American Muslim leaders. Taking more than one wife is still part of the culture of some African immigrants and is encouraged in the ideology of a few African American sectarian groups as an antidote to the reality that black families often have absent fathers. Polygamy is projected by some as a means of saving African American society by providing caring homes in the context of U.S. aid policies that favor single mothers. Some new studies project that polygamy in the black community may actually be on the increase. It appears to be practiced among some immigrants from West Africa, in which cases the marriages are not recorded.

Despite the background of feminism that many African American converts bring with them, Carolyn Rouse insists that there is still an assumption of essential gender difference that pervades their general understanding. The underlying belief is that women are better suited to be in the home with the children than in the workplace, though circumstances do not always allow this. African American women, says Rouse, respond very favorably to sermons delineating the gender roles, due particularly to their desire to sustain the success of the family unit. Rather than feeling threatened by the lack of certain rights, they are concerned with the overall balance and functioning of the family. Aminah McCloud also notes that many women view themselves as "recovering" the role of mother, wife, and homemaker in a positive sense. African American women are keenly aware of the breadwinning responsibilities that black women have had to assume, she says, and welcome the chance to play the traditional roles of wife and homemaker.

Concerns within the American Muslim Family

Many second- and third-generation Muslim families in America seem to have more or less come to terms with the ways in which traditional Islamic concepts of the family must be modified in the Western context. Those who are more recently arrived, or are dedicated to maintaining traditional familial structures, find the pressures of American society very complex. Some American Muslims advocate that women should become increasingly independent and participate in public life rather than "just stay at home." Others are increasingly arguing that the importance of "family values" may mean the adoption (or re-adoption) of more traditional models of family relationship, often ones in which women do not work outside the home and major decisions are still made by the men of the family. Muslims mirror these alternative patterns in their own decisions about how families should operate.

Muslim families today face many issues and concerns. They are often forced to find their communal relationships in nonfamilial structures, a new experience for many immigrants and even for African Americans. Muslim leadership is working to defend the right of Muslims to define their relationships according to their own norms. On the one hand, Muslims are challenged to paint as positive a picture as possible of the advantages of living Islamically, particularly in light of current anti-Islamic feeling in the West. On the other hand, they are also recognizing that the only way to counter some of the problems faced by Muslim families and in particular women is to acknowledge those problems and move actively toward their solution, since often such problems are no different from those faced by other Western families.

One important issue that many women must come to terms with, and one that clearly has ramifications for their families, is whether or not they should seek outside employment. The question has many nuances: whether or not it is appropriate for women to work outside the home, what kinds of work (and what working hours) are advisable, whether the work environment is appropriate, and who makes those decisions. While many traditional Muslims believe that women's work is in the home, in reality women "staying home" was a luxury only the middle classes in Muslim societies could afford. In America most Muslim families look favorably on women's outside employment because it allows women to use their educational training, brings in extra income, and gives women an opportunity for professional fulfillment. Some feel that employment for women is acceptable so long as it meets such Islamic restrictions as permitting the woman to wear Islamic dress, not placing her in a situation in which she has unnecessary contact with men, and does not expose her to *haram* (forbidden) substances such as alcohol, drugs, or pork products.

Muslim women who choose to work in the public arena are faced with a range of choices, often not unlike those many other American women need to deal with. If a woman's husband or family does not want her to go to work and she does want to, should she abide by or ignore their wishes? What if her husband objects to her choice of employment, saying it is not an appropriate setting for a Muslim woman? Conflicts can become particularly painful when objections must be set aside in view of the need of a family for more income. The mobility of individuals and families characteristic of American society, with no child care available from extended family members, also presents problems for many Muslim women who want to work.

On the whole the career versus family decision for most American Muslim women is not a choice of one over the other, but an attempt to determine whether any kind of employment will interfere with (or somehow even supplement) their responsibilities as full-time parents. Of course questions of women's employment cannot be divorced from the economic needs of families and are framed differently according to social and economic class, status (including, as in the case of some refugees, limited skill in English), and professional abilities. In general these concerns are not different from those faced by other Americans; the necessity of facing them, however, may be more pressing for Muslims newly arrived on the American scene.

For many Muslim women in the United States, of course, concerns about whether or not it is appropriate to go to work are irrelevant—they are well educated, fully able and eager to participate in the professional workforce, and face no family opposition to doing so. Nonetheless they often do decide that they will interrupt their careers so as to be home while their children are growing up. In some instances women who have advanced professional training choose to take time away from their work to raise their families, often resulting in their inability ever to rejoin the workforce. "I know that my staying home for a number of years is a major sacrifice," said a Pakistani physician. "I will be out of touch with all the new developments in my profession. But for me there is no choice—I refuse to be out of the house while my children are growing up."

Aging parents present new concerns for Muslim families in the American context. Traditional cultures generally support the elderly through the context of the extended family, providing an atmosphere in which elders enjoy more respect than they do in American culture. A young married woman living under the general authority of her husband and the control of her mother-in-law in traditional Islamic societies at least has been able to hope that her own later years, with the marriage of her sons, will bring status, respect, and power. The preponderance of the nuclear family, the different Western cultural expectations, and the need for more family members to be employed outside of the home raises new and serious problems for the older generation of American Muslims. The elderly, usually women, are often lonely, isolated, increasingly frail, and in many cases psychologically separated from younger people in the family whose new ideas and ideals they may not understand.

Islamic tradition has no place for isolation of the elderly into special homes separate from the family. "I would never dream of putting my mother or father in a nursing home," says an immigrant Muslim speaking for most in her community. "No matter what kind of burden they might be, their place is at home with their family." But the choice is sometimes unavoidable, and Muslims face not only the pain of separation but the intense guilt of needing to "send their loved ones away" to be even more lonely and isolated. Recently, a few of the larger Islamic Centers in the country began considering programs devoted especially to the elderly, and two are working on plans for constructing special senior housing near a mosque or Islamic center. ISNA has plans to open a Center for Aging, Support, and Counseling (CASC). The Center, to be owned and operated by Muslims, will provide elder care facilities for Muslims as well as others in need of assistance. The January 2004 issue of ISNA's bimonthly journal *Islamic Horizons* is dedicated to the topic of "The Final Stages: Living and Dying with Dignity."

Other traditionally "hushed-up" topics gradually being addressed through academic research, in popular Muslim journals, and via the Internet include women's mental health concerns, spousal abuse and abuse of children, homosexuality, and the possibility of AIDS in a family. Many Muslims still want to insist that such things do not occur in the Muslim family, while others recognize that the only way to find help is to openly acknowledge their reality and seek to provide Islamically-guided (and sometimes state-supported) assistance.

Abuse within the family, usually of spouses but also of children, has been the subject of a number of serious studies. Research has identified the importance of such factors as women's fear of reporting abuse by their husbands, stereotypical and discriminatory treatment of Arabs and Muslims by police, and the failure to include Muslims on task forces dealing with violence against women. Qur'anic verse 4:34, cited above, interpreted as granting authority of men over their wives, also appears at first view to give men the right to physically reprimand recalcitrant wives. There is no question that in many cultures, in many parts of the world, and today in America, some Muslim men have taken this verse as justification for what American society interprets as physical abuse of their spouses. Many Muslim representatives, spokespersons, and organizations in America are actively disavowing the validity of any such interpretation. "Small steps forward are necessary to counter regressive forces," says Canadian author Sheema Khan, "some of which apply narrow, hateful interpretations to the (Arabic) text of the Koran." Yet some influential scholars still insist that a husband may resort to mild measures in disciplining their wives. Jamal Badawi, for example, author of numerous books and featured in many videotapes on Islam, describes this action as a gentle tap "like the touch of a feather."

However, despite the strong statements made by many in the Muslim community, including imams and others in leadership positions, it is often difficult for women to speak out against abuse by their own husbands. Several recent studies note the incidence of domestic violence among South Asian Muslims in the United States and Canada. Some wives, especially of immigrants from traditional societies, believe that they deserve to be beaten if they argue with their husbands or deny them sex. Many may be uncertain as to what the Qur'an really does sanction, and often tradition (including both immigrant and African American) has trained them simply to accept what their husbands say and do. Traditions that many Muslims believe are spuriously attributed to the Prophet insist that all wives are going to hell if they do not obey their husbands, a theme repeated in some conservative mosques. Other women may be clearer that indignities and even injustices are occurring, but are embarrassed to tell other family members or friends what is going on: "Do you think I would ever admit that I don't have enough control over my husband that I can't stop him from being a little physical sometimes? What would that make me look like?" Many women fear that if they talked about their home situation with a friend, or even the imam of their mosque, it would soon become public knowledge.

Women also worry that if they report abuse to non-Muslim law enforcement agencies there is the real possibility that their husbands may be incarcerated or, since 9/11, that they may be deported. Several communities have set up support systems to deal with this issue, but the security cordon around Muslims and the fear of deportation has led the community to counsel against reporting such actions. Abuse within the family is more easily accepted and put up with by those who have recently come from traditional Muslim societies that sanction such behavior, and by women who are less educated, than by second and third generations or those who have a good understanding of Islam. Muslim women in general are increasingly familiar with, and responsive to, the attention now being given to wife abuse as an evil in American society that must no longer be tolerated.

Specific efforts are being made in various parts of the country to provide assistance to victims of family violence. In June 2004, for example, Pillars Community Services, a non profit agency in Summit, Illinois, aided by Muslim women activists, began airing radio and television announcements, running newspaper ads, and putting posters in bus shelters alerting women in Arabic and English as to how they can find help. The goal is to help victims by providing therapists who understand the Arab culture and its concept of honor and the importance of a woman's chastity. "It's going to be: 'O my God, people are talking about it!'" said the president of Arab American Family Services in Palos Hills. "Some people will be relieved. Other people will be in denial. But we want them to know that help is there." The Islamic Circle of North America (ICNA) has established Muslim Family Services to provide aid to battered women.

More recently Muslims have begun to discuss matters of sex and sexuality more openly. Until now they have tended to avoid sexual issues, insisting that they do not pertain to the Muslim community. AIDS, for example, until very recently was never seen as a disease that could afflict Muslims—some literature, in fact, has identified it as God's punishment on the West for a variety of social and political reasons. While a few young Muslims are identifying themselves as gay or lesbian, and are establishing Web sites for conversations with each other, homosexuality is unacceptable for the vast majority of American Muslims, and those who admit to such an orientation may well find themselves ostracized from their families and communities. The Spring 2003 issue of *Azizah* magazine, a journal devoted to Muslim women, courageously provided a feature article on AIDS and ways in which Muslims can and must begin to address the problem. Organizations such as the National Muslim Aids Institute ("A Project of Health Force: Women and Men Against Aids") sponsored by the Bronx Community College of the State College of New York represents one of the first efforts to educate American Muslims on the issue of HIV/AIDS.

Some Muslim families are now being forced to acknowledge, at least to themselves, that it is possible that their children may be gay and may even be adopting an openly gay lifestyle. Such a realization is anathema to most Muslims, who believe that the Qur'an specifically identifies homosexual activity as unacceptable. A Muslim imam in Ohio, when asked at an interfaith discussion whether he knew any gay Muslims, responded that he certainly did not and that there was no such thing as a homosexual Muslim. Challenged as to what he would do if a member of his congregation admitted he was gay, the imam responded that he hoped this hypothetical person would keep quiet about his inclinations. One Muslim man put in a personal ad that he is looking for a lesbian friend, one whom he might even want to marry, because of pressure from his family to find a wife. "I feel like a rag doll in the middle of a tug-of-war," he confessed, "and for all of you who are in the same boat, you know what a difficult position this is. So if you are a lesbian Muslim in a similar situation I'd love to hear from you. Maybe we can help each other out."

The Internet may have done as much as anything to bring the issue of homosexuality into the open. Several gay Muslim groups such as Queer Jihad based in West Hollywood, the gay-lesbian-bisexual-transgender (GLBT) organization al-Fatiha, the South Asian Gay and Lesbian Association, and groups in Washington, New York, Toronto, and elsewhere offer Web sites to help young women and men who think they may be gay to know that despite the official Islamic position on homosexuality there are others who share their concerns. Chat rooms allow them to enter freely and still anonymously into conversations about matters of sexuality.

American attitudes toward sex and sexuality also have affected the responses of some Muslim mothers and fathers toward public school education. Especially difficult for some is the way that issues of gender and sexuality are dealt with in public schools. They have long objected to the mixing of girls and boys in certain school-related activities such as field trips and extracurricular events, and many have insisted that their girls be allowed to wear modest uniforms that cover the whole body (and boys to cover to the knees) as an alternative to the more revealing gymsuits or swimwear that girls wear for athletic activities. Very creative designs have been developed to allow girls to participate effectively in sporting events at the same time that they are appropriately covered.

In the last several years increasing attention has been given to the concern of some parents for the ways in which sexual education is provided. Such programs generally include boys and girls in the same sessions, which share detailed descriptions of human anatomy, methods of contraception, and models for various kinds of sexual orientation. Many parents object keenly to such instruction and refuse to let their daughters participate on the grounds that they propagate values that are substantially different from what the girls are taught at home, possibly even promoting promiscuity through knowledge of condoms and other methods of birth control. In a pioneer study of sexuality among Muslim immigrant girls, Aida Orgocka has discovered that the concerns of Muslim mothers that knowledge about sexuality may in fact lead to promiscuous activities has caused them to withdraw their daughters from sex-education programs provided in the schools. The girls are therefore kept from getting important information as well as better understanding of what sexual maturity means. Orgocka has discovered that in reality, conversations about sex between girls and their mothers is often negligible due to feelings of embarrassment on the part of the older Muslim women and deep concern that their daughters will somehow bring shame on the family and most specifically on them as mothers. Girls themselves report that they do not think their mothers are able to talk with them about the physical and emotional changes they are undergoing. Appropriate sexual education for girls, and whether it should take place at home or in special school programs, is emerging as an important item on the agenda of family concerns. The American Association of Health Professionals found in a recent survey that Muslim youth often feel that their parents do not understand how things are in America, the pressures young people feel to "fit in," and that girls are especially angry with their parents when they see their brothers treated more leniently. They are also disturbed that their friends think they are "weird" because they do not date.

Traditionally Muslim women have either kept their personal problems and concerns to themselves or shared them only with closest family members. More facilities are now available for counseling and other kinds of assistance to Muslim women, but getting them in the door remains a big problem. Many are simply too shy or concerned that if neighbors and others discovered that they had what are called mental health problems they would be somehow shamed. They also recognize that few mental health workers, despite their best intentions, know a great deal about Islam or about their particular cultural customs and needs. Language can be a significant barrier in a woman's ability to express her problem or the caregiver's ability to understand what is being expressed. Some women fear that if others discover they are worried or depressed blame may fall on the husband, who may then take it out on his wife. It is also the case that many pious Muslim women feel strongly that if they are perceived as having serious problems it might be interpreted as a weakness in their faith, a giving-in to the temptations of Satan and a failure to pray effectively. New concerns are raised in the post 9/11 climate in which women fear that the very fact of their being Muslim may prejudice the health-care worker against them. Shahina Siddiqui, an experienced Canadian para-professional in the field of social work and a volunteer spiritual counselor with Muslim women, tells the story of a hospitalized female patient who was sus-pected by the staff as having obsessive-compulsive behavior. The problem, it turned out, was that she had insisted on special hygienic requirements and on taking time out from her treatments to do her five daily prayers.

Despite these concerns, important steps are now being taken in the spheres of public and mental health to ensure that the particular circum-stances of Muslim women with physical and emotional needs are addressed in appropriately contextual ways. Many hospitals and physicians understand that Muslim women often find it personally difficult or culturally inappropriate to have their care provided by male physicians or other personnel. Special efforts are increasingly being made to provide privacy for Muslim women and treat-ment by women physicians and caregivers and to otherwise understand that attention to religious and cultural appropriateness may be as important as the correct medical care. Part of this care involves the recognition that women need the active support of their families and that special efforts must be made to allow family members to visit and share in the caregiving whenever possible. One of the first attempts to collate information about Muslim women and men needing counseling advice is Ahmed Kobeisy's *Counseling American Muslims*. Kobeisy, Director of ISNA's Center for Aging Support and Counseling, in-cludes specific recommendations concerning the special needs of women at home, in the workplace, and in recuperative facilities. A new *Journal of Muslim Mental Health*, edited by Abdul Basit, identifies the mental-health needs of Muslims. American imams are discovering new definitions in their respon-sibilities that include family counseling.

Serious issues, often related to the question of what it means to be Muslim in the West, face Muslim families in America. Cultural affiliations are being negoti-ated, and the strength of allegiance to one's original country, language, and particularities inevitably fade with length of time in America. These changes have a direct effect on relationships within the family and most particularly on women's roles in regard to their husbands and other family members. Male authority in the family is being challenged and negotiated, and women are increasingly assuming public roles beyond the confines of the home, generally with the support of the community. New patterns of social interaction, including mate selection, are developing for Muslim children and young adults, often leading them away from the close circle of family domination. African Ameri-cans, Latinas, Caucasians, and others often must deal with family concerns both as Muslims and as members of extended non-Muslim families.

Voices within the Islamic community, as well as pressures from American society at large, are making it necessary for Muslims to deliberate carefully the role of the family and to reappropriate in new forms some of its traditional responsibilities. Many aspects of the Muslim family in America, therefore, are now open to negotiation—definitions, role responsibilities, cultural presuppositions, and relationships with the broader Western culture of modernization and secularization. What seems not negotiable, however, is the reality that American Islam is rooted in the structure of the family and the respective roles of women and men within it. Family relationships and responsibilities are on the agenda for interfaith dialogue between members of the Muslim and Christian communities in many areas of the country. Muslims hope that as they are informed by Western norms and inevitably (if reluctantly) are modified by them, they in turn may play some role in helping redefine and strengthen the institution of marriage and family in American society.

6

Muslim Women
in the Crucible

Maysa Mounla-Sakkal was elated when she was notified in July of 1994 that she was accepted into Western Reserve's Pediatric Residency Training Program in Cleveland, Ohio. With a medical degree from Aleppo University, she had spent nine years as a medical researcher and nurse in her husband's practice in Syria. As she went through her monthly rotations at Western Reserve, physicians on the teaching staff of the pediatric department completed evaluations of her performance. At the end of her first year, Dr. Mounla-Sakkal's residency was not renewed. She brought a lawsuit against the pediatric department alleging religious and national origin discrimination, harassment, and retaliation. Her suit was dismissed before trial because of a lack of direct evidence, although her deposition shows that before she was hired the teaching staff had made comments about her Arab origin and wanted to know her position with respect to the Arab-Israeli conflict. A female physician on the teaching staff told Mounla-Sakkal that if she wanted to continue to second-year residency, she could not pray in public and would have to take off her headscarf, adding that "babies are afraid" of the headscarf. The attending physician allegedly commented to other clinicians that Muslims ride camels and are backward thinking, that Muslim women walk behind their husbands, and that Islam is inferior to Christianity. Although the incidents that Mounla-Sakkal could point to were clearly inappropriate, under the law they were considered neither frequent nor harsh enough over the course of one year to constitute harassment.

How is a society that is based on the principles of tolerance and egalitarianism supposed to accommodate the demands of an increasingly heterogeneous public? In the United States this question lies at the heart of multicultural accommodation of religious and ethnic minorities. There has been a growing trend toward the acceptance of myriad cultural practices and identities as legitimate forms of self-expression. But at some critical points of intersection between "mainstream" society and its component parts, important trade-offs ensue. For instance, while tolerance of difference is a valued concept, so is the equality of women. When the precepts of a so-called "foreign" belief system appear to offend mainstream perceptions of the equal rights of women, which is to hold sway? According to contemporary American legal standards, the civil rights of women by and large trump the civil liberties of religious or cultural minorities whose inherited traditions, perhaps incidentally, result in sexist or discriminatory treatment.

Tensions between Islamic traditions and practices and American concepts of women's rights continue to be engaged, argued about, harmonized, negotiated, and renegotiated in varying ways. Unfortunately, prevalent in this dialogue are views that tend to be reductionist—ones that discredit Islam as a peculiarly sexist religion, or Western feminism as a hazardously ideological movement that pits women against men. Such attitudes have not been particularly helpful in working through the controversies that in fact reflect the complex nature of both Islamic and Western societies. These contests are apparent nowhere more than in American courts of law. As Muslims become more confident and assertive of their rights as members of a religious minority in American society, a struggle to balance the sometimes clashing requirements of religious law and secular law ensues. Besides inevitable conflicts that arise between Muslims and non-Muslims—such as Dr. Mounla-Sakkal's complaint against her employers—American courts of law are also more frequently drawn into disputes among Muslims, often on issues of Islamic family law. Some Muslims are pressing American courts to apply Islamic legal rules in instances of family law, making the resolution of disputes arising from the realities of Muslim life in the United States an important although complex part of the American legal terrain.

For many Muslims, the stipulations and directives redacted from the Qur'an and Sunnah still prevail in many Muslim countries, particularly in relation to matters of personal status law and marriage (which in Islam is contractual, not sacramental), treatment of women within the family, divorce, and maintenance of children. While Muslim family law is one of the main targets for Islamic reform in many countries of the world today, for many practicing Muslims in the West it is accepted as the essential core of what makes a society Islamic. The details of the law (differing slightly among the four prominent Sunni schools) are too extensive to treat fully here. Shi'ites have their own legal codes, along with directives from their Imams and Ayatollahs.

Fiqh, jurisprudence, is very important to observant American Muslims trying to understand what regulations genuinely apply to persons living in non-Muslim majority countries. The implementation of Islamic law in everyday circumstances actually becomes more important in a non-Muslim environment, where it is easy to slip into Western ways without societal constraints based on Qur'anic injunctions. With no school of law predominant in the United States, and with traditional Islamic notions of family relations often at odds with prevailing American ideologies and practices, Muslim leaders are spending considerable time and attention in helping their constituencies understand what is right, appropriate, legal, or not legal in the American context.

In this chapter we explore the following areas of law as they affect the lives of Muslim women in the United States: protection from anti-Muslim discrimination, discrimination and accommodation in the workplace, school dress codes, and marriage and divorce. The experiences of Muslim women in American courts have been highly productive. In their work on gender, power, and identity among evangelical Christian and Muslim women in the United States, sociologists John Bartkowski and Jen'nan Ghazal Read point out that religion has provided unique cultural repertoires which enable women to affirm their religious values while refashioning their convictions to fit their post-traditional lifestyles. We would add that the law—whether sacred or secular—also helps women to negotiate their place in American society. They are able to stay current and engaged with broader social trends (such as prevailing gender norms) while simultaneously tailoring their own religious identity.

Protection from Anti-Muslim Discrimination

The problem of anti-Muslim discrimination, complicated as it is by the historical relationship between Muslim societies and the West, has become especially pronounced in the United States since the September 11 attacks. The FBI, along with local law enforcement agencies, has reported a huge increase in harassment of Muslims and Arabs, as well as violent crime against their persons and their property. In monitoring workplace discrimination, the Equal Employment Opportunity Commission (the EEOC) has documented hundreds of complaints annually since 9/11 from individuals who allege backlash discrimination because they are—or are perceived to be—Muslim, Arab, Middle Eastern, South Asian, or Sikh. Homes, businesses, and places of worship have been firebombed or vandalized. Individuals have been attacked with guns, knives, fists, incendiary devices, and words.

Many of these cases involve women, most commonly their wearing of a head covering. Women in *hijab* (loose clothing and headscarf) are targets of strong anti-Muslim feeling ranging from hate crimes and violence to discrimination in employment and education. Women wearing headscarves have been spat upon, shoved, and beaten. School children have been harassed by their teachers and classmates and by the parents of other children. The following cases illustrate some of the ways in which this discrimination has been demonstrated, some of them recording incidents that took place even before the 2001 attacks.

On September 30, 2002, the EEOC sued Alamo Rent-a-Car Company because a customer service representative in its Phoenix office, Ms. Bilan Nur, was denied permission to cover her head with a scarf during the Muslim holy month of Ramadan. Alamo had granted Ms. Nur permission to cover during Ramadan in 1999 and 2000, but in December 2001—just three months after the terrorist attacks—the rental company refused to allow her to observe her religious beliefs in relation to dress. Alamo subsequently disciplined, suspended, and eventually fired Ms. Nur for failure to remove her scarf. Several cases like Ms. Nur's have been brought to the courts to adjudicate claims of anti-Muslim discrimination in the context of the workplace and beyond. Women and girls who wear the headscarf or more concealing *niqab* (full covering, including face veil) for religious reasons have long been the subject of discrimination lawsuits; such suits have multiplied since 9/11.

A highly publicized post-9/11 bench trial in Florida, *Sultaana Lakiana Myke Freeman v. State of Florida*, involved a Muslim woman who wished to have her driver's license issued either without her photo on it or with a photo of her wearing dress that covered her entire body except for her eyes. Citing post-9/11 security concerns, the state of Florida insisted that the woman's driver's license is her primary form of identification and that law enforcement personnel ought to be able to determine the woman's identity efficiently with the aid of her license. A photoless license would not be very helpful in this endeavor, the state argued. The judge in this case agreed with the state, writing in her ruling that while the woman "most likely poses no threat to national security, there likely are people who would be willing to use a ruling permitting the wearing of full-face cloaks in driver's license photos by pretending to ascribe to religious beliefs in order to carry out activities that would threaten lives." The upshot of the court's ruling was that a Muslim woman was associated with the threat of terrorism simply on the basis of her appearance. While *she* is not a terrorist, the court said, others who intend to plot terrorist attacks might take advantage of the liberties protected by the Constitution to dress like this woman in order to disguise their identities. The reasoning on which this decision is based justifies state infringement of a fundamental liberty as a means to prevent a hypothetical crime in the future.

The ACLU has taken up the cause to fight against anti-Muslim "backlash" discrimination since September 11. The civil liberties organization is defending persons charged under the Patriot Act and other federal intelligence-gathering laws with crimes related to espionage and terrorism. It has also defended Muslim women who have been discriminated against. For instance in June 2004, the Nebraska chapter of the ACLU filed a civil rights lawsuit against the city of Omaha on behalf of Mrs. Lubna Hussein, a Muslim woman who was told she would have to take her headscarf and cloak off if she wanted to accompany her children at the municipal swimming pool. Pool employees told Mrs. Hussein that she could not be in the pool area with her "street clothes" on, even though she was not planning on swimming; Hussein observed that there were others in the pool area in street dress.

Some incidents of anti-Muslim behavior actually involve violence or intrusive behavior on the part of the perpetrators. Amani al-Diffrawi, originally from Egypt, lived with her husband and four children in Torrance, California. She and her two daughters wore long dresses and headscarves when outside of their house. On September 27, 2000, al-Diffrawi's husband was out of town, and she and her children went to bed at 9:30 P.M. Soon thereafter she was awakened by loud pounding on her front door. Neighbors roused her to alert her that her house was on fire. Amani ran outside to discover a fire under the kitchen window of her house. Her neighbors helped her to douse the fire with a garden hose. Neighbors reported seeing a white male run up the driveway of al-Diffrawi's home to throw a Molotov cocktail, or incendiary device, against the house. The perpetrator, a Mr. Barrett, quickly escaped the scene in a white Ford pick up truck and was apprehended soon after by police. When they arrested him the perpetrator called the police officer a "nigger" and, when in the patrol car, made more racist remarks that were recorded on tape. He said, "I don't like other than whites and I will never change...." When brought to trial the perpetrator testified that he disliked minorities. Asked how he felt about people from the Middle East, he said, "I wish they'd go home. I don't know any." He denied being the person who firebombed el-Diffrawi's house. Barrett was convicted of a hate crime by a jury.

The case of Samar Kaukab, a twenty-three-year-old U.S. citizen of Pakistani ancestry, born and raised in the United States, is worth examining in detail. Kaukab, who lives in Columbus, Ohio, and works for the national service program Volunteers in Service to America (VISTA), was detained at O'Hare Airport in Chicago on November 7, 2001, while passing through airport security. In accordance with her religious beliefs, she covers her hair and neck with a scarf at all times in public. At the airport she was wearing pants, a long sweater, and ankle-length boots as well as her *hijab* and carried a purse and a small bag.

While she was waiting in the security line, Kaukab noticed that occasionally someone would set off the metal detector. When this happened, the security staff did a quick, relatively nonintrusive additional search with a hand-held metal detector and then the person was allowed to go on his or her way. Kaukab saw a woman wearing a scarf on her head, and some people with baseball caps, walking through the checkpoint without being stopped or asked to remove their headgear. But none of these people, according to Kaukab, appeared to be of South Asian or Pakistani descent or wore clothing that would identify them as Muslim. Eventually, Kaukab sent her bags through the x-ray machine and walked through the metal detector without setting it off. When she went to retrieve her bags, however, a National Guardsman working for airport security instructed the security staff to stop and search her.

The security staff surrounded Kaukab as if to prevent her from leaving the checkpoint, and at the direction of Mr. Vargas, the National Guardsman, they searched her multiple times with a hand-held metal detector. A female security staff person passed the wand of the detector over Kaukab's head and upper body, down her legs and her crotch, and stuck the detector into her boots (while she was wearing them). She then conducted a pat-down, pulled the hooks and straps of Kaukab's bra, and asked Kaukab to lift her sweater. Despite numerous and extensive passes over Kaukab's head and body, the detector produced no audible signal. With a crowd beginning to gather, Kaukab felt embarrassed and humiliated.

After the female security staff completed the pat-down, the three staff members, after conferring with Vargas, ordered Kaukab to take off her headscarf. Kaukab explained she could not remove it in public for religious reasons. The staff insisted, and Kaukab stated that she would remove her headscarf in a private room or behind a screen and only in front of a woman. Her request was not honored. Feeling upset and violated, Kaukab repeatedly stated that for religious reasons she would not take off her *hijab* in public or in front of a man. After a lengthy discussion among the staff with Vargas, a male security guard ordered Kaukab to follow him to a room where he insisted that he search Kaukab while his female colleagues stood outside to guard the door. Kaukab, feeling harassed and frightened, repeated her objections. Finally the security staff agreed that Kaukab would go into the room with the two female security guards.

One guard then conducted what Kaukab calls a "demeaning and overly intrusive" search of her head. When told to remove her *hijab* Kaukab complied. Then the security guard ran her fingers through Kaukab's hair and rubbed her scalp and neck. Despite Kaukab's compliance with the order to remove her *hijab*, the security guard proceeded to perform a complete body search, including removing Kaukab's sweater and placing her hand inside of Kaukab's bra, as well as unbuttoning and unzipping her pants to place her hands inside her pants and check her crotch. During the entire search, the other female security guard watched. Finally dressed again, Kaukab was allowed to leave to catch her flight. Vargas and the security personnel had found no weapons or contraband.

Kaukab sued the commander of the Illinois National Guard and the private airport security service provider contracted with United Airlines. She alleged that defendants violated her First Amendment rights to practice her religion, her Fourth Amendment right to be free from unreasonable searches, and her Fourteenth Amendment right to equal protection under the law. She also claimed that, because of her race, ancestry, color and/or ethnicity, the defendants deprived her of the full enjoyment of all the privileges, benefits, terms, and conditions of her passenger contract with United Airlines. Finally, she complained that the defendants falsely imprisoned her and committed battery against her.

Kaukab's complaint against the senior officer of the Illinois National Guard centered on the officer's responsibility to ensure the adequate training of Guard member. Although Kaukab traveled between Columbus and Chicago seven times between November 7, 2001, and June 24, 2002, she was actually improperly detained and searched only once. The lawsuit, filed on behalf of Kaukab by the ACLU of Illinois, sought unspecified financial damages, plus a federal injunction to require airport guards to be trained not to base searches solely on religion or ethnicity. Ms. Kaukab said at a press conference announcing the lawsuit, "The entire experience was degrading. I felt as though the security personnel had singled me out because I didn't belong, wasn't trusted and wouldn't be welcomed in my own country. Nothing like this ever happened to me before. When it was over, I went to the restroom to gather my emotions and telephoned my mother. I was just so humiliated." Kaukab's case was settled out of court for an undisclosed amount. The case illustrates that since 9/11 the right of a person to be free from being profiled for purposes of search and seizure based on her or his apparent Muslim religion or apparent Arab ethnicity must be guaranteed and that a balance between legitimate security concerns and personal freedoms is still in the process of being formalized.

Discrimination and Accommodation in the Workplace

How our personal and professional lives intersect is never more complicated than it is in the realm of religion. While the free exercise of religion is enshrined in the U.S. Constitution, the very expression of religious belief in daily life evokes consternation when it overlaps with work. When an employee displays a scriptural passage in a work space, or reads the Bible or the Qur'an at lunch break, or starts a conversation about religion with co-workers, red flags are raised in a way that rarely happens when an employee talks about the hometown professional baseball team. Religion is a sensitive area of life that makes many people uncomfortable, and the issue of religion in the workplace is not an easy one to handle. The regulation of religion in the workplace often leads to litigation. On the one hand, an employee who is censored in her religious expression at work may bring a lawsuit against her employer for infringement of her First Amendment rights or for discrimination on the basis of religion (which is prohibited by civil rights laws). On the other hand, an employer who liberally allows religious expression—say, by permitting someone to wear a crucifix or a Star of David in the workplace—may face a religious harassment lawsuit from employees who are made uncomfortable by its implications. What is more, if the employer is a part of the public sector (for example, in a public school), then an opening is created for a lawsuit based on the establishment clause of the First Amendment, which prohibits the "endorsement" of religion by the state.

In the face of such liabilities, what is an employer to do? In 1997 the federal government released guidelines on religious exercise and expression in the federal workplace. The standard articulated in the guidelines presents a high threshold: Restrictions on religious expression are allowed only in cases where an employee's interest in the expression is *outweighed* by the government's interest in efficient provision of public services. In addition, if a government employer allows nonreligious speech (such as, "How'd Barry Bonds do last night?") that has a negative effect on productivity or efficiency in the workplace, then it must also allow similar religious speech even if it reduces workplace efficiency. To put it another way, if public employees gather at the water cooler to discuss baseball scores and their supervisor does nothing to put an end to it, employees with a religious message must also be permitted the same liberty as long as it does not slow down their productivity any more than the discussion of baseball did.

The 1997 federal guidelines point out that some forms of religious expression do not amount to harassment of other employees, even though they may not want to hear or see such expressions. For instance, keeping a Qur'an at one's desk to read during breaks, or discussing religious views with co-workers in the cafeteria or the hallway, or wearing religious jewelry, does not in most circumstances amount to harassment of other employees. According to these guidelines, to qualify as religious harassment the speech must reach the level of religious *intimidation*, ridicule, or insult (for example, "My god is better than your god"; "Believe as I do or else!").

How does one know the difference between protected expression and harassment? Some employees, in both the public and the private sector, have gone to the courts to receive guidance about what constitutes religious harassment in the workplace. In *Venters v. City of Delphi* (seventh Circuit, 1997), a federal appellate court reasoned that religious harassment is analogous to sexual harassment for the purposes of determining legal liabilities. In other words, previous court decisions that have delineated what constitutes *sexual* harassment in the workplace can be helpful in determining what kinds of behaviors constitute *religious* harassment as well. Thus, employees' claims of both the "quid pro quo" and "hostile work environment" variety of harassment have been accepted in the courts for evaluation. Quid pro quo religious harassment may take the form of a supervisor requiring an employee to engage in an unwelcome religious activity in order to keep a job or a job benefit. For instance, a supervisor who requires attendance at prayer meetings as a condition of employment can be said to be harassing his or her employees. In one case, a Muslim employee claimed that her supervisor told her she could choose to live her life either God's way or Satan's way, and that she could not continue to work for him if she chose to follow Satan's way. This constitutes a "quid pro quo," or an arrangement whereby satisfaction of a sexual (for sexual harassment) or religious (for religious harassment) demand is a condition of continued employment.

In comparison, a "hostile work environment" claim of religious harassment can occur when an individual employee makes disparaging remarks about another employee's religious beliefs, or places literature that insults her religious beliefs in her mailbox, or threatens an employee with physical harm. In these cases the work environment is poisoned by the hostility of a co-worker or supervisor. However, because the perception of what constitutes a "hostile" work environment is subjective—every individual has different levels of tolerance for unwanted pressures—the courts require that the complainant show that not only does she find the harassment severe, but that a "reasonable person" in her shoes would have found the work environment hostile (an objective criterion). Moreover, the courts have held that the *occasional* utterance of distasteful comments or hateful epithets that an employee may find offensive is not enough to create a hostile work environment. The *totality* of circumstances has to include evidence of severe and pervasive conduct, which means that the sheer number of overtly hostile comments or behaviors has to be frequent enough to allow a jury to believe that the harassment interfered with the employee's work performance or created an intimidating working environment.

Various examples of charges of discrimination in the workplace that could not be successfully prosecuted can be cited, including the one with which this chapter began. Another is that of *Sheveka Gibson v. The Finish Line, Inc., of Delaware* (2003). A Muslim woman sued her former employer, alleging claims of a hostile work environment and wrongful discharge (that is, she was improperly fired) because of her religion. Ms. Gibson worked as a cashier for a sporting-goods store in Kentucky called The Finish Line, and in March of 2000 she began to talk about the possibility of her religious conversion from Baptist to Islam. On April 2, 2000, she informed a co-worker that she had learned more about the Nation of Islam, was attending services at a mosque on a regular basis, and was closer to deciding that she wanted to be a Muslim. The assistant manager of the store was within earshot of this conversation and out of Gibson's presence discussed with the manager what she had overheard. The assistant manager, who was white, said that she perceived the Nation of Islam to be a racist organization, "worse than the Ku Klux Klan," and that she did not feel comfortable continuing to work with Gibson. Gibson pressed charges, but the federal court held that Gibson had failed to show that the conduct of the assistant manager of the store in which she worked had created a hostile work environment. The court held that the assistant manager's single comment, made to employees other than Gibson and not in Gibson's presence, was not objectively hostile. Neither the frequency nor severity of the discriminatory conduct met the definition of a hostile work environment.

Yet another unsuccessful case is that of Firoozeh Butler, a practicing Muslim of Iranian descent, who has worked for a software company in various capacities since 1993. During the first few years of her employment she consistently received favorable performance evaluations. However, she says that after she complained to the Human Resources department in 2000 and 2001 about derogatory remarks made by co-workers concerning her ethnicity and religion, management "engaged in a calculated and deliberate effort to malign [her] job performance, to target her for termination, and to ostracize her from her fellow employees." She was demoted from senior software engineer to software engineer II in June 2001, with the reasons for this job action never adequately explained. Butler also alleges that her supervisor threatened to terminate her health benefits, suggested she resign, contacted her physician without authorization, and placed a bogus verbal warning in her personnel file while she was on short-term disability leave for a stress-related condition. Fellow employees, she says, "ridiculed her religious beliefs and national origin by inquiring whether she was to blame for terrorist activity and by referring to her as a 'camel jockey.'" In 1997 her supervisor commented to Butler that Iranians are crazy and put dirty laundry on their head, while the supervisor's manager is alleged to have remarked that Middle Eastern people smell. Butler sued, claiming a hostile work environment and discrimination according to national origin, race, and religion under Title VII of the Civil Rights Act of 1964, as well as intentional infliction of emotional distress. The case was tried in 2003, and the jury returned a verdict in favor of the employer.

While most employers maintain and regularly train employees on their antidiscrimination and antiharassment policies, employers' enforcement efforts have not traditionally focused on prevention of discrimination on the basis of national origin or religion, although these claims are mentioned in the policies. While the cases cited here were not successfully prosecuted, it may be that awareness of the potential for discrimination or harassment on the basis of national origin or religion is growing, particularly as employers see that such actions may well result in the same sorts of penalties as discriminating on the basis of race, gender, and disability.

School Dress Codes

If dress is an issue involving considerable controversy in the workplace, it is also very important in the context of American public schools where religious symbols are banned because the school is considered an instrument of the secular state for the public education of its future citizens. From this perspective, the absolute prohibition of religiously inspired attire such as the headscarf strengthens the boundaries of the secularized public sphere against any religious interference and upholds the separation of church and state.

Some of the cases that have reached the courts involve schoolgirls wearing Islamic dress. Nashala Hearn, a sixth-grade student at Ben Franklin Science Academy in Muskogee, Oklahoma, for example, was suspended twice from school for wearing a religious headscarf, in violation of the school's dress code banning bandanas, hats, and other head coverings. Her parents filed suit against the Muskogee School District in October 2003, and in March 2004 the Justice Department filed a motion in federal court in support of Hearn's position. According to the government's civil rights attorney, "No student should be forced to choose between following her faith and enjoying the benefits of a public education." The government alleged that the school district violated the equal protection clause of the fourteenth Amendment, which bars states from applying dress codes in a discriminatory manner. (This position, incidently, moves in the opposite direction of that taken by the government of France, which has banned Muslim headscarves in public schools by adopting an "anti-veil" law in March 2004, as have several German states.)

Nashala said, "I didn't know it was going to be a problem because on August 18, 2003, my first day of school last year, I explained to my homeroom teacher that I am Muslim and I wear a *hijab* and that I also pray between 1 and 1:30. She said that was fine and that she had a room for me to pray in. From that day forward, I received compliments from other kids as well as school officials." All that changed, however, when another teacher approached Nashala in the cafeteria and said her *hijab* looked like a bandana or a handkerchief, both head coverings banned under the school system's dress code. She was suspended from school until the U.S. Justice Department interceded and had her reinstated in March 2004. Two months later the Muskogee Public Schools reached an agreement to settle the lawsuit filed on the girl's behalf by the Rutherford Institute, a Virginia-based civil liberties group. The school district agreed to change its dress code to accommodate attire worn for religious reasons. Testifying before senators in a U.S. Senate Judiciary subcommittee hearing in June 2004, Nashala said her insistence on wearing the headscarf set off "a battle between being obedient to God by wearing my *hijab* to be modest in Islam versus school dress code policy." At the Senate hearing she testified to feelings of depression and humiliation as a result of the episode.

In another incident, a high-school teacher in the Jefferson Parish public school system in Louisiana was suspended on religious harassment charges. In January 2004, the teacher allegedly pulled off the headscarf of a Muslim student, Maryam Motar, saying to her, "I hope God punishes you. No, I'm sorry, I hope Allah punishes you." According to Motar, the teacher also said, "I didn't know you had hair under there." The remarks were part of a number of ethnically charged jokes that the teacher reportedly used in his world history classes, this time directed toward Motar. Although the superintendent of the school district recommended that the teacher be fired, the school board decided to temporarily suspend him, transfer him to another school, and require him to attend and pay for sensitivity training. Ms. Motar separately filed a legal complaint against her teacher in court, but the criminal charges against him were dismissed after she failed to show up for the trial for the second time.

Other cases involve the dress of teachers. The case of Alima Delores Reardon in Pennsylvania provides an interesting example, one that unfolds in a series of developments. In 1984 Reardon, a Muslim who believes that her faith compels her to wear a headscarf and long, loose dress in public, was fired from her job as a substitute teacher in Philadelphia's public schools pursuant to Pennsylvania's "religious garb" statute. The statute prohibits any public school employees from wearing religious dress, marks, emblems, or insignia while performing their duties. It was enacted in 1895 on the heels of a very unpopular Pennsylvania Supreme Court ruling that allowed Catholic nuns to wear traditional religious habits in public schools as long as they were not doing any religious instruction during school hours. The new statute prohibits any public school teacher from wearing anything indicating that he or she is an adherent of any religious group. Any public school principal who fails to suspend or fire an offending teacher is subject to a criminal penalty.

Ms. Reardon had been working in the Philadelphia school district for twelve years when she decided in 1982 that her religious beliefs required her to adopt the *hijab*. She continued teaching after 1982 while wearing it and received no complaints from either the community or the school administration for about two years. At the end of 1984, however, she was told on three separate occasions, by three principals, that she could not teach while wearing the *hijab*. Three times she was sent home because she refused to take it off.

In November 1984 Reardon filed a Title VII complaint with the EEOC against the school district of Philadelphia, claiming discrimination on the basis of religion. The EEOC found the complaint to be valid and attempted reconciliation meetings with the school board. Reardon was reinstated as a teacher in November 1985 and was allowed to teach full-time as a substitute in the Philadelphia school district while wearing the *hijab*. However, she was not awarded back pay, and the school board refused to concede that the religious garb statute was applied in a discriminatory fashion. As a result, the U.S. Justice Department (on recommendation of the EEOC) sued the Philadelphia school board in federal district court, alleging that the school district, by failing to accommodate the religious beliefs of people who wear certain dress, discriminated against them.

Initially Reardon's case was successful. The district court held that Title VII of the 1964 Civil Rights Act prohibited the enforcement of the religious garb statute, and Reardon received her back pay. The court said that the school board's application of the religious garb statute to Reardon was "selective and disparate treatment," because several others in the school system wore religious symbols or garb without incident and there was no evidence that any student saw it as an endorsement of a particular religion. The school board was prohibited from continuing the enforcement of the religious garb statute.

But on appeal, the Third Circuit Court of Appeals overturned the lower court ruling in favor of Reardon. The appellate court accepted the school board's argument that accommodating Reardon's religious practices would constitute an undue hardship for the school district in two ways. First, it would put school principals in the position of violating a valid state law, thereby exposing them to the risk of criminal prosecution, fines, and the loss of their jobs. Second, it would require Pennsylvania to sacrifice a compelling state interest in preserving the secular character of its school system. The two reasons combined were enough to persuade the higher court to reverse the lower court ruling, saying that the 1964 Civil Rights Act does not prevent the school board in Philadelphia from denying Reardon the opportunity to teach while wearing the *hijab*. In fact, the ruling implies but never explicitly holds that Title VII's requirement of accommodation of religious practices in the workplace might place the public official at risk of violating the establishment clause of the First Amendment by creating the impression of official endorsement of religion.

Marriage and Divorce

While some Muslims in the United States ignore Islamic law altogether and choose instead to rely exclusively on secular American law, many selectively combine key provisions of Islamic law with American conventions on marriage. For example, in addition to getting an official marriage license from city hall, some couples have the marriage religiously sanctioned in accord with Islamic law, which treats marriage as a matter of contract. Not all of the Islamic traditions relating to marriage, supported by Islamic law based on the stipulations of the Qur'an, are observed in the West. Traditional legal stipulations, such as that allowing Muslim men to marry up to four wives at one time, are not observed because they contravene the laws of the state.

Other regulations, such as those dealing with the payment of the *mahr*, or dower, often are observed in American Muslim marriages, if only symbolically. Islamic law stipulates that the husband pay a *mahr* for the right of intercourse. Before getting married the couple negotiates an Islamic marriage contract in which it is spelled out that the groom will pay to the bride an immediate *mahr*—an honorific sum of money, jewels, or gold, and even in some cases nonmonetary gifts—when the marriage takes place, and will also commit to pay a "deferred" *mahr*—another specific sum of money—in the event that the marriage ends in divorce. The couple may customize their marriage contract by adding stipulations that generally guarantee the rights of women vis-à-vis their spouses. For instance, women frequently add a clause that guarantees that they keep their finances separate from their spouses' and control their own investments. Women can reserve the right to work outside the home without getting their husbands' permission, to initiate divorce, and to use contraception. They can even stipulate that they will not cook or clean the house!

Some American Muslims, such as attorney Azizah al-Hibri, are working to help women understand how to protect themselves through careful wording of the marriage contract. Islamic marriage contracts, in fact, can exceed the guarantees provided for married women under American law. Women's rights, al-Hibri states, are unrecognized and therefore underutilized by Muslim women, and the right to insert conditions into marriage contracts, to modify conventional marital relations in a manner that enhances women's freedom, is chief among these. Facsimiles of a Muslim marriage contract that would serve these purposes can be found on the Internet at the Web site of the Muslim women's human-rights organization KARAMAH.

One of the important issues now being addressed is whether an American court of law, in the name of pluralism, should substitute the *mahr* provision for the usual provisions of alimony and child support, or for the equitable division of community property called for in state law. If a married couple has signed an Islamic marriage contract—either as U.S. residents or in another country before immigrating to the United States—should the provisions of that contract supersede existing state laws governing the dissolution of the marriage? To appreciate the potential economic and social inequalities that could occur in such cases, we need to keep in mind the purpose for which the *mahr* is practiced.

Historically, the ostensible purpose of the *mahr* provision has been to protect the wife in the event that the husband decides suddenly to divorce her. It is meant to compensate for the fact that women are vulnerable in marriage to the man's privilege to execute a *"talaq"* divorce. The husband traditionally can divorce his wife without her being present at the divorce "proceeding" or even knowing about it. All a man needs to do is to pronounce "I divorce you" three times, sometimes done in quick succession or even at one time. Women traditionally had virtually no recourse to this method of repudiation. (Several Islamic countries now have created legislation that limits this right.) Thus, the *mahr* provision serves as a cushion, a guarantee of maintenance, in the event of divorce, particularly important for women who have no private wealth. Attorney Asifa Quraishi suggests that the record of Muslim marriage litigation in the United States shows evidence that Muslims generally do continue to include the *mahr* provision in their contemporary marriage contracts, making the question of whether *mahr* is valid under civil law a relevant one.

Some of the marriage contracts into which Muslim couples in the United States have entered illustrate that the definition of *mahr* reflects a wide range of personal interests. They include such provisions as a dollar amount of $35,000; a copy of the Qur'an and an eight-volume set of hadith after one year of marriage and a prayer carpet after five; a new car, $20,000, and a promise to teach the wife certain sections of the Qur'an; $1 at the time of the marriage and $100,000 in the event of a divorce; Arabic lessons; a computer and a home gym; a trip around the world including stops in Mecca, Medina, and Jerusalem; a leather coat and a pager; and a wedding ring up front and one year's rent for the deferred *mahr*.

Whatever form it takes, it is important to keep in mind that a *mahr* does not serve the same purpose as a prenuptial agreement under American law. In the United States, marriage law falls under the jurisdiction of each of the fifty states, and each state sets out its own laws governing prenuptial agreements. Prenuptials are meant to define and preserve the assets that existed before the marriage as well as to define what happens to assets accumulated during the marriage. The most common use of the prenuptial agreement is to protect the separate character of property owned before marriage. It is applied only in instances where there is a substantial disparity in the wealth of two people about to marry. In contrast to *mahr* provisions, which are created in order to protect women from the harsh effects of unilateral divorce under Islamic law, the prenuptial agreement is used to draw an enclosure around the assets of an individual in order to protect her or him from the potentially acquisitive grasp of the individual's partner. While the *mahr* is gender specific, providing maintenance for the wife, the prenuptial agreement is gender neutral and can be used by either spouse to protect his or her property.

What would happen if American court officials were asked to apply the Islamic rules of marriage and divorce instead of existing state law on the dissolution of marriage? In many cases courts have treated the *mahr* provision as if it were a prenuptial agreement. This, however, is a misapprehension of what the *mahr* is intended for. Should the *mahr* replace the usual provisions for alimony or the fair division of marital assets, as stipulated under community property rules? Ultimately, in the case of the dissolution of the marriage, the question of whether the *mahr* provision should be honored in American courts turns on this question: Would the woman be economically worse off than she would be under state laws governing the dissolution of marriages?

Following are brief synopses of some U.S. court cases resulting from litigation of Muslim divorces. Focusing on *mahr*, they illustrate the typical problems that have arisen in state courts of law and their solutions. The question often is whether women accept the legal opinion of the court or see the Islamic marriage contract as binding. It is important to keep in mind that both sets of American civil law that have a bearing on Islamic marriage contracts—laws on marriage and divorce and contract law—fall under state jurisdictions in the United States. Because of the independence of the fifty states (plus the District of Columbia), the outcomes of litigation in courts are a mixed variety of rulings that are supportive of Islamic legal claims in some states and prohibitive in others. The landscape that emerges, therefore, is neither consistent nor predictable.

Several courts appear to have accepted the binding nature of the *mahr* contract. In the case of *Odatalla v. Odatalla* (2002), the couple had been married in an Islamic ceremony conducted by an imam (religious leader). Before their marriage, the families of the bride and groom negotiated the terms of the marriage contract, including the terms of the *mahr*, which was written by the imam and signed by both the bride and the groom. The husband was to pay the wife one gold coin during the marriage ceremony, and a deferred *mahr* of $10,000 in the event of a divorce. In this case, in addition to the *mahr* notation in the Islamic marriage contract, the negotiations between the two families prior to its signing had been videotaped as part of the marriage ceremony, and two witnesses signed the agreement. Several years later, the wife filed for divorce and sought enforcement of the *mahr* provision in a New Jersey court. The husband objected, arguing that enforcement of the *mahr* would violate the establishment clause of the First Amendment by putting public officials in the position of implementing what was essentially a religious agreement.

The trial court rejected the husband's argument, and held that the enforcement of the *mahr* provision of an Islamic marriage contract would neither excessively entangle the court in questions of religious doctrine nor violate the "free exercise" rights of the husband (both infringements of First Amendment guarantees). While included as part of a religious ceremony, the *mahr* provision of the contract had a secular purpose, the court reasoned, because it was intended to address the financial support of the wife after the marriage ended. The award of the *mahr* to the wife was within the judicial authority of the court and did not breach any constitutional prohibition against the entanglement of the state with religion. The *mahr* provision also complied with New Jersey standards for contract law and thus was enforceable.

In New York, the state supreme court accepted the concept of the *mahr* provision in the case of *Habibi-Fahnrich v. Fahnrich* (1995), ruling that in general it is enforceable in a state court of law. Nevertheless, the court held that the specific *mahr* provision contested in this case was not legally valid, because the terms of the payments were simply too vague to be enforced by a court of law. The immediate *mahr* was a ring and the deferred *mahr* was to be half of the husband's possessions. However, since no specific means were presented in the contract to determine which assets were under consideration, calculated at what time during the marriage, the court found the terms to be too indefinite and thus a violation of the state law on frauds. The court ruling emphasizes that Islamic marriage contracts need clearly written terms if they are to stand up in courts.

In the case of *In Re Marriage of Shaban* (2001), the couple divorcing had been wed in Egypt in the early 1970s. Their marriage contract provided for an immediate *mahr* of 25 piasters (about one American dollar). The deferred *mahr*, to be paid in the event of a divorce, was equal to about thirty dollars. At the time of the marriage, neither spouse anticipated that the couple would emigrate to California. Once there, the husband became a successful physician and the couple subsequently divorced. Had the court found that the deferred *mahr* was a valid agreement, the wife would have received only $30 instead of half of the $3 million estate she shared with her husband. In this ruling the court refused to substitute the *mahr* for the equitable division of community property under California divorce law.

At other times, however, courts have recognized the *mahr* as superceding the provisions of state law. In *Chaudry v. Chaudry* (1978), a New Jersey court held that the *mahr* superseded any alimony or division of the property of the husband, who also was a millionaire physician. The court based its decision in part on the fact that the husband had gone back to Pakistan and obtained an Islamic divorce. In accordance with the international rule of comity—which says that decisions rendered procedurally in foreign courts will be upheld in American courts unless they fly in the face of U.S. public policy—the court viewed the *mahr* agreement as a waiver of the Muslim wife's right to equitable distribution of the couple's jointly-owned property under state law in the American legal system.

A 1996 Florida case, *Akileh v. Elchahal*, provided another instance in which the state court accepted the *mahr* as a legitimate device for settling the property claims of a divorce. Here the Muslim wife had been denied the *mahr* by a lower court. On appeal a higher Florida court overturned the ruling, concluding that the *mahr* was enforceable and avoiding any legal discussion of the division of the couple's marital property. One year after the couple had married, the wife discovered she was infected with a venereal disease. The only possible source of the infection would have been her husband, who failed to inform his wife of the infection prior to the marriage. The wife moved out, but continued to try to save the marriage by insisting on counseling. She filed for divorce only after learning that her husband was intending to leave the state. This case is unusual, because in receiving the *mahr*, the wife was better off than she would have been under Florida's rules of community property. She received a deferred *mahr*, worth $50,000, that was valued at more than half of the couple's jointly owned assets.

The difficulty in applying Islamic family law, as with any body of law, is that it is not a fixed and unitary structure of meaning. It is rather a fluid body of kaleidoscopic forms, subject to differing interpretations and doctrinal controversies. Several Islamic legal schools of thought and different cultural and class traditions influence the interpretation of the law's proscriptions and prescriptions. What prevails in one legal approach or interpretation is not necessarily recognized in another context. So, for example, a couple who marries in Egypt may have been influenced by, and intended to adopt the meanings of, the particular understanding of Islamic legal norms that prevailed in that country at the time the marriage took place. According to some (but not all) interpretations of Islamic laws on marriage and divorce, when a wife initiates a divorce she forfeits any claim to the deferred *mahr* stipulated in her marriage contract. That the *mahr* provision is invalid in these circumstances renders the provision indeterminate and not always predictable. In some cases, courts have viewed the *mahr* provision with skepticism, rejecting it if it allows the wife to profit from a divorce. To call the *mahr* a "financial incentive" to file for a divorce when it can easily be made void—depending on which Islamic legal doctrine is chosen to apply—is inaccurate and illogical. One might just as well argue that the risk of losing the deferred *mahr* would serve to deter a wife from filing for divorce even in cases where the husband is unfaithful or abusive.

Thus in a case decided in California, *In Re Marriage of Dajani* (1988), a Muslim couple married in Jordan had agreed to a *mahr* equivalent to about $1,700 in case of divorce. The California Court of Appeal struck down the agreement because it clearly provided for the wife to profit by a divorce—in other words, there was a financial incentive for her to initiate the divorce, despite the fact that the *mahr* was not worth very much. This presumes, however, that a wife does not forfeit the *mahr* if she initiates the divorce, which is not an altogether valid presumption. The important point about this case is that the court found that the *mahr* was not enforceable because it contradicted secular public policy in the United States in general and in California in particular.

Western distortions and unfavorable portrayals of Islam and Muslims have been replete in popular culture and officialdom in the United States for many decades. Is a less-than-hospitable reception of Islamic legal norms in the courtrooms and law offices of the United States yet another example of this? Any Western discussion of Islamic family law necessarily begs the question of whether it condemns or misapprehends Islam as a religion and *shari'ah* as a body of law. As more Muslims immigrate to the United States, and more Muslim Americans take seriously the role that their religion might play in shaping their marriages and family life, American courts will be faced increasingly with instances of people blending or traversing between Islamic and domestic/civil sources of law. A desire by the courts to give Islamic law due respect draws the courts along the inevitable path of deciding what constitutes the appropriate interpretation of Islamic law to fit the particular circumstances before the courts, on a case-by-case basis. This may force courts into the impermissible terrain of violating the establishment clause, asking government officials to determine the content of religion.

Cases of divorce, discrimination in the workplace and schools, hate crimes, and passenger profiling in the aftermath of September 11, are all instances that display tensions between individual freedom and the authority of the state. The law is central in determining the relationship between the individual's right to religious liberty and the state's power to protect and promote such general interests as national security and gender equality. In some instances, we can see the state occasionally protecting a woman's right to wear a particular mode of dress despite resistance on the part of employers or schools who seek to promote other objectives. In other cases the state has acted in a manner that jeopardizes a woman's right to self-expression, by singling her out for extraordinary scrutiny and by making religious freedom secondary to competing interests. The practice of "veiling" is not the only issue that places women in the crucible of American domestic law—we have also seen examples of American courts applying Islamic rules of marriage and divorce. Issues such as domestic violence, child custody, inheritance, and female genital cutting raise further questions about women's rights under Islamic law. Do these offer potential sites for a collision between secular and religious laws in American courts? For now, the *hijab* has made an easy symbol, both for the growing presence of Muslims and the increasing pluralism of public life in the United States. It may yet prove to be a harbinger of increasing toleration in the halls of justice.

7

Claiming Public Space

"Hands off my Hijab!" read the large placard raised by a group of American Muslim women rallying in support of their Muslim sisters in France who are facing recent French antiveiling laws. These young protestors, also holding "Diversity is Beautiful" signs, were reflecting their concern that such restrictions may come to apply in the United States. Public demonstration and claiming their rights as Muslims and as American citizens are ways in which American Muslim women are making themselves seen and heard in public places. Voices of concern, protest, and mutual support are also being raised through the media, in the press, and on the Internet, and are coming from a wide range of perspectives. "I am a young liberal Muslim Arab," said Lebanese-born Alia Fattouh in a Web message entitled "An Arab liberal's anguish." Fattouh stressed that she wears jeans and miniskirts and no veil, watches "Sex and the City" and "The Simpsons," and plans to pursue a career in international affairs. But right now, she says, "I feel deeply estranged from everything the government is trying to do.... The U.S. seems not to understand who we are."

The public roles being adopted by Muslim women are vital in the process of defining, and redefining, the meaning of American Islam. Not only by their presence in a variety of professions, but publicly by giving voice both to the pain that the community is currently experiencing and to the kind of commitment that they represent, these women are changing the face of Islam as it is seen both from within the various Muslim communities in this country and by those Americans who struggle with perennial images of Islamic women as oppressed and forced into seclusion. Muslim women are journalists, educators, artists, politicians, chaplains, and founders of literally hundreds of organizations dedicated to a better understanding of Islam— often with different ideas of what that Islam is—and to the service of women and others in their communities.

The Key to Progress Is Organization!

Hadia Mubarak, studying for a master's degree at Georgetown University, ran uncontested for the position of president of the Muslim Student Association. The MSA had never before had a woman president and was not to have one after that election either, because women students got together at the last minute and backed an immigrant male to oppose her. No surprise—the man won. Now, however, after having been nominated by MSA chapters in several different universities, Mubarak has won the presidency and is both the first woman and the first American-born student to be MSA president. Mubarak is working to overcome what she describes as the obstacles created by the differences between the immigrant mindset and the American-born frame of mind. For the latter, the priorities are domestic issues such as homelessness, civil rights, elections, social justice, and social security reform, whereas the pertinent issues among the immigrant students tend to be foreign policy concerns, gender interaction, and the position of women. Talking about the greater participation of women in general in MSA activities, often involving strenuous physical labor, she says, "Everywhere it is the sisters who are holding up the organization—even doing the heavy lifting!" In 2004 Hadia Mubarak was one of three recipients of CAIR's Islamic Community Service Award.

The MSA president is not the only woman to be featured as head of a major Islamic organization. Since the mid-1990s, Muslim groups whose members are both male and female have been springing up in the United States. Some, like the MSA, are specifically religious in nature, most notably the Islamic Society of North America (ISNA). This association has moved from an original conviction that Muslims should avoid any more involvement in American society than necessary to advocating active participation for both women and men, although on Islamic terms and by Islamic definitions. New leadership roles are at issue. In 2001, ISNA for the first time elected a woman, Ingrid Mattson, to serve as vice president. Mattson's election to this office signals an important attempt on the part of ISNA to fulfill a pledge made publicly by many public Muslim groups and persons, namely, to bring women into positions of genuine national leadership.

Mattson, a Canadian Muslim who served as advisor to the Afghan delegation to the UN Commission on the Status of Women in 1995, teaches at a Christian seminary in Connecticut. She has been an occasional invitee of the White House to participate in public events such as fast-breaking ceremonies and to join other Muslim leaders in helping government officials understand the perspectives of Muslim Americans. She is looked to by young Islamically-observant women as an example of someone in a position of power who wants to make public witness to her faith. Mattson, who has served on ISNA's Shura (consultative) Council, acknowledges that most Muslim women have experienced repression and discrimination on the part of some male Muslim religious leaders. It is urgent for women to be Islamically-educated, she argues, particularly in the interpretation of scripture and law, so that they can effectively make the case for legitimate leadership roles for women. Renewal, she says, is an Islamic paradigm for legitimate social change.

Notable as the achievements of Mubarak, Mattson, and other women may be, it is patently clear that men still hold the vast majority of leadership positions in Muslim religious, social, and political organizations. At a meeting of Muslim leaders several years ago, sponsored by the "Muslims in the Public Square" Pew Charitable Trusts study, only one woman was present in a room of some twenty-five men. She turned out to be a secretary. Embarrassed when questioned about the absence of women, a male participant commented that he did not know of any women who were heading up Islamic organizations. The Islamic Circle of North America, second in size among Muslim groups to ISNA, has determined that gender parallel, rather than integrated organizational structure, best reflects its Islamic commitment, and for many years has had a separate group operated by and for women. The male branch is the public face of the organization, and male leaders participate in public events. The first time the Islamic Circle allowed a woman to speak at its annual convention was in 2002. In 2001 it would not allow the female vice mayor of the city where the convention was held to welcome the participants because some in its leadership, as well as its rank and file, believe that a woman's voice is sexually seductive. Some observers believe that the fact that at least small numbers of women are now becoming more visible in leadership capacities reflects the current concerns of the Muslim community about government investigations, invasion of privacy, and general policing of Islamic activities. "Let the women take the heat up front," such an attitude might suggest. Most Muslims women, however, point to increasing roles of women in "up front" positions as a positive and hopeful sign of the parity in roles that they believe an egalitarian Islam should always strive to promote.

Some women continue to work within what remain primarily male organizations, quietly pursuing both their own ends and the aims of their particular group and hoping to ensure that more women actually serve in leadership positions. Others have decided that it is more important, and ultimately more productive, for women to form their own organizations. Networking with other Muslim women, while it carries different connotations in

America than in traditional cultures, is a natural move for many immigrants who have always had strong bonds with other women in the community. It is also a structure of cooperation that fits well into the community-oriented focus of many women of color. The informal nature of this networking activity is now being augmented by more formal structures, such as women's groups and structured networks. They are new in a number of ways, not least in the heterogeneous nature of their composition, sometimes including both immigrant and indigenous women.

Women's groups and agencies differ widely in purpose. Some help promote a better understanding of the faith, such as Sisters in Islam (initiated in Malaysia but represented in the United States by such advocates as Amina Wadud), which reinterprets Islamic principles and practices in light of the Qur'an. Others, like the Rahima Foundation, founded in 1993 by Habibe Husain as a nonpolitical charitable and educational organization in the San Francisco–San Jose area of California, provide goods and services to Muslim women and families and serve as women's support groups. Muslim women's centers can be found in most major cities of the United States and Canada. Women work with each other in nongovernmental organizations (NGO's) and civic groups, health, and educational agencies. Many have grown up participating in Muslim youth organizations and are extending their experience and training by taking their place in the leadership of the American Muslim community.

The list of formal organizations for Muslim women, both national and international, grows daily, many dedicated to bringing about better understanding of rights, responsibilities, and opportunities for women. *Windows of Faith*, edited by Gisela Webb, provides an excellent and lengthy listing of most of the national and regional organizations in which Muslim women, for a variety of purposes, now participate. Many of these groups have more personal goals, such as helping women find sisters with whom to congregate or helping promote a better understanding of what it means to be a Muslim woman in the context of contemporary America. Others, such as KARAMAH: Muslim Women Lawyers for Human Rights, are designed to provide information about women's legal rights. Some differences naturally exist between organizations that favor *da'wah* as a primary activity and those more interested in women's rights per se; women who choose to be involved have a diverse range from which to select.

The American Muslim community lost one of its most prominent activists with the death of Sharifa Alkhateeb in the fall of 2004. Alkhateeb spent her life working to educate America about Islam and to demonstrate her faith by working as a grassroots advocate for those in need. The daughter of a Yemini father and a Czech mother, she matured during the feminist movement of the 1960s and determined how best to work for the betterment of women within the context of Islam. Her strategy was to organize. From her home base in Northern Virginia she founded the North American Council of Muslim Women (NACMW), a nonprofit, educational, legislative, policy, and advocacy group. She served as president of the Muslim Educational Council, a mid-Atlantic not-for-profit organization designed to educate schools about Islam, and in 2000 she created Peaceful Families, a nationwide family violence awareness program funded by the U.S. Department of Justice. Alkhateeb also served as youth advisor to large Muslim youth organizations such as the Muslim Student Association (MSA) and the Muslim Youth of North America (MYNA).

Some organizations are designed specifically for political purposes, and have grown in prominence in recent years as Muslims have attempted to advocate for their rights in the political arena. The Muslim Women's League, founded in 1999, is a nonprofit Los Angeles-based organization that works to implement Islamic values in American society and to reclaim the status of women as active contributors. It participates in global efforts to improve women's lives, networks with numerous organizations, publishes materials about alternative perspectives on issues of concern to Muslim women, promotes a range of educational forums, and supports spiritual/study retreats and dialogue. Spokesperson and past president of the MWL is Leila al-Marayati, a physician who has been vocal in fighting for women's access to places of power in relation to politics, media, and other public positions. About efforts to counter the relative absence of Muslim women's voices from the public discourse, she says, "We're sort of clawing away at the edges." Al-Marayati was a Presidential appointee to the U.S. Commission on International Religious Freedom, serving from 1999 to 2001. Her courage in speaking out against perceived injustice was evidenced in an article she wrote in *Counterpunch* (December 16, 2002), in which she accused fellow committee member Elliot Abrams, head of the Commission, of deep bias in favor of Israel and of alienating those whose support the United States needs in order to fight terrorism effectively.

Al-Marayati is an interesting example of someone who wore the *hijab* when she was in her early twenties, but took it off after completing medical school and residency at UC—Irvine. She was told that certain faculty members had opposed her acceptance to the medical school because she wore Islamic covering. The *hijab* had reduced al-Marayati to a stereotypical image, so she stopped wearing it when she finished medical training to "avoid the discomfort of the attention the scarf attracted." Despite the fact that she experienced what can be described as competing identities—a professional, a Palestinian, an American, a Muslim—al-Marayati says she does not find them to be in conflict. "The yardstick I measure by is my faith; everything else falls into place. My identity is an American Palestinian who is a Muslim."

Also active on the West Coast is San Franciscan attorney Asifa Quraishi, who has been a prominent voice calling for redress of such abuses suffered by

Muslim women as domestic violence, lack of child custody, lack of access to education and employment, pornography, and inadequate maternity leave policies. Quraishi is critical of Muslim leadership that she says is fixated on upholding an idealized image of Muslims, ignoring the welfare of individuals and the community. She advocates the use of the Internet as a forum in which Muslim women can ask questions openly without fear of being harassed, interrupted, or silenced. Quraishi approves of Muslim women working with Western feminists toward the achievement of common goals and argues strongly that the Muslim community needs to overcome taboos against women holding significant leadership positions.

Formed in 2003 in Richmond, Virginia, the Association of Muslim Women in America, Inc. (AMWA) is working to achieve representation of Muslim women from a wide range of backgrounds, ethnic and cultural identities, disciplines, and political positions. It is based on the exchange of women from already-established organizations, those from mosques and Islamic groups, and those with professional and academic standing. Of immediate concern to AMWA are such issues as delivery of adequate social services for Muslim women, working toward gender equity, crisis intervention, work place empowerment, and social and economic development.

A few female-initiated groups are Islamic in conception, but specifically open to all women. Sisters United in Human Service, Inc., for example, is dedicated to "working in the spirit of sisterhood to promote, support, uplift and serve human concerns." With a governing board of both men and women, interfaith and interracial, the Sisters United organization fosters cooperative projects such as collecting and distributing food and clothing to the homeless, annual interfaith health conferences, interfaith programs and events, and youth leadership, and development. Sisters United is based in Decatur, Georgia.

The proliferation of women's Islamic organizations in Canada and the United States reflects to a great extent the opportunity for access to instant information and communication. Most Islamic journals have sections or articles about or for women, with clear instructions as to how to connect with other women or to find assistance with particular problems, and the number of journals specifically for women is growing. Many are available on-line.

Another way in which Muslim women are "claiming public space," although their efforts are not yet represented in organizations as such, is through participating in, and sometimes initiating, different kinds of interfaith dialogue and exchange. One notable effort highlights the attempt to promote understanding between Muslim and Jewish women in America. Mahnaz Shabbir, a first-generation Shi'ite American Muslim of Indian parentage, has formed a friendship with Sheila Sonnenschein, a first-generation American Jewish woman whose father emigrated from Latvia. Finding commonality in their experiences of being "different" in the context of middle-American

Kansas, the two women have written a book together about ways to bring their families and communities to better understanding of each other. *Person to Person: That's Where Peace Begins* talks about the journey they have undertaken in sharing their personal, cultural and political affiliations and identities. They now speak publicly together to religious and civic organizations as a model of women's interfaith cooperation and friendship.

Players in the Field of Politics

In November 2004 Saudi-American Ferial al-Masri ran for U.S. House of Representatives on the Democratic ticket in the thirty-seventh electoral district in California. She hoped to challenge the Republican stronghold in the area and to be the first Muslim woman from the district to serve as a member of the House of Representatives. While she lost the election, al-Masri won a major victory for the participation of Muslim women in the American political process, proving her readiness to fend off any attacks made on the grounds of her Saudi heritage or her religious affiliation. Like many Muslim women, being actively interested in politics came after American involvement in the First Gulf War. Al-Masri teaches American history at a Los Angeles high school and was named "Person of the Week" on Peter Jennings' *ABC Nightly News*. "I was the first Saudi woman to appear on a newspaper cover without a veil," she says, noting that she has become "a media darling" in her homeland. Meanwhile her boast that her son was serving in the American military in Iraq has alienated her from other Arab Americans.

Another unsuccessful candidate whose determination has not been allayed by her electoral loss is Afifa Syeed, who ran for the Board of Supervisors in Loudoun County, Virginia, in 2003. Syeed is the daughter of the executive secretary of ISNA, who is originally from Kashmir. As she says, "I lost the election but not my enthusiasm for politics." Syeed, who is Director of the Muslim Education Resource Council, Inc., and Principal of Al-Fathi Academy in Sterling, Virginia, is working to get the Muslim community activated and empowered. In 2003 she gathered a group of Muslim women to go together to the Capitol to talk to legislators about raids on Muslim homes and facilities after 9/11 and to argue for repeal of the Patriot Act. Some of the women, who had emigrated from police states and were afraid to confront the government, nonetheless followed Syeed's lead. "They say that 'it takes a village,'" Syeed says. "Well, it also takes an Ummah [Muslim community] to effect change!"

Successful in her bid for political office has been African American Muslim candidate Yaphett S. El-Amin. Elected to the Missouri House of Representatives in 2002 and still serving, El-Amin, a native of St. Louis, was featured on the cover of *Azizah* magazine in the winter of 2002. She has served on committees dealing with tourism and cultural affairs, job creation and economic development, health and social services, education, and urban issues. America's first female Muslim to be appointed to a judgeship in American courts is Zakia Mahasa, Master Chancery in the Family Division of the Baltimore City Circuit Court. Mahasa, who became a Muslim while an undergraduate at the University of Maryland, presides over some ten to thirty domestic cases every day. She wears her Islam confidently, asserting that the best way to propagate the faith is by example. On March 11, 2005, a Muslim woman, Shirin Tahir-Kheli, was selected by Secretary of State Condoleezza Rice to be her senior advisor and chief interlocutor on UN reform. Tahir-Kheli, a U.S. citizen of Pakistani origin, served as special assistant to the President and senior director for democracy, human rights, and international operations at the National Security Council from 2003–2005.

Not all Muslim women interested in the political process in America, of course, run for political office or participate in such public ways as the women noted here. For virtually the first time in the history of Islam in America, women along with men are being strongly encouraged by Muslim organizations and spokespersons to exercise their right to vote at the local and the national levels (although Muslim and Arab women did form a coalition for the campaign of Jesse Jackson for President). During the run-up to the Presidential elections of 2004, young women were often to be seen outside of mosques or at Islamic organizations encouraging others to register to vote. As Garbi Schmidt has found in her work with youth in the Chicago area, some young Muslim women are involved in high-scale political lobbying. Generally, she says, there is a direct correlation between the degree of political activism of a young person and the number of generations his or her family has been in America.

African American Muslim women are taking active roles both in working for community justice and in publicly defending Islam. Sister Bahija Abdus-Salam, for example, served as Islamic Coordinator for the Million Mom March Against Gun Violence in Washington on May 14 (Mother's Day), 2000. "I am here to represent the Muslim woman," she said, "and to let people know that we are not oppressed. We are a part of this society and we have a place in this society!"

Muslim youth are learning the effectiveness of working in collaboration with other young people. Girls for Change, a group operating out of San Jose, California, brings together teens of various backgrounds to work on community problems and projects. Girls in *hijab* participate alongside those with spiky colored hair and pierced body parts to address issues such as rape, runaways, drugs and alcohol abuse among teens, and to involve the city in fostering legislation to address such problems. Under the guidance of women professionals, girls design, lead, and find funding for innovative projects to bring about change in their neighborhoods. Najeeba Syeed-Miller, executive director of the Western Justice Center Foundation in Pasadena, California, works with schools, courts, and communities in the area of conflict management and resolution, helping administrative agencies achieve justice and equal access.

The Arab American community, those fighting for equal opportunities for women, and the world of academia all lost a highly esteemed member when civil rights activist Hala Salam Maksoud died in the spring of 2004. Born in Beirut, Lebanon, Maksoud emigrated to the United States in 1947, and as an American citizen struggled to fight for Arab women's rights in the international arena and for better understanding of Arab and Muslim women in her new country. She lectured, wrote, and made numerous radio and television appearances speaking out against misperceptions of Arab women that she believed contribute to stereotyping and discrimination and was a founding member of the American Association of University Graduates and the American Council for Jerusalem. Maksoud also helped U.S. Senator James Abourezk of South Dakota found the American-Arab Anti-Discrimination Committee (ADC) in 1980, and she served as its powerful and dynamic president from 1996 until 2001, when illness prevented her from continuing. Maksoud received a lifetime achievement award from the American Immigration Law Foundation.

Women as Educators of Children and Youth

The American Muslim community as a whole recognizes the heavy responsibility it carries for making sure that its children are well-educated. Those who are professionally successful want to guarantee that their children are able to maintain their standards of economic achievement, while those in the lower economic classes want to take advantage of America's promise of education for all. A number of parents are also concerned that their young people receive the kind of Islamic education that will allow them to understand the fundamentals of their faith and its practice.

Many Muslims are looking with increasing concern at the state of affairs in the nation's public schools, particularly those located in heavily populated urban areas. They worry that proper education is being sacrificed in the struggle to keep order in the classroom and that schools are too often the locus of guns and drugs and other undesirable elements of American culture. More conservative Muslims believe that the too-easy interchange between young women and men can lead to contact in ways that they feel are both inappropriate and potentially dangerous. As a result some Muslim families are looking for alternate ways to provide for the full education of their children, ways that will train them in the social and physical sciences as well as the humanities and will also provide certain elements of Islamic instruction.

If most Muslim children receive any Islamic education outside of the home, it takes place in after-school programs or in special weekend religious training in mosques and Islamic centers. Muslim women in America today carry the heaviest responsibility for making sure that the young people of the community are familiar with the basics of Qur'an and Sunnah, as well as the elements that make up their responsibilities as Muslims. While men, of course, also function as teachers, administrators, and authors of literature used in children's education, women are at the forefront of managing after-school programs, educational hours at the mosque (normally held on Sunday morning and called weekend school or Sunday school), and teaching in the small but growing number of Islamic schools in the country.

There are now over 200 full-time Islamic schools and charter schools across the nation, of which most are kindergarten through sixth or eighth grade, and no more than a dozen are high schools. Recent estimates are that some three quarters of the teaching staff of these institutions are women, a fairly recent development in Islamic education. Many women also serve as school principals. Muslim educator Susan Douglass, author of teaching resources for elementary and secondary Muslim schools as well as public schools, says that among the reasons for the predominance of women in these teaching capacities is that low salaries make it difficult for heads of households to provide financially for their families. Many women are therefore teaching part-time, often in schools in which their children are students or which have on-site day-care facilities and flexible sick-leave policies. Women are also at the forefront of the necessary efforts to make schools function, from cleaning to gardening to fundraising, in addition to the ordinary work of a school. Professional services from male members of the school community range from construction and repair to technology services and financial support.

At the Al Noor School in Brooklyn, the largest Islamic private school in the New York area, enrollments are soaring. This is also the case in many of the other twenty-three Muslim institutions in the New York City, Long Island, and New Jersey area today. In nearby Queens, the Al Iman elementary and high school, like its sister institutions, insists on uniforms for students: long dresses and headscarves for older girls and blue sweaters and gray pants for boys. Cosmetics, nail polish, and jewelry are forbidden, and students receive demerits for "flirtatious" behavior. Young women interviewed at the school feel strongly that rather than being unpleasantly restrictive, such rules help them to avoid the dangers of lax behavior that characterize many public schools.

While some of the Islamic schools in America are mixed-gender, others stress the need for keeping girls and boys separate as they pursue their education, at least in upper elementary and secondary schools. The need for girls' schools is particularly felt by members of immigrant communities who fear the consequences of having boys and girls in too-close proximity. They insist that learning can take place better without the temptations of interacting with members of the opposite sex. In addition, Muslims have recognized recent trends in research indicating that single-sex education in secondary grades is more conducive to the academic and social development of both genders. Institutions designed especially for girls provide a viable alternative for some families to sending their daughters back home for their education.

Occasionally schools are unable to accommodate all of the families who would like to have their children enroll. The Tarek ibn Ziyad Academy in Inver Grove Heights, Minnesota, for example, found as it began its second year as a charter school in 2004 that there were 765 applicants for only 215 seats in grades K–5. About half of the teaching staff at Tarek, mainly women, are conservatively dressed Muslims, while the others are primarily Christians. More than eighty Islamic charter schools are now open in the United States.

Among the few Islamic high schools in the United States, and the first in Massachusetts, is the Al-Noor Academy in Mansfield. Its building was originally St. Mary's Roman Catholic Church. After seventy-five years of activity, the church was closed for nearly two decades. Now it is again a hive of activity as young Muslims learn on the first floor and worship on the second, which has been refurbished to serve as an area for prayer. Unlike many Islamic schools it is coeducational, hoping soon to triple the current enrollment of around fifty students drawn from the surrounding community. The curriculum includes both standard high school courses and more specialized offerings on Islam, the Qur'an, and Arabic. While its superintendent is a male, many of the teaching faculty are women. Other Islamic high schools are growing up rapidly, including the Universal School in Bridgeview, Illinois, Al-Ghazali School in New Jersey, and the Universal Academy in Tampa, Florida. Chicago alone has as many as five Islamic high schools.

Until fairly recently, efforts at Islamic education were scattered and often doomed to failure. While new schools were opened, others were forced to close for a variety of reasons. Observing that some strategy was desperately needed to connect schools with each other, and with organizations that could provide help and support, four women and three men in 1998 founded the nonprofit Islamic Schools' League of America, incorporated in Virginia. Its stated purpose is "working in partnership with Muslim educators and Islamic organizations to foster the development and growth of quality education in an Islamic environment for Muslim children...." One of the founders, Karen Keyworth, now serves as director of the League, whose current board of education advisors is made up entirely of women.

Keyworth observes that one of the most important issues for Islamic schools is deciding what the curriculum should be. Most often schools choose curricula used in local districts and even use the same textbooks for convenience, for financial reasons, and to make it easier for students to make the transition to public high schools. Subjects such as music and gym are often dropped in favor of adding Arabic language instruction and Islamic studies. Keyworth is at the head of a growing movement to encourage parents and educators to work together to make curricular decisions, observing that Islamic schools now range from a co-op structure with the deep involvement of parents to one in which parents are more interested in fund-raising than in substantive curricular issues. Muslims in America, she argues, must design a curriculum that prepares Muslim children to live in America.

Among a number of other Muslim women who are working to provide better structures for the Islamic education of children is Yasmeen Qadri, whose presentation at a February 2002 ISNA Education Forum argued for new leadership models for Islamic school principals. Board members and administrators must work together to achieve the goals of the school, she said, and more attention must be given the importance of educators rather than simply focusing on the donors who make such education possible.

The founder of the Noor al Iman School in South Brunswick, New Jersey, is the daughter of an early immigrant from Yugoslavia. She cites the necessity of "knowing who you are" in order to survive in American society as one important rationale for the establishment of Islamic schools. Thus, many of those responsible for the founding and running of Islamic schools see their efforts as part of the overall initiative of American Muslims to provide structure and identity for young Muslims, in addition to education. They support the efforts of their young people not only to stay in touch with their respective and various cultural roots but to reach beyond national origins to discover the unity that helps them to work for their own rights and interests in an increasingly multicultural and multireligious American society.

Many families may not have access to or be able to afford to send their children to an Islamic school or may not find themselves in agreement with the particular orientation that an Islamic school available in their area offers. After-school or weekend training is an option for some, while for others it may appear insufficient. Another alternative for these parents is home schooling. In most cases it is women who function as stay-at-home parents/teachers, aided by the growing number of resources now made available for home-style instruction. Cynthia R. Sulaiman of Massachusetts founded the Muslim Home School Network and Resource and was a pioneer in Internet-based information on curriculum, instructional resources, and legal issues for Muslim home school families.

Some Muslims have been aided by conversation and cooperation with conservative Christians with whom they share the same concerns about public schooling. The Christian-based Homeschool Legal Defense Association has worked with Muslim families to do the proper paperwork that will allow them to teach their children at home. "We need to work together as people representing all faiths," said one Hispanic mother, "to preserve our right to educate our children as we think is appropriate."

Home schooling for Muslim children, while growing, is still a small movement. The U.S. Department of Education, in a study done just before

2000, determined that only about 2 percent of Muslim children are receiving this kind of education, although Muslim home-school organizations argue that the number is considerably higher. In any case, over the past several years a wide range of Muslim-specific home-school networks, e-mail and print resources, and other aids have been developed to assist in the task of adequate home education. In 1999 the Muslim Home Educators Network in San Antonio, Texas, began e-mail communication with Muslim families across the country. In some areas families of home-schooled children come together for social activities, trips to museums, and even community-service activities to affirm and support their identity as Muslims and also their location as part of Western culture. While the concerns of parents who send their children to public schools are often focused on too much socialization with non-Muslims, those who opt for home-schooling have the opposite concern—that their children may become too insulated. Some women, therefore, are creating new opportunities in which their children can play with and come to know children from a range of other religious traditions.

Rethinking Islamic Leadership: Muslim Women as Chaplains

As Muslims in America increase in number, and Muslims at the local and national levels become more organized and more involved in both secular and religious organizations, the need for trained leadership is increasingly being acknowledged. Islamic spokespersons place leaders who are grounded both in law and theology and in an understanding of American culture at the top of their list of priorities for the immediate future. Although the understanding of most Muslims is that women technically cannot be imams, Muslim women are helping meet the need for trained leadership by serving as chaplains in various kinds of institutions, including prisons, universities and colleges, and hospitals.

One of the major problems in training Muslim women for leadership is the lack of solid support from the community. Muslims are unused to the idea of a leader being anything other than a male imam. Many do not even understand the need for special imam education, and it is even harder for them to think about training women for positions of religious leadership. Financial support for training is also a serious problem. Since 9/11 many of the financial resources of the Muslim community have gone into legal defense and social action to protect Muslims rather than to leadership training programs. Despite these difficult realities, women are finding ways to become educated and trained to assume leadership positions.

The Islamic Society of North America in the summer of 2004 began a core training and pilot program intended to help identify the needs for Muslim leadership and to develop resources for strengthening imam and chaplain training in the Muslim American community. The Summer Leadership Institute included three courses focusing on (a) leadership skills, (b) American society and institutions, and (c) practicing Islam in North America. The program targeted imams, chaplains, community leaders, and active members of Islamic centers, and the students were diverse in terms of gender, race, and leadership responsibilities. Plans are underway for strengthening the institute and for continuing to develop others facets of ISNA's Muslim leadership training program.

Muslims have served in the military for decades, but unlike Christians and Jews have enjoyed very little in the way of officially endorsed religious guidance. Even today there are only fourteen designated Muslim chaplains in the three branches of the military, and as yet none of these is a woman. The first Muslim woman in the U.S. military was an American born of Lebanese parents from Quincy, Massachusetts, who joined the WAVES. After the Vietnam War and with the end of the draft more women, mostly African American but also some South Asians, Arabs, and Caucasians, joined the military. No Muslim females have graduated from the military academies, although they have been commissioned through ROTC and the Officer Candidate School (OCS), starting in 1972. Muslim women have served as aviators in the Army and the Air Force, flying F-16s, and in a variety of capacities have worked close to the front lines. Currently the highest-ranking female officer is a white American who converted to Islam after an assignment in Tajikastan. An African American lieutenant commander in the Navy, now retired, was the first female Muslim to be commissioned as a line officer in the Armed Services. Since the 1970s Muslims in the military have been given certain privileges, such as space on military bases for worship, Islamic education, and time off for Ramadan and other religious activities. While some commanding officers allow servicewomen to wear *hijab*, the issue is still under formal discussion.

Despite the fact that there are now over 4,000 Muslims serving in the military, there remain very few opportunities for Muslims to receive the kind of adequate formal training necessary for their endorsement as military chaplains. Only two American educational institutions offer a degree in chaplain studies for both women and men. The School of Islamic and Social Sciences in Virginia is one, but it does not have formal academic accreditation. A small but growing number attend Hartford Seminary's accredited chaplaincy training program for Muslims. Despite the special need for spiritual leadership and counseling of the more than 500 Muslim women in the military, as yet they have access only to very limited religious leadership, and all of it is male.

One woman is trying hard to change that situation. U.S. Army Major Shareedah Hosein, a recent graduate of Hartford's chaplain training program, is waiting to be designated a chaplain. "There is a concern that by making me a chaplain the Army would be telling the conservative Islamic world that the

U.S. is trying to change Islam from the inside out," she said in an interview with the *Boston Globe* on May 2, 2004. Hosein has been in the army for twenty-five years, serving mainly in administrative positions. The Army itself will not discuss whether or not it plans to create a chaplaincy position for Husein or when a decision will be made. After graduation Husein was stationed in Kuwait and is now located in Boston while she waits for a decision. Shareda reports that some of the other women in her unit in Kuwait, used to seeing her take out her prayer rug five times each day, looked to her for spiritual guidance and conversation, regardless of their own faith.

Universities are gradually coming to recognize the need not only for Muslim student organizations on campus but also for chaplains to work with students as advisors and counselors. Most often these persons are men, but gradually Muslim women are breaking into the ranks of college and university chaplains. In a few instances small colleges without funding for a full-time chaplain position find other ways to meet the needs of their Muslim women students. Khalilah Karim-Rushdan, currently psychotherapist and chaplain at Smith College in Northampton, Massachusetts, has worked in various forms of community service for a number of years, including being a criminal investigator in Mississippi. She says she enjoys being able to do the two things she loves most, namely *da'wah* and psychotherapy. Having begun her work at Smith in 2000 as adjunct faculty to the Office of Chaplains, she found her role expanded after the events of September 2001. "I have learned how to understand and work with people from all walks of life," she says, "and have always had some form of leadership position in the Muslim community." Karim-Rushdan is currently president of the New England chapter of The International League of Muslim Women, Inc., and sits on the Mosque Cares Office of Education, Special Team, which is part of the ministry of Imam Dr. W. D. Mohammed. Among her duties at Smith is conducting Friday congregational prayers for women, doing pastoral counseling, and helping provide the college with the moral and ethical voice of Islam.

Another field beginning to open up to female chaplains is ministry in the nation's prison system. Incarcerated Muslim women have generally needed to rely on the ministry provided by Christian chaplains, some of whom are making special efforts to educate themselves about Muslim practices and special needs. Now a few Muslim women themselves are working in women's correctional facilities. Mumina Kowalski, since 1999 Muslim chaplain at the State Correctional Institution in Muncy, Pennsylvania, is the first woman to work in that capacity in the Pennsylvania system. Her responsibilities are to conduct religious services, distribute Islamic literature, counsel inmates in terms of their personal and religious needs, visit inmates in the various infirmaries and hospital units of the prison, do group religious counseling, and in general to relate to people of faith who are not Muslim. Kowalski sees herself as a resource person rather than an authority and tries to be a mediator between inmates. She is working hard to stock the Muslim library at the institution with literature that is broad-based, normative, translated from Arabic or other languages, or written in English. "If we can construct successful educational and service programs for Muslim inmates," she says, "we will be performing a great service to both incarcerated Muslims in particular and to our society in general." Among her greatest wishes is that more Muslim women would serve as volunteers in prison programs.

Pakistani-born Ghazala Anwar, active in the American Academy of Religion, has also served for a year as a volunteer chaplain at the Philadelphia Industrial Correctional Center. Anwar, who is a both a practicing Sufi and a self-acknowledged lesbian, chose not to reveal either identity to the inmates with whom she worked out of respect for the many concerns with which they were already dealing, knowing that both would be difficult for them to accept. Anwar's goal was to create a safe space where sisters could explore their understanding of Islam without fear of reprisal. The inmates with whom she worked were almost all African American. Incarceration, she says, removed any pretenses about adhering to generally accepted standards of Islamic behavior and opened the door for a level of exchange about matters of religion that may not be possible under other circumstances. Among the concerns that she tried to help inmates and/or the institution address, or redress, during her time at the facility were hygiene, training of correctional officers, rehabilitation programs for drug abusers, library facilities, and daily meeting times for religious instruction.

Creativity and the Arts

"On my street, mercy resides. Spiders get carried out of houses in Styrofoam cups, gently airlifted to safety.... On my block church bells ring early on Sunday morning and every prayer is for another. The Lord's Prayer mingles with the sound of the *adhan* [call to prayer] floating from the nearby mosque. On my street we want for nothing, but *salaam* [peace], long for nothing, just *rahman* [mercy]." Dima Hilal, author of these verses from her poem "Ar-Rahman Road" (cited in *Aramco World* magazine), was born in Beirut and raised in California. Her poetry has been featured in a number of publications, including Nathalie Handal's *The Poetry of Arab Women: A Contemporary Anthology*. She teaches poetry workshops and lectures on contemporary Arab poetry. Hilal, whose work is featured at numerous cultural centers, stages, museums, and conferences, is one among a growing number of Muslim women who are choosing the arts as a way of speaking in the public forum.

Muslim women are displaying their literary creativity in a great variety of ways, including poetry, novels, plays, and film and video scripts. Some are writing as Muslims who want their work to be seen as an Islamic contribution;

others are working to blend the traditional writings of their heritage with new interpretations and styles; still others are simply literary artists who happen, usually by accident of birth, to be Muslim. Art has been a crucial medium of expression throughout the history of Islam, although different racial and cultural groups have differed about what subjects are appropriate for humans to portray. American Muslims owe much to the very public efforts of Lamya (Lois) al-Faruqi, wife of former Temple University professor Ismail al-Faruqi, to underscore the links between religion and the various media of artistic expression. Her efforts culminated in the publication of the extensive work *The Cultural Atlas of Islam* in 1986, which she co-authored with her husband.

A few brief sketches of some of the American women working today in the broad area of arts and communication will serve to illustrate Muslim women's growing contributions in this broadly defined field.

A young Muslim woman poet whose work seems to be increasingly controversial is Mohja Kahf, assistant professor of literature at the University of Arkansas. Kahf, author of the widely publicized *Western Representations of the Muslim Woman from Termagant to Odalisque*, has published her poems in a number of different venues. Much of her verse is modeled on early Arabic love poetry. She is also a regular contributor to the progressive Islamic Web site *Muslim Wakeup!*. Conservative Muslims, who respect the fact that Kahf always wears a headscarf, are shocked both at the nature of some of her original poetry and at her regular Web site column in which she addresses such topics as premarital and oral sex. She also uses the medium of short-story writing to help counter what she sees as too-rigid conservative Muslim attitudes toward sex.

Writing narratives that are directly or indirectly autobiographical is another genre in which Muslim women are beginning to make their mark. Take, for example, Egyptian-born Samia Serageldin, who immigrated with her family to the United States in 1980. Serageldin is perhaps best-known for her novel *The Cairo House* (2000), which traces three decades of political developments in Egypt, including the assassination of President Sadat and the rise of Islamic feminism. In a 2000 article for the *NC Writer's Newsletter* Serageldin describes her life in a "happily hybrid culture" of Egyptian cuisine and French governesses which was shattered by the repression of the Nasser regime, and her own move to the United States where she saw her sons playing soccer in North Carolina. "There was no room in this brave new world for my memories of jasmine and dust," she writes. "I locked away my photography albums of Egypt in the attic and blended into my new environment like a perfect chameleon." It was her effort to recover her lost voice, to reconcile her present with her past, that engendered *Cairo House*. She confesses that the only way she could overcome her natural reticence was to hide behind "the fig leaf of fiction." Serageldin has helped forward the cause of Arab and Muslim American writers in numerous articles and contributions to anthologies.

Fiction's fig leaf was not necessary for the quite similar work of Egyptian Harvard Professor Leila Ahmed called *A Border Passage: From Cairo to America— A Woman's Journey*, published in 1999. Ahmed, on the faculty at Harvard Divinity School, writes elegantly about her growing-up years in Cairo, the 1952 revolution and issues of Arab nationalism, her experiences in Europe, and what it has been like teaching in America. She describes how she and her nanny used to spend time on the roof of their Egyptian home, looking for angels. The author of the now classic *Women and Gender in Islam*, Ahmed in the autobiographical *Border Passage* talks about her own transition from criticizing her Arabic-speaking mother for her traditional style of life to coming to a deeper appreciation of how Egyptian women with relatively little education live with calmness and dignity.

"I am an American Muslim, a woman who freely chose Islam as my personal path to spiritual power," writes Eisa Nefertari Ulen, who teaches literature at Hunter College in New York City. "I am also African-American, instilled with a legacy of activism since childhood" (*Essence*, January 2000). Nefertari Ulen, who has received awards for fiction writing and journalism, saw her first novel published in 2005, which she describes as a novel for adults. This work, called *Fatima's Move*, tells the story of a girl who moves with her family from Philadelphia with its large and visible Muslim population to tiny Harrisburg, Pennsylvania. Fatima has just started to wear *hijab*, and she must face the consequences of that decision in a school where she is the only Muslim student. She has also contributed a chapter in a text for middle school readers in which a Muslim and a non-Muslim girl become best friends. Her 2004 article in the *Encyclopedia of African American Relations* is titled "Hip Hop Women." Women of all faiths, she stresses, must unite to protect the ideal of American freedom.

In January 2004 a group of Muslim women dedicated to presenting and promoting "positive Islamic fiction and non fiction reading materials," as its Web site proclaims, formally established the Islamic Writers' Alliance. Membership is open to newly published and, as yet, little-known authors and writers of talent. The proclaimed goal of the Alliance is to help new writers find publishers, to increase public awareness of works by Muslim women writers who are already published and to promote creative fictional Islamic works for Muslim children.

Another medium in which Muslim women are starting to make their mark is the creation and production of films. Winner of the National Association of Muslim Women's Best Film Producer of 2003, for example, is Farah Nousheen for her film *Nazrah: A Muslim Woman's Perspective*. Nazrah provides the viewer an opportunity to see a diverse group of Muslim women who live in the Pacific Northwest—community activists, lawyers, mothers, and teachers—engage in an open dialogue about Islam, stereotypes, and current political events. The film begins personally as Nousheen shows photos of herself at age four, a time when children in the Indian Muslim community in which she was raised begin to recite the Qur'an. Nousheen, who serves as writer, director, and producer of *Nazrah*, sees the film-making as an opportunity to share her own views on what it is like to be a Muslim at a time when Islam is in the international spotlight.

Zarqa Nawaz, born in Liverpool, England, and raised in Toronto, uses the medium of film not as documentary but to present her message through fiction. She works with humor and even ventures into the absurd in her two videos that were premiered at the Toronto International Film Festival. *BBQ Muslims*, done in 1995, is an offbeat story of two Muslim brothers who experience a backyard barbecue mishap and are accused by neighbors of being terrorists. The film is intended to highlight the irony of the conviction of a white American for the 1995 Oklahoma City bombing after the media had unquestioningly accused the North American Muslim community. *Death Threat*, a satire from 1998, tells the story of a young Muslim woman who has written a bad Harlequin type novel and is struggling to find a publisher. Frustrated and depressed after getting many rejections, she decides to exploit cultural stereotypes to catch the eye of a publisher, a ploy that badly backfires as she becomes the victim of the same stereotypes. Zarqa currently lives in Regina, Saskatchewan, and has recently completed a feature-length screenplay.

Muslim women are also making names for themselves in the performing and the visual arts. Poet, writer, and singer Fawzia Afzal Khan, for example, has composed musical scores and played in a number of international music festivals. Her original performance, entitled "A Sufi Madwoman from Pakistan? You Better Believe It!" was presented at the Asian-American Writers Workshop in 2003. Illustrative of the many visual artists born overseas and now living and working in America are the following:

- Ghada Amer from Cairo and currently living in New York, whose aim is to study intersecting cultures and women's respective positions. Amer's work, which shows Islamic influence through use of passages of the Qur'an, is sometimes criticized by conservative Muslims as being too suggestive. Her embroidered "paintings," for example, weave pornographic images into what at first seem to be abstract expressionist creations.
- Salma Arastu, born in Ajmer, India, and living in Bethlehem, Pennsylvania. Arastu's medium is clay sculpture, papier-mâché, and print. She has worked extensively with calligraphy and now offers a greeting card line, "Your True Greetings," to serve American Muslim communities.
- Shirin Neshat, born in Qasvin, Iran, and now working as an artist in New York City. Neshat explores issues of her native Islamic society

through photography and video. She uses symbols of the veil, female forms, Arabic texts, and guns to show her feelings about Iran's transformation after the revolution of 1979.

- Halide Salam from Bangladesh, currently professor at Radford University in Virginia. Through drawing, painting, and teaching, Salam explores the connections between knowledge and belief and between the spiritual and physical worlds. Author of two books, she encourages her viewers and her students to perceive intuitively and creatively.
- Shahzia Sikander from Lahore, Pakistan, now living in Texas. Sikander specializes in miniature paintings evolved from the Mughal Muslim dynasty that ruled in India from 1526–1857. A practicing Muslim, she is interested in the interplay between Hindu and Muslim influences on the miniatures.

These are only a few examples of the many women who are expressing themselves through a variety of art forms. Additional information about American Muslim women artists is available at IMAN (International Muslima Art Network).

Another way in which Muslim women are exercising their creativity is through journalism. In some cases they are moving into important positions in already-established journals. Ayesha Mustafa, for example, for some time has served as editor of *The Muslim Journal*, a periodical featuring the ministry of Warith Deen Mohammed and his followers. Other journals are created specifically by and for women. The women's branch of the Ahmadi sect annually publishes a magazine called *The Ayesha*, and a Shi'ite woman's group in Queens puts out a journal entitled *al-Zehra*. Perhaps the most noteworthy journalistic endeavor by Muslim women, however, is the eye-catching, recently created journal called *Azizah*.

Founder, publisher, and editor-in-chief of *Azizah* is Tayyibah Taylor, who says the magazine is "for the woman who doesn't apologize for being a woman, and doesn't apologize for being a Muslim." As its Web site proclaims, *Azizah* is designed to present the issues, accomplishments, and interests of Muslim women in North America. It is more than a magazine, says the page, "It's a catalyst for empowerment!" That claim may not be unreasonable. Since the first issue appeared in 2002, the journal has elicited excitement on the part of many Muslim women and genuine interest from non-Muslims. Its graphics are engaging, the photos of Muslim women in a great range of dress styles are often alluring, and the articles are sufficiently substantive to provide some important information about topics of interest to the Muslim community and especially its females. Since the initial publication, *Azizah* articles have discussed such issues as breast cancer, inheritance laws, helping women survive in Baghdad, refugees in America, ID theft, women marathoners and practitioners of Taekwondo, power networking tips, and hypno-birthing.

While *Azizah* is clearly conceived and designed for the practicing Muslim woman, its editorial staff, writers, glossy color spread photos, and articles represent a wide range of racial and ethnic identities as well as topics. Taylor, who was born in Trinidad and raised in Toronto and did a six-year study program in Saudi Arabia, says that *Azizah* "melds perfectly my passions for Islam, reading and composition." She chose the name for its connotation of a Muslim woman with nobility, strength, and dignity who is "dear" to herself and others. Following what she believes was the Prophet's model of encouraging discussion and questioning, she has not been afraid to tackle subjects that are often considered taboo, such as the disabled community, women and depression, and AIDS. *Azizah* regularly features models of all ethnic identities showing creative fashions for the woman who chooses to dress Islamically. Asked why every issue shows a woman with *hijab* on the cover, Taylor replied, "You can find lots of magazine covers featuring women with uncovered heads. What other publication would regularly feature a Muslim woman who covers?" To date, the answer is none. Taylor contemplates an international edition of *Azizah* sometime in the future.

The myth that Muslim women are incarcerated in their homes, without access to the public domain, is obviously untrue for most of those who live in America, as it is generally untrue in other Western countries and, to some extent, for Muslim women in other parts of the world. American Muslim women are visible, whether or not they want to be immediately recognizable as Muslims, and are playing roles not only in the areas described above but also in business and commerce, industrial work, medicine and other health professions, architecture, environmental organizations, and a range of other activities. While some immigrant families are reluctant to have women involved in such public ventures, their numbers are dwindling as Muslims inevitably find themselves more Westernized, more Americanized, and—as those who want to highlight their Islamic identity would argue—more aware of the emphasis that a rightly interpreted Islam places on the full participation of women in society.

8

Competing Discourses

Muslim women who have emigrated to America over the last
five decades have brought with them a range of cultural, social,
ideological, and religious expectations, formed and influenced by
the variety of societies from which they have come. They have also
joined an already existing Muslim population made up of African
Americans, second- and third-generation immigrants, and others
who have been part of an American Muslim population that has
grown up for over a century. One piece of the baggage carried by
Muslim immigrants on their arrival to the West is their experience
of colonial hegemony during Europe's domination of the Muslim
world and the national myth propagated by the state and inculcated in
schools to create a consensus among the citizens. Thus, they come
with varying conceptions of national and ethnic identity but also with
an awareness that the West has subjugated Muslims and usurped
their resources under the guise of civilizing them and "liberating"
their women. In the process, Westerners tend to look at Muslim
women as the "other." Muslim women's historical consciousness
is one that reflects not only the impact of the Western incursion itself,
or its concomitant stereotyping, but also the defensive mechanisms
and apologetics developed over two centuries of the most intimate
of encounters.

For many Muslim women from nations that achieved
independence from Western colonialism, the twentieth century has
been a time of struggle both *against* colonial occupation and *for*
what has been termed "the liberation of women." The transformation
of their role in society was seen as one of the necessary cornerstones

of development. In the minds of many, these two forms of struggle have been inextricably bound together. In the struggle for political liberation women fought for and won their place in society. They envisioned many possibilities as part of the professional workforce: serving as teachers, doctors, engineers, nurses, in the military and other public spheres. The expectations of some women were raised as the project of nation building took hold and they imagined and dreamed of the potential new roles necessary for them to play in that project.

Many were disappointed when, in the postindependence period, the nation-states decided to put their societies on a "fast track" for development emulating the socialist system. Most of the governments nationalized women's organizations even as they nationalized industry and agriculture. In the process, women's liberation became an instrument of nation-building (a move that tended to put women's issues on hold while the state bureaucracies grappled with the economic and political problems they were facing). It generated disappointment among some, and anger and deep frustration on the part of many early advocates of changes in the role and status of women, many of whom came from among the elite in society.

Significant changes have occurred over the last century in the tone and content of Islamic traditionalist literature. While texts published in the nineteenth century instructed men on how to be householders, caring for the needs of their wives, twentieth-century texts began to emulate Victorian norms describing women as homemakers. Some medieval texts had warned against the education of women on the grounds that it would make them argumentative, thus leading to family discord. And even at the beginning of the twentieth century the debates focused on whether women should be educated. Today the right to education is affirmed by traditionalists, as by others, to be a Qur'anic prescription. The debate in the Islamic literature has shifted to what subjects women should study, whether they can attend co-educational institutions, and what contributions they can make to society. Instances in which Muslim parents do in fact impede the education of their daughters are said to be due not to Islam but to the residue of tribal and social customs of patriarchy.

Another phase in advocacy for women's rights came as a consequence of the rise of Islamic consciousness after the 1973 Arab-Israeli war, when Islamic movements called for the transformation of women in Islam, but not in the model of radical Western feminism. As an alternative to Western paradigms of gender, whether capitalist or socialist, the movements promoted the emulation of Islamic models of womanhood. Emancipation, they argued, can only be achieved within the faith through surrender to the truth of the Qur'an and living in accord with the Shari'ah.

The apprehension of those who were secular in outlook, holding a nationalist or socialist worldview, increased in the wake of the Islamization project that gained momentum after the revolution in Iran that brought to power the Islamic Republic of Ayatollah Khomeini. While many Muslims celebrated the revolution as validating the promise of the Qur'an that commitment to Islam brings victory against the greatest of tyrants, secularists feared that the achievements they had attained in various Muslim countries were now going to be reversed. As for the several émigrés who left Muslim countries for the United States, the new environment they encountered offered both a challenge and an opportunity.

Women arriving in the United States from Muslim countries brought with them varying ideas about the role of women in Islam. For most of those who came from traditional societies, the cultural assumptions had ingrained in them the notion that a good wife is one who is obedient to and supportive of her husband and that her sphere of activity should be confined as much as possible to the home. Such an orientation also characterizes many in the recent Islamist movements. But for the many who are considered liberal nationalists, socialists, and secularists, the infinite possibilities of redefining women's roles in Islam, even dreaming of being the vanguard of an empowered generation that could pioneer a new path for Muslim women worldwide, seemed within reach at the close of the twentieth century.

The most prominent feature of Islamic literature written during the twentieth century on the role and status of women is its dialogical and/or apologetic nature, regardless of the gender or ideological orientation of the author. It is stamped with the imprint of the disruptive impact of the colonial experience not only in the economic, military, and the political spheres but more importantly in the social and cultural areas, where Western ideas have had an enormous impact on Muslim society and the understanding of the role of women for over a century. Most discourse on the topic of refuting Western paradigms, adopting them wholesale, or integrating them into local customs, appears to be beholden to everchanging Western models and norms. It tends to mirror Western discussion about the role of women and to provide a comparative perspective while at the same time affirming that Islam offers the best means to liberate women. The Qur'anic text grants women the right to live, to be educated, to conduct business, to maintain their property, and to keep their names, rights that Western women have had to struggle to achieve. This literature demonstrates the strides that have been achieved in developing the paradigm of Muslim woman.

This does not mean that some of the traditional restrictive views have not survived. They continue to be preached not only in some Islamic countries but also by conservative imams in America who maintain that a woman's work should be confined to the home, raising children and pleasing her husband. Her role is to be a mother and wife, providing comfort and love and maintaining Islamic culture in the home. The Qur'an clearly affirms that men and women are created from the same cell, that both (in the person of Adam and his mate) were tempted in the Garden and expelled for their disobedience, and that both will equally be held accountable on the Day of Judgment. It also insists that there are differences between the genders. Interpreters have understood these differences to be both biological and emotional, which has determined social and political distinctions between the two genders. The Qur'an, for example, stipulates that the witness of one man is equal to that of two women, often understood to be due to the fact that women are emotional while men are rational. Each gender has been assigned a distinctive role in life. Males are distinguished because they are the protectors of and providers for women (Qur'an 4:34), a difference often interpreted to imply man's superiority. Males and females together, in their divinely dictated separate but complementary roles, have been charged with creating a cohesive virtuous society.

The discourse generated overseas on women's roles and status has an impact on Muslim women in North America. Ideas flourishing in Muslim nations are readily available for Muslim consumption worldwide through publications, the media, and the Internet. At the same time, America has created arenas for debate and celebration in which many Muslim women, whether observant, essentially secularist, or somewhere in between, have begun to reflect on circumstances for women both in the United States and in their homelands. Ideas and practices women bring with them, or fashion from Islamic materials in North America, move in a circulatory pattern, engaging with the discourse generated elsewhere and probing far deeper into the cultural arguments of identity than ever before. While what is meant by the term "Muslim identity" is subject to multiple interpretations, particularly in the West, it is in fact critical to understand the conflicting pressures to which women of Muslim faith are subjected in the United States. It is the goal of this chapter to look at the different kinds of literature and writing, by and about women, that have become part of the "competing discourses" both allowed and supported in the American environment.

Speaking with a Conservative Voice

Before World War II, Muslims in America were still small in number and geographically dispersed across the expanse of the United States. Little effort was made to think about what it means to be Muslim in a Western context. Most were concerned about economic survival and generally tried to live according to the norms of the societies they left behind and to adhere to the traditions inculcated by their parents. The few texts available in the West about Islam and Muslim women were written by Orientalists and missionaries, and virtually none was provided by and for Muslims on how to live in the context of the West.

The first books written in English by Muslims that provided instruction on the role of women and the family were published overseas and exported to the West, such as those provided by the Ahmadiyyah Movement in Islam reflecting South Asian traditionalist views. Outlining the parameters of Islamic life, they appear to have had a profound influence on converts to Islamic movements in the African American community. When texts about Muslims in America did begin to appear, some of the earliest dealt with the issue of women and again promoted conservative interpretations. Muhammad Abdul Rauf, a graduate of al-Azhar in Egypt and of the University of London, for example, was among the first to try to define women's roles and responsibilities. At one time imam of the Islamic Center of Washington, D.C., the "showcase" mosque of America built in the 1950s, Abdul Rauf was one of a very small number of Islamic scholars to provide leadership for the few mosques that were functioning. In his two books, titled *The Islamic View of Women and the Family* and *Marriage and Islam*, Abdul Rauf promoted traditional values while affirming that Islam does not discriminate between men and women and that the Qur'an teaches equality.

Abdul Rauf appears to have believed that males have an exclusive right to interpret the Qur'an and that females should not try to innovate because they lack the innate abilities essential to the task. In a public encounter at the American Academy of Religion in the 1970s, between Abdul Rauf and Riffat Hassan, one of the early prominent Muslim female academics in the United States whose scholarly work was the exegesis of the Qur'an as a document affirming equality between men and women, he chastised her publicly for not having the authority to do such exegesis. He even suggested the inherent deficiencies of women at a seminar at the mosque in Washington when he remarked that they are created "from a crooked rib" and that they menstruate.

The contributions of Abdul Rauf were very influential not only on the Muslim immigrants but also on African American converts seeking instruction concerning women's proper roles in the family. His conservative understanding of women's rights and roles has been echoed by a number of male interpreters whose writings continue to be highly influential, such as al-Azhar graduate and Princeton University professor Hammudah Abd al-Ati, author of *The Family Structure in Islam* and *Islam in Focus*. Another important male author who helped set the "discourse of the mosque" in North America on the understanding of the role of women in the contemporary world is Professor Jamal A. Badawi of Canada. Through his writings and audiotapes— such as *Gender Equity in Islam: Basic Principles*; and "The Status of Women in Islam"—he has had an international impact.

American Muslim leaders who favor a more traditional model of Islamic life continue to teach and preach the importance of conforming to traditional Islamic values in regard to women. Concern for maintaining these traditional values is also evident among Salafis as well as in mosques with imams who belong to the South Asian Barewli or Tableeghi Jamaat interpretation of Islam. They tend to stress the exclusion rather than the inclusion of women in community public affairs, often worrying about losing their identity and their faith in light of pressures toward integration into current American culture. American Muslim women often find themselves the focal point of external and internal pressures facing Muslim religious communities. Externally, they feel the push to be homogeneous, to find a place for all Muslims despite their differences, and to find consensus on issues of morality, social interaction, and standards of personal dress and conduct. Internally, they may still feel the strong pull of those things that serve to differentiate them, from culture to ideology to the degree to which they want to affiliate with religiously observant Muslim communities in America.

In the 1970s the nascent Muslim Student Association (MSA) began to publish material to guide new immigrants coming to the West, much of it related specifically to women. One of their most important publications, considered an authoritative text for a quarter century, was *Parents' Manual: A Guide for Muslim Parents Living in North America*, prepared by the Women's Committee. This material was later augmented by publications of the Islamic Society of North America, the International Institute for Islamic Thought and the Islamic Foundation in Britain (publishers of Kurshid Ahmad's book *Family Life in Islam*) affirming the superiority of the Islamic worldview. These texts have received worldwide distribution and tend to reiterate Islamist views developed overseas as a response to what is experienced as the cultural onslaught of the West. They have been sold in a variety of venues, through mail order, on the Web at sites such as Amazon.com and Barnes & Noble, at annual Muslim conventions of regional and umbrella organizations, and at mosque bookstores; their instructions have been propagated from mosque pulpits and discussed by women in a variety of forums, including study circles.

In addition to the works of religious scholars writing specifically for an American audience, the Muslim community in America has continued to be influenced by *fatwas* issued in Egypt, Iran, Iraq, and other centers of Islamic authority. Many in the younger generation are turning to the Internet to find answers to their questions about daily living as Muslims, and are finding fatwa Web sites. In most cases these are by men giving their opinions about what is appropriate for women within the Islamic context. Increasingly, however, conservative Muslim women are also engaging in the debate by writing books, articles, tracts, and Internet opinions in support of an Islam that is immutable and whose core teachings do not need to change with the flow of history and the reality of new times and cultures any more than absolutely necessary. They believe that the basic teachings of Islam, articulated in the *fatwas*, injunctions, and interpretations of many Muslims on the international scene as well as by conservative propagators of the faith in America, are mandatory on all believers.

Among the most influential American Muslim women writing from a conservative or traditionalist perspective have been Caucasian converts. Maryam Jameelah (formerly Margaret Marcus), an orthodox Jew who adopted the faith after studying the historical relationship between Jews and Arabs, has been writing about Islam for a number of years. An essayist and journalist, Jameelah often cites her correspondence with popular Pakistani revivalist Maulana Maududi as influential in her formation as a Muslim. In her most recent and well-publicized interview, published in *Women Who Have Embraced Islam*, she repeats her argument that many American women are disgusted with the way women are treated in the West and that they seek the peace of Islam. Jameelah's writings are augmented by a number of audio- and videotapes in which she argues passionately for her interpretation of Islam and women. Also influential on the thinking of many American Muslims has been the work of Lamya (Lois) al-Faruqi. A specialist in Islamic art, in 1986 she was murdered with her husband, Palestinian professor Ismail al-Faruqi of Temple University, himself a very influential conservative interpreter of Islam. Lamya al-Faruqi's *Women, Muslim Society, and Islam* provides an overview from a conservative Islamic understanding of the role of women in Islam. Al-Faruqi argued that the goals of Western feminism are culture specific and therefore not relevant for women in other societies. She insisted that they are not an exportable commodity precisely because Muslim women view Islam as their best supporter while the Western feminist movement views religion as one of its enemies. Furthermore, she insisted, for feminism in the Muslim world to succeed, it must benefit both men and women. Most importantly, Islam, in order to be able to confront alien influences, must govern all aspects of human life.

Conservativism is only one kind of response available for American Muslims. Because the population of the United States is so very diverse, including immigrants, converts, and American-born, second-generation, and sojourner Muslims, many different ways of affirming Islamic identity are possible and indeed are in evidence. Ethnic affiliations, class and educational levels, professional involvements, tolerance for diversity, and many other factors reflect differences in the kinds of Islamic discourse being fostered by American women. To this diversity must be added the reality of the freedoms available in the Western cultural context, which, particularly in the case of women, provides new opportunities for interpretation.

At the opposite end of the spectrum from those conservatives described above is a sizable, growing, and very articulate body of Muslim women who generally represent a more nuanced understanding of Islam. They see themselves as Muslims who may or may not observe all of the ritual requirements and who do research and writing on women's issues in Islam in a way that is not conditioned by the doctrinal formulations articulated by medieval jurists. They may identify themselves as "modernist," "progressive," "secular," or sometimes even "feminist," working to challenge the patriarchy that they see as dominant in most Muslim societies through the centuries and to help bring about reform both within the religion of Islam and in the secular structures of states in which Islam is dominant. The Qur'an, for these women, while always a "mercy to humanity," is seen not as rigid and unchanging but as flexible and open to different interpretations that address the exigencies of changing times and circumstances.

Women as Scholars and Academics

Parallel to the discourse of the mosque, a new genre of writing about Muslim women began to develop on American campuses in the last decades of the twentieth century, pioneered by Muslim women who were beginning to achieve prominence as scholars in American academia. They were usually recent immigrants, most of whom were educated overseas first and then acquired graduate degrees at American universities. They represented the modernized secularized Arab women who identified with the national aspirations of the Arab world. For the most part they were products of the nationalist-socialist discourses taking place in their home countries after the demise of colonialism and were influenced by the modernization paradigm then in vogue among social scientists in the United States. They tended to look at the situation of women in their home countries through the prism of development. Former colonies were expected to emulate the achievements of Europe and the United States by following a similar trajectory and replicating the national secular nation-state and its policies in relation to women. When in the 1970s the American feminist movement began to raise questions about the treatment of women in America, Arab American women joined them in seeking similar goals for women not only in the United States but also in the Arab world.

In making their assessment these scholars joined Arab Muslim women who have been itinerant lecturers at American universities such as Nawal Sa'dawi, former Minister of Health in Egypt, and Moroccon sociologist Fatima Mernissi. Identifying and challenging patriarchy in Islam and working for reform both within the faith and within the secular structures, they have provided new insights on women's roles and rights and validated the necessity of having women themselves contribute to the debate. Mernissi and Sa'dawi identified the problems of patriarchy as belonging to societal systems rather than to the religion of Islam. A few of the first-generation Muslim women academics, such as Professors Leila Ahmed and Ghada Karmi, have even argued that, contrary to the opinion of most Muslim interpreters, Islam's egalitarian "ethical vision" concerning women has never been actualized in practice. Ahmed does not advance the simplistic argument that women are better off either before or after the introduction of Islam; instead, in her widely-read 1992 book, *Women and Gender in Islam*, she argues that early Islam brought notable changes in the status of Muslim women, including the right to inherit property and to be treated as legally competent, while in other respects it actually curtailed women's freedom and worked to subjugate them to men.

Among the early Muslim scholars to make her mark in American academia was Afaf Lutfi al-Sayyid Marsot, an Egyptian and the first Muslim woman to be elected president of the Middle East Studies Association of North America. In her numerous writings on Egypt Marsot insisted that the position of women in society is a result not of religion but of social practice. She argued that the injunctions of the Qur'an, for example, actually favor women's financial rights, but that family and social practices have gotten in the way of the realization of those rights. By analyzing the documents, she discovered that modernity undermined rather than enhanced the role of women.

Georgetown professor Amira al-Azhari Sonbol, through her research in court documents and archives, has demonstrated that historically Islamic law was flexible and in many cases served to work in favor of women's full participation in the economy. Distinguishing between legal discourse and actual practice, she shows that modern legal reforms initiated during the period of colonial hegemony were generally fashioned after Western nineteenth-century philosophy of gender. The scholarship of Sonbol and her cohort groups in Muslim countries not only has challenged prevailing paradigms of historical interpretation but has served to liberate women from the constraints of the discourse of modernization theory imposed by colonial as well as national expediency. It has set them free to create new paradigms that are intrinsically Muslim and are based on Islamic scholarship, precedence, and judicial interpretation. It poses another challenge to the Western presupposition that modernization and Westernization are necessarily good for women while Islamic law is archaic and repressive and impedes progress. These arguments parallel those of women scholars overseas engaged in similar research who have been instrumental in promoting changes in contemporary laws in Egypt, Jordan, and other Muslim countries based on new understandings of what was historically true and verifiable within the Muslim historical experience. In this way they are affirming their right to define themselves with a special awareness that change comes from within. By recovering the past, they are eager to point out that one model of womanhood should not be privileged over another.

The Iranian Revolution precipitated the emigration of a number of scholar-activists to the United States. Their initial impact on the American academy and women's studies programs was the perpetuation of the development paradigm given their attitude toward religion as an impediment to women's progress. Among those whose work is influential in thinking about women in Islam are Shahla Haeri, Afsaneh Najmabadi, Guity Nashat, Nayereh Tohidi, Haideh Moghissi, and Nesta Ramazani. They generally pursue their research with a focus on Iran, hoping that their analyses will have serious implications for Muslim women in general in a variety of cultural contexts. Postrevolutionary developments in Iran, which have empowered women and produced feminist interpretations of the Qur'an, have moderated their intellectual production and provided a nuanced interpretation of current developments. By means of teaching, writing, and public presentations they are important voices in the articulation of what it means to be Muslim in the American context.

Similarly, a number of South Asian women who are now located in North America are studying the situation of women in their home country. Some have emphasized the existence of patriarchy both within South Asian households and within Western state systems and are critical of both. Shahnaz Khan, for example, is a Canadian Muslim of Pakistani origin who takes on issues she sees as having been used by Western feminists to essentialize Muslim women, or that have been co-opted by Orientalist discourse, and reframes them in non-Orientalist terms. She re-examines practices and issues that have been classified or discussed in purely religious terms—such as *zina* (adultery) and women's punishment in Pakistan—and demonstrates that they are in fact products of economic, political, and patriarchal conditions unrelated to religion, or at least having less to do with Islam than is portrayed in the West. Khan promotes an international discourse that examines women's conditions and the problems they face in terms of economics, politics, and education rather than simply in terms of gender, culture, and religion.

It is probably not surprising to find that many Muslims who consider themselves more traditional in their interpretation of Islam tend to look on these scholars, whom they sometimes call "secular feminists," with growing suspicion. Their concern is not so much that these women academics are not publicly affirming their Islamic identity through word and dress but rather that when they criticize Islamic traditions they are feeding into and therefore reinforcing already existing (and growing) anti-Islamic American prejudice. "Secular feminist" writers are accused, therefore, of complicity in undermining their own Muslim sisters by the very fact that they are appropriating Western discourse and modes of critique. Even worse, they are seen as falling into the Western trap of portraying Islam (at least as it is preached by those who are more traditionalist) as rigid and "essentialized," a once-for-all religion that can never be updated. Paradoxically, their very attempts to show the mutability of Islam are seen by more conservative Muslims as enhancing the rationale for neocolonialist Western domination of Muslim societies. Thus the secularists are viewed as complicit in undermining the solidarity of Muslims worldwide, seen as necessary for a final liberation of Islam from the influence and dictates of the Western powers.

Islam and Feminism

While to many Americans the term Islamic feminism may sound like an oxymoron, some Muslim scholars and activists both in the United States and overseas see it as the focus of their identity. It has become more of an umbrella definition for anyone who advocates a different discourse outside the purview of traditional Islam. It has thus acquired a variety of meanings as scholars attempt to classify and analyze the range of interpretations. Some see Islamic feminism as more radical than its secular counterpart because it is not centered in a liberal rational assessment of society. Rather, it affirms its vision as a divine mandate grounded in an eternal immutable Qur'an and modeled after the example of the life of the Prophet Muhammad. These scholars have generally abandoned the efforts of the earliest Muslim secular feminists in the Arab world and their cohorts in the United States to compare the condition of Muslim women with Western norms emulating colonial bureaucrats and missionaries; rather, they have opted to address the issues from within the heritage and to seek to reconcile Islam and feminism. They attempt to ground their gender paradigms of equality and liberation in the Qur'an and in Islamic jurisprudence and are examining traditional narratives of Islamic history, legal precedents, and court decisions in order to reconstruct history.

A number of factors contributed to the developing understanding of feminism and Islam. Islamization was beginning to take hold overseas, and many of the new immigrants to the United States were socialized on its ideology, especially in the post-Khomeini era. In response, feminist scholars such as Mernissi began to write on the traditions in order to bring about change from within. Mernissi became, in effect, the foremother of a wave of Muslim women in the Muslim world and in the diaspora who have become convinced that it is crucial for women to participate in creating Islamic knowledge to meet the demands of the twenty-first century. Islamic knowledge, they affirm, should not be the exclusive and private domain of male scholars pontificating on the topic through their patriarchal prisms. These women are convinced that change can come only through the full participation of women in the discourse.

Another important contributor to the feminist discourse was the publication of Edward Said's *Orientalism*. Said debunked the modernization theory that undergirded secular feminism as part of the Western hegemonic effort to dominate Third-World countries by defining them as less than civilized and in need of Western civilization. His work had a great impact not only on literary studies but on the way scholars construct knowledge in Islamic studies, the social sciences, and women's studies.

Thus far we have highlighted several general alternatives of Islamic discourse about women, namely traditionalism, conservatism, Islamic modernism or secularism, and feminism. There is, of course, a range of interpretations among these alternatives. Many women professionals who are affirming their deep faith in God and allegiance to the Qur'an also believe that the text and traditions are dynamic, flexible, and susceptible to new interpretations. Some may consider themselves feminists by an Islamic definition, while others eschew such an identifier. What they hold in common is the conviction that Islam is eternally valid at all moments in history but that it contains an inherent flexibility that allows it to be applicable to changing times and circumstances. While the principles of the Qur'an are eternal, and reflect the unchanging nature of God, local interpretations can vary. Thus they do not question the validity of the Qur'anic text but its interpretation by male scholars. The term "gender *jihad*" has been appropriated by some as defining a way of categorizing the efforts of these women who are contesting the prescriptions of the traditionalists, the reactionaries, and the fundamentalists but who are clearly working with a mandate to affirm the divine message of the Qur'an and the ultimate viability of the Islamic system.

Those who promote "gender *jihad*" are engaged in fashioning new and viable interpretations of Islam grounded in the Qur'an and the example of the Prophet, opening the discourse as well as human endeavors to new possibilities of individual interpretation and collective consensus. They are trying to provide legitimate interpretations that break out of the confines of scripted and prescribed molds, looking for ways in which to make an Islamically valid contribution to twenty-first-century thought and life. They want to create an attractive alternative to both dogmatic traditionalism with its constraining patriarchal overtones, on the one hand, and on the other to secular liberal feminism that appears to have given up on Islam and succumbed to the changing whims and values of a West that appears unable or unwilling to appreciate Islam. Affirming God's guidance for all humanity in all times, they base their discourse on the assumption of an Islamically validated modern lifestyle.

Islamic feminist discourse in general has been formulated as a way of responding both to what we are calling Islamic traditionalism and to the claims and judgments characteristic of Western norms and Western feminism. It is the result of many years of encounter with various forms of Western colonialism, as well as what have been understood in the West to be universal models of womanhood as they have been formulated and promulgated by the feminist movement in America. Western attempts to make these models "fit" Islamic cultures, and what often appears to be intolerance of deviation from the feminist paradigm developed in the West, have led Muslim women to conclude that the solidarity they sought with American feminists is not necessarily in their best interests. What has been labeled Muslim feminist discourse in the West is the result of exposure to and influence by Western liberationist discourse and postmodernist analyses, blended with the recognition that Muslim women face their own circumstances that may not fit with Western feminist models. Sometimes the urgency of seeing Islamic feminism as inherently different from that espoused in the West obscures for Muslim women scholars the fact that Western feminism itself has evolved and changed into a variety of forms of expression and interpretation. Thus, some Islamic discourse posits Western feminism as the antithesis of both Islamism and Orientalism, which permits the creation of "new" space for Muslim women related to but not identified with either.

One of the tasks to which modern Muslim "feminists" are called is a reinterpretation of certain verses of the Qur'an. Believing that Islam is a dynamic faith and one that constantly calls for interpretation to meet new circumstances, they reject male-dominated traditional commentaries in favor of an exegesis that shows the Qur'an to have been a pioneer in affirming women's rights. They know that the context in which the Qur'an was revealed was a patriarchal society and that exegesis through the centuries has been done by men who are themselves looking at the world through the lens of patriarchy. They deny, however, that the text of the Qur'an itself is patriarchal or that it places women at any disadvantage in relation to men. It is rather a whole and autonomous unit affirming God's oneness and human—male and female—responsibility to God and to each other. No verse can be understood out of context of the whole text. A single verse or passage that might alone be seen as privileging males over females must be seen in light of the overall Qur'anic affirmation of God's absolute justice.

Sudanese American Muslim scholar Hibba Abugideiri provides an insightful summary of the last several centuries of Arabic commentaries on the Qur'an in the *Encyclopedia of Women and Islamic Cultures*. She concludes that these texts conceptualize woman basically as a relational being—most specifically mother and wife—rather than a person in and of herself. Man is thus the primary reference around which women's rights and roles are understood. Such relationality, Abugideiri argues, sets the scene for a division of labor that is supported by the ideas of equity and complementarity rather than equality (interpreted as "the same" roles for men and women). This distinction is a major element in much contemporary Islamic discourse. Abugideiri calls it "the Qur'anic pretext" for giving man authority over the economic maintenance, protection, and leadership of the family, while the wife is limited to home responsibilities. She cites Surah 4:34 of the Qur'an as one of the most obvious verses in support of that distinction, calling the general interpretation of this verse a "body-based methodology" for interpreting Islamic rights that ultimately upholds a system of gender inequality. Typical of much of the work being done by female Qur'an interpreters today, Abugideiri says that understanding the Qur'an must be seen in light of Western imperialism and Western attempts to argue that Muslim women are subjugated and repressed. Islamic emphasis on the family, she insists, is one way to actively resist

Westernizing change. Unfortunately it has also served to promote the notion that female rights are understood only in the context of home and family responsibilities.

One of the pioneers in reinterpreting verses of the Qur'an dealing with women has been Pakistani American scholar Riffat Hassan of the University of Louisville. For over three decades Hassan has argued that if one holds as a basic principle that (a) the Qur'an is the word of God and (b) God is just, it is logically impossible that anything in the Qur'an could be understood to support the unjust (and unequal) treatment of women. Hassan, who is working actively for the rights of women in her home country of Pakistan, was one of the first of the feminist scholars to argue that religion is used as an instrument for the oppression of women rather than a way of freeing them from unjust legal and social systems. She has long recognized that most Muslims simply find it obvious that women are unequal to men and have basically never been challenged to reconsider that supposition by "correct" Qur'an interpretation. She sees that assumption to be based on three passages of the Qur'an that, in her opinion, have been incorrectly interpreted. These are:

1. That God's primary creation is man (not in the generic sense) and that woman came from man's rib;
2. That woman is primarily responsible for the fall from the Garden of Eden; and
3. That not only was woman created "from" man, but that her existence is "for" man and not of significance in itself.

Hassan challenges these interpretations by careful analysis of what the Qur'an really says about these issues, and discovers (a) that man and women are created from one soul and that the rib story has no Qur'anic basis but is based on traditions copied from Jewish literature; (b) that Adam and Eve (unnamed in the Qur'an) were equally responsible for the fall and that, again, only oral tradition talks about Eve as responsible for expulsion from the Garden; and (c) that men and women were created from one soul to be mates to each other and that woman was not made to be in service to her husband. Hassan's work, including both her basic assumptions and her careful scriptural analysis, has served as an inspiration for a new generation of young women scholars interpreting the Qur'an as a document of justice and equality for both women and men.

Another woman scholar of the Qur'an whose work has served as the basis and inspiration of a generation of Muslim women is Amina Wadud, cited in chapter 4, "Practices of the Faith," for having recently led the prayer for a mixed-gender congregation. Wadud, in her widely-read *Qur'an and Woman*, argues strongly for the importance of women becoming directly involved in what she calls the "crucial strategy of identity development," meaning alternative exegesis of the Qur'an. She identifies both neotraditionalist strategies (one conservative and one reactionary) on the one hand and secularist approaches being taken by Muslim women on the other and severely criticizes both. Neotraditionalism is popular because it affirms that Islam is perfect. Secularists, on the other hand, she sees as having given away the store by becoming antitradition, pro-Western, and ignorant of the importance of Islam and Islamic spirituality as a dimension of identity for women. Wadud advocates instead a new perspective that understands Islam not as a historical phenomenon that happened once and for all but a dynamic process constantly being created in accord with the cosmic order established by God.

Wadud has put up a challenge for all women (and men) who are engaging in exegesis of the Qur'an. Women have traditionally been voiceless in the task of *tafsir*, Qur'an interpretation, which has created a major gap in understanding. This gap, she argues, cannot be closed by simply repeating the rhetoric that says equality is basic to the Qur'an and the religion of Islam. It will require a major intellectual effort on the part of women, or men, who are willing to employ new exegetical understanding. If and when this is done it will constitute a major contribution to the debates currently taking place in America over the status of women. She thus argues for a new approach employing the principle of what she calls an alternative *ijtihad* (engaging in individual interpretation of the text). This is no easy task, as Wadud understands it, and must include the continual and radical rethinking of the text of the Qur'an. It is not that only the Qur'an has Truth, she says, or that it contains itself all Truth, but that it establishes a vision of the world that can lead to certainty.

One scholar who has taken up the challenge raised by Amina Wadud is Asma Barlas of Ithaca College. Barlas was once a member of Zia al-Haqq's government in Pakistan. Her comprehensive book *"Believing Women" in Islam: Understanding Patriarchal Interpretations of the Qur'an*, written in 2002, aims to recover the scriptural basis of sexual equality in Islam. While many analysts have condemned the notion of Islam as a patriarchal religion, she argues, she is the first to come up with a working definition of patriarchy (a politics of sexual differentiation that privileges males by transforming biological sex into politicized gender) with which to analyze the entire Qur'an. Acknowledging that the scripture was revealed in the context of a traditional patriarchy, she sets out to discover if the text itself supports this kind of patriarchy. She poses two sets of questions. The first is whether the Qur'an is a patriarchal or misogynist text that supports sexual inequality or the oppression of women. Secondly, she asks whether the Qur'an permits and even encourages liberation for women. Recognizing that Muslims have read and continue to read the Qur'an in more than one way, she concludes after lengthy analysis and argumentation that the answers to the two questions are, respectively, a resounding no and yes.

Acknowledging her debt to previous scholars such as Wadud, Barlas tries to demonstrate a number of points about the Qur'an: (a) that it does not represent God as male, (b) that while it addresses patriarchy it does not condone it, (c) that it does not see men as ontologically superior to women because God created humans from a single self, (d) that while it clearly acknowledges biological differences between men and women it does not suggest sexual and gender inequality, and (e) that while it does make distinctions between men and women with respect to some particular issues it does not establish them as unequal. The reason Muslims have not seen the Qur'an as a basically antipatriarchal text, she says, is because it has been men who have read and interpreted it, and they have done so in patriarchal contexts and without paying proper attention to hermeneutical and theological principles that the Qur'an itself advocates for its own reading. Understanding how important it is that Americans understand Islam in today's problematic world, she urges Muslims to strive for egalitarian readings of the Qur'an and the religion as part of the effort to know one another.

Increasing numbers of African American Muslim women are also getting actively involved in the study of the Qur'an. As Carolyn Rouse puts it, women are "negotiating gender" through exegesis of the text, providing the context in which women and men can meet and come to terms and through which new members can become familiar with the text and its emerging interpretations. Rouse refers to the ways in which women use interpretation of the Qur'an to redefine their duties as "engaged surrender"—not to their husbands, but to the text itself, to a truth in which they believe absolutely. They find in it complete affirmation not only of their own validity as women but also of their empowerment as African Americans. Amina McCloud also refers to the many study groups and classes engaging in exegesis that are now underway among African American women. McCloud was among the first to identity the distance African Americans feel from other Muslim groups, and her findings support Rouse's contention that because African Americans feel marginalized from mainstream Islam they turn quickly to the Qur'an as the ultimate support and affirmation. She is somewhat less sanguine than Rouse that men's thinking will actually be changed through these efforts, while the latter writes that interpretations communicated at these female gatherings, and found to be valid, can circulate in the community and eventually become accepted by both women and men. Both scholars, however, recognize that power in the community still rests with males, and that effecting changes in attitudes and understandings is no easy task.

Scholar-Activists

A small but important group of American Muslim female academics are those who fall under the category of "scholar-activist." Among them, for example, is Mahnaz Afkhami. Afkhami had played a prominent role in Iran before the

1979 revolution, serving as Minister of State for Women's Affairs from 1976 to 1978. With other scholars who supported the Shah, she emigrated to the United States after his fall from power and the establishment of the Islamic Republic by Ayatollah Khomeini. Since coming to America she has concentrated her efforts on working for justice for Muslim women and has written extensively on women's human rights, the politics of participation, and global feminism from a Muslim perspective. For five years she headed The Sisterhood is Global Institute, an international NGO with consultative status to the United Nations. Founded in 1984, the Institute attempts to facilitate strategies to address women's rights, freedoms, and power. Afkhami then became president of the international NGO, Women's Learning Partnership for Rights, Development and Peace, which provides leadership and programs for literacy campaigns and economic development for women in the Third World.

Currently, highly visible among Muslim scholar-activists representing a "Muslim feminist" approach is Azizah Y. al-Hibri, professor of law at the University of Richmond and founding editor of *Hypatia: A Journal of Feminist Philosophy*. Trained as a corporate lawyer and a philosopher, al-Hibri has long been engaged in gender activism. She was a member of the National Organization of Women, which has criticized Islam as a patriarchal religion. She and other Arab American feminist members of the organization were disappointed when the leadership of the American feminists refused to condemn the Israeli invasion of Lebanon that led to the death of 20,000 civilians and precipitated the massacres of Sabra and Shatila. Some of these women (both Christian and Muslim Arab Americans), continued to work for feminist causes as secularists and founded the journal *Mizna* to propagate their ideas. Al-Hibri chose to continue her activism within the Islamic discourse. She is perhaps best known for having founded KARAMAH: Muslim Women Lawyers for Human Rights. As president of the organization she has written and spoken at length about such topics as Islam and democracy, Muslim women's rights, domestic violence, and redefining women's roles. Al-Hibri sees one of the basic assumptions of the Qur'an to be the elimination of hierarchy in human society, including gender hierarchy. Patriarchal thinking, she says, has informed the interpretation of the Qur'an over the ages. Her program of action calls for dismantling patriarchal societies and using *ijtihad*, or individual interpretation, to promote an equitable interpretation of the Qur'an and a re-examination and reinterpretation of Islamic law. Al-Hibri, like others, rejects what she calls "outside" impositions of international declarations of women's rights and calls instead for the establishment of an International Muslim Women's Human Rights Commission. In an article entitled "Tear Off Your Western Veil," al-Hibri has accused Western feminists of being veiled by the very stereotypes through which they see Muslim women.

Among the pioneers of the field of visual anthropology is Fadwa el Guindi, former professor at the University of California at Los Angeles.

El Guindi, who is past president of the Society for Visual Anthropology, is working on a long-term ethnographic study, including visual research, of Arab-Americans. Her work includes experimentation with ethno-theater in the representation of ethnic cultural identity. Her popular play *Mahjar* identifies some of the issues immigrant parents have to deal with when their American-born children assert their independence. A frequent commentator on Arab and Muslim Americans, El Guindi has written extensively on veiling practices in Arab culture. In her book *Modesty, Privacy and Resistance* she calls attention to the need to rethink veiling from the perspectives of the socioeconomic and cultural contexts out of which women choose to veil. El Guindi was the only anthropologist among a select group of scholars to meet with President Clinton for a discussion of U.S. policy in the Middle East. She was elected president of the Los Angeles chapter of the Arab American Anti-Discrimination Committee during a time of political crisis.

The Appeal of Sufism

A few Muslim women have turned their scholarly attention to the examination of Sufism in its many forms and permutations in the West. Most of these women are advocates of a Sufi path that is defined as the personal engagement with the divine and claim a personal interest and involvement in it as a practice or as a philosophical orientation. They affirm that Sufism allows them to maintain their Islamic identity in a personal and quietist way that does not draw them into the struggles with society that so many of their sister scholars are experiencing. They find in traditional mystical treatises and practices a way to transcend the mundane and to engage with the divine on a level where all creatures are more or less equal and issues of gender equality do not need constantly to be argued.

Some scholars, like Marcia Hermansen, are interested in looking at the many ways in which Sufism has taken root in America. Hermansen has used the metaphor of a garden with its various kinds of plants—perennials, annuals, hybrids, etc.—to suggest the array of Sufi movements available. She highlights what elements in the various Sufi traditions allow for the engagement of women and how the practice of Sufism in the West often opens doors formerly closed to female participants. The work of Gisela Webb of Seton Hall University on the Bawa Muhaiyaddeen Sufi community in Philadelphia, and its particular appeal to women, is also in this genre of descriptive literature on American Sufism.

Other scholars writing from the American context, like the late prolific German scholar Annemarie Schimmel of Harvard and Bonn Universities, have talked more generally about both women's participation in Sufism worldwide and about the female principle expressed in Sufism. Schimmel, who often referred to herself as a Sufi, was critical of Western feminists who attacked Islam without understanding its many traditions, cultures, and languages. In her small book *My Soul is a Woman: The Feminine in Islam* she demonstrates the equality of women and men in the Qur'an, in the traditions of the Prophet, and in the feminine language of the mystical tradition. With examples from a wide range of cultures, especially the Indo-Muslim, she shows how physical love between woman and man gives expression to the highest forms of the mystical understanding of God.

Another kind of Sufi writing looks at the psychological effects of involvement in Sufi movements. *Sufi Women of America: Angels in the Making*, by Laleh Bakhtiar, chronicles seven American women who have joined the popular Naqshbandi Sufi Order. Bakhtiar, who is with KAZI Publications in Chicago, describes the experiences of these women who have chosen to be Sufis. An American Muslim of Iranian heritage who grew up in the West, Bakhtiar is trained in both philosophy and psychology. In *Angels* and other works she tries to demonstrate that classical Islamic training provides a viable alternative to modern methods of psychological treatment, showing how the traditional Muslim emphasis on ethics and morality is essential to sound mental health. One of her primary goals is helping women and girls, especially teenagers, deal with their problems through classical Islamic methods. In a three-volume work she explains traditional psychology and the Islamic Sufi origins of the Anagram.

The Debates Continue

The production of knowledge about Islam and women has become an important and highly contested industry not only in the academy but also in more public arenas. With the move of the American population as a whole into the "e-information age" the discourse has taken on new dimensions. Within the past decade cyberspace has come to provide a new forum for the exchange not only of information but of very strongly held views about Islam and Muslim women. The Internet has made interpretations, conversations, debates, and even polemics instantly accessible at the touch of a key. Vast Web sites have become the playground of Muslims and non-Muslims, all eager to have an input in the debates about women. Among those anxious to join the conversation are radicals and conservatives, fundamentalists and pro-Western feminists, those speaking as apologists for traditional interpretations and those who are blatantly anti-Muslim. Serious attempts at education get mixed in with off-the-cuff opinionating by those who may know very little about Islam, and the rate of exchange is extremely rapid.

The most popular topics in relation to women are the teachings of the Qur'an and Sunnah about gender issues, stories about the early Muslim community and male-female relations, the wives of the Prophet as models for female behavior and initiative, and discussion about contemporary family law in Muslim countries. What are called "*fatwa* [legal opinion] sites" feature responses to questions about all kinds of relationships between men and women, including dating, marriage, sexual concerns, and how best to live an Islamically-oriented life in America. Women and men living in the West can turn to recognized legal authorities around the world to find answers to the most personal kinds of concerns. Such a situation could never before have been imagined, and both the opportunities and the potential dangers are readily apparent. In a random sample of material from over twenty sites, a graduate student was asked to sort out what sites advocate an Islamist ideology and which ones are more generally liberal. The result of the exercise was sobering. It became quite clear that it is hard for the uninitiated to distinguish between the various discourses. The debates have become so involved that the women and men engaged in them even adopt each other's language and disputations in order to prove their point.

Publication of books on women in Islam has increased dramatically in the last few years. It is hard for the uninitiated to make an informed judgment about the truth of some the claims made by the various contending discourses. Causing a considerable stir among members of the Muslim community, particularly those who are more conservative in orientation, is the work of Canadian writer and journalist Irshad Manji. Calling herself a kind of Muslim gadfly who wants to encourage reflection and reform on the part of her co-religionists, she has labeled her efforts "Operation *Jihad.*" Manji, whose family came originally from Uganda, is the author of a highly publicized book titled *The Trouble with Islam: A Muslim's Call for Reform in Her Faith.* She openly identifies herself as a lesbian, calling on Muslims to show more tolerance and understanding of this issue. Currently she works as producer-reporter for Queer/Television in Toronto. Manji is producing a documentary about young Muslim women and plans to create an Institute for Independent Thinking in Islam, which has grown out of her book. One of Manji's most controversial contentions is the possibility that the Qur'an may not be completely "God-authored." She argues for more flexibility in scriptural interpretation, for the embrace of tolerance and pluralism, and for new opportunities to empower women such as economic initiatives and more participation in media organizations.

Also writing in an autobiographical style, although somewhat less controversial than Manji, is second-generation Pakistani American author Asma Gull Hasan, who in two well-publicized books has tried to convey to the American public what it means to have been raised in a "liberal" Muslim family. Referring to herself as a "Muslim Feminist Cowgirl," Hasan chronicles her growing-up days as a Pakistani in Colorado. Hasan's first work, *American Muslims: The New Generation*, was written in 2000 and tries to illustrate that one can be a believing Muslim without veiling, following strict regulations, or being a stay-at-home woman. Hasan, who is now a practicing attorney in San Francisco, has published in a variety of newspapers and journals and made appearances on CNN, *Fresh Air, Morning Edition, Fox News* and many other media programs. In 2004 she published her second book, *Why I Am a Muslim*, which is again partly a personal memoir and partly an effort to describe an Islam that she understands to be tolerant, diverse, and affirming of women's rights. Hasan's style is chatty and casual and is intended to bring the reader into conversation with her. Being Muslim, she insists, has allowed her to be a better American.

A recent arrival into the forum of competing and complementary discourses on and by American Muslim women is an organization known as the Progressive Muslim Union (PMU). Among its guiding principles, formulated in 2004, are the affirmation of the equal status and equal worth of all human beings regardless of religion, gender, race, ethnicity, or sexuality. Members of the PMU affirm that justice and compassion are the essential characteristics of God and thus are incumbent on human beings. They reject authoritarian, racist, and sexist formulations as antithetical to principles of justice and compassion. Among the founders and now on the board of the PMU is Sarah Eltantawi, writer and media-commentator on American Muslim affairs and Muslim women. The main scholarly production of the PMU is a volume edited by Omid Safi and entitled *Progressive Muslims: On Justice, Gender, and Pluralism*. Women contributors to the volume are Tazim Kassam on the risks and responsibilities of being a female Muslim scholar, Sa'diyya Sheikh on women and gender justice, Kecia Ali on a progressive interpretation of marriage and divorce law, Gwendolyn Zohara-Simmons on a radical reordering of the Islamic discourse on women, Amina Wadud on race and ethnicity, and Marcia Hermansen on youth culture and identity. The progressive Muslim project, as the editor states in the introduction, is dedicated to a new *ijtihad*. Its premise is that true justice for Muslims must be for all, and that includes Muslim women. While many in the Muslim community think that PMU is going too far in some of its analyses, those who call themselves progressive Muslims believe that they are just getting started.

Muslim women are speaking about Islam, and about their role as females within the ongoing tradition, from a great range of perspectives: as immigrants or converts; American-born or women bringing with them the heritage of a non-American and usually colonized culture; as scholars and recognized authors and academicians and as those who are newly finding their voices; as women who speak from a position of deep piety and practice; and as those for whom the religion of Islam is only one of a range of identities that claim their allegiance. Added to all of these voices are the opinions and interpretations of others: Muslim men defining the role of Islam in the West; Muslims from other cultures attempting to make sense of new developments in American Islam; and non-Muslim scholars, critics, and concerned citizens recognizing the new reality of a growing Muslim population in the United States.

In this chapter, and in this volume, we have attempted to reflect at least some of the range of voices in the emerging conversation, as well as the very different ways in which American Muslim women are responding to the challenges of being citizens and participants in what many people still claim is a secular Western culture. The scene is constantly shifting with new developments, new movements, and new contributors to the dialogue. No word, it seems, is either definitive or final, and no single study can begin to do justice to the opinions and activities of the many individuals who make up the growing body of American Muslim women. The reader is advised to avoid generalizations, to try to see the big picture, and to "stay tuned" to the new developments that are unfolding virtually every day. That changes will continue to occur is inevitable—and equally inevitable is the reality that some Muslim women will welcome them while others will fear for the integrity of their religion and their tradition. The question is whether they will choose to be the gatekeepers who uphold the norms and defend against innovation and engagement with America, or become cocreators of a new future. In this range of responses they share commonality with members of all of the religious traditions that have come to find a home in the constantly evolving culture of America.

Glossary

Adab al-Qur'an   Right intention, position, and ritual purity when reciting the Qur'an

Agha Khan   Leader of the Isma'ili Shi'ite community

Alimah   Woman educated in the Islamic sciences

Burqa   All-encompassing black cloak

Dars (pl: *durus*)   Study circle

Da'wah   Call to Islam; propagation of the faith

Dhikr   Congregational Sufi ceremony of remembering God

Du'a   Private, personal prayer of supplication

'Eid   Religious holiday, or ceremony ending a major Islamic holiday

Fiqh   Islamic jurisprudence; codification of Shari'ah or Islamic sacred law

Hadith   Traditions that record the words and deeds of the Prophet Muhammad

Hafizah   Woman who has memorized the Qur'an

Hajj   Pilgrimage to Mecca and Medina required, if physically possible, once in a lifetime and performed during pilgrimage month

Halal   Legally permissible

Halaqah   Study circle

Haram   Forbidden in Islamic law

Hijab   Head covering worn by Muslim women as a sign of piety and Muslim identity

Iftar   Daily breaking of the fast during the month of Ramadan

Ijtihad   Individual interpretation of Islamic law

Imam   For Sunnis, a leader (of the prayer); for Shi'ites, the hidden leader who will return at the end of time

Jilbaab   Robe

Jinn   Mischievious spirit

Jum'ah   Friday congregational prayer

Khadijah   First wife of the Prophet Muhammad

Khutbah   Sermon delivered at the Friday congregational prayer

Madrasah   Islamic religious school

Mahr   Amount a groom pays his bride, stipulated in an Islamic marriage contract

Mahram   Male guardian or protector

Majlis (**pl.** *majalis*)   Religious gathering

Milad   Birthdate observance of an Islamic saint

Mosque   Muslim house of worship

Muharram   First month in the Islamic calendar; sacred month for Shi'ites

Mut'ah   Rare form of marriage contracted for a specific length of time

Niqab   Full-face veil

Polygyny   Practice of men marrying multiple wives at the same time

Qur'an   Scripture or Holy Book of Islam

Salat   Formal prayer performed at five designated times each day

Shahadah   Affirmation of the oneness of God and the prophethood of Muhammad

Shalwar khameez   Loose tunic and trousers

Shari'ah   Islamic law based on divine revelation

Sufism   Practice of schools of Islamic mystical thought

Sunnah   Way of life exemplified by the Prophet Muhammad

Tajwid   Recitation of the Qur'an

Talaq   Repudiation or divorce

Tarawih   Ritual worship prescribed for nights during the month of Ramadan

Ummah   Muslim community

'Umrah   Lesser pilgrimage to Mecca and Medina performed at any time

Zakat   Alms payment; charitable tax

Sources

CHAPTER I SETTING THE SCENE

AbiSaab, Rula. "Women, Gender and Sectarianism." In *Encyclopedia of Women and Islamic Cultures*. 2: 721–724. Leiden: Brill, 2004.

Alvi, Sajida Sultana, Homa Hoodfar, and Sheila McDonough, eds. *The Muslim Veil in North America: Issues and Debates*. Toronto: Women's Press, 2003.

Bagby, Ihsan. "The Mosque and the American Public Square." In *Muslims' Place in the American Public Square*, edited by Zahid Bukhari, Sulayman Nyang, Mumtaz Ahmad, and John Esposito, 323–246. Walnut Creek, Calif.: AltaMira Press, 2004.

Barlas, Asma. *Islam, Muslims and the U.S. Essays on Religion and Politics*. Delhi, India: Global Media Publications, 2004.

Bullock, Katherine. "Hijab & Contemporary Muslim Women." *The Message International* (February/March 2004): 8–11.

Dannin, Robert. *Black Pilgrimage to Islam*. New York: Oxford University Press, 2002.

Haddad, Yvonne Yazbeck, and Jane I. Smith, eds. *Muslim Communities in America*. Albany: State University of New York Press, 1994.

———. "Women in Islam: The Mother of all Battles." In *Arab Women: Between Defiance and Restraint*, edited by Suha Sabbagh, 137–150. New York: Olive Branch Press, 1996.

———. *Muslim Communities in the West: Visible and Invisible*. Walnut Creek, Calif.: AltaMira Press, 2002.

Haddad, Yvonne Yazbeck, Jane I. Smith, and John Esposito. *Becoming American: Immigration and Religious Life in the United States*. Walnut Creek, Calif.: AltaMira Press, 2003.

El-Halawany, Hanan Salah El-Deen. "Highly Educated Egyptian Women's Response to Gender Role Challenges in Post 9–11 America." PhD diss., University of Pittsburgh, 2003.

McCloud, Aminah Beverly. "African-American Muslim Women." In *The Muslims of America*, edited by Yvonne Yazbeck Haddad, 177–187. New York: Oxford University Press, 1991.

———. *African American Islam*. New York: Routledge, 1995.

Mernissi, Fatima. *Beyond the Veil: Male-Female Dynamics in Modern Muslim Society* (Revised Version). Bloomington: Indiana University Press, 1990.

Rouse, Carolyn Moxley. *Engaged Surrender: African American Women and Islam*. Berkeley: University of California Press, 2004.

Smith, Jane I. *Islam in America*. New York: Columbia University Press, 1999.

———. "Patterns of Muslim Immigration." In *Muslim Life in America*, 14–19. Washington, D.C.: U.S. State Department: Office of International Information Programs, 2002.

Waugh, Earle H., Baba Abu-Laban, and Regula B. Qureshi, eds. *The Muslim Community in North America*. Edmonton, Alberta: The University of Alberta Press, 1983.

Newspaper and Magazine Articles

Khan, Sheema. "Don't Misread the Koran." *Globe and Mail*, February 14, 2001.

Malik, Nadia. "Looking Beyond the Veil." *Daily News Herald*, Arlington Heights, Illinois, February 25, 2005.

CHAPTER 2 PERSISTENT STEREOTYPES

Adeney, Miriam. *Daughters of Islam: Building Bridges with Muslim Women*. Downers Grove, Ill.: InterVarsity Press, 2002.

Ahmed, Leila. "Western Ethnocentrism and Perceptions of the Harem." *Feminist Studies* 8, no. 3 (1982): 521–534.

Burton, Richard. *Personal Narrative of a Pilgrimage to El-Medinah and Meccah*. London: Longman, Brown, Green, and Longmans, 1855–1856.

Delacroix, Eugène. *Algerian Women in Their Apartments*. 1834. Musée du Louvre, Paris.

Flaubert, Gustave. *Flaubert in Egypt: A Sensibility on Tour; a Narrative Drawn from Gustave Flaubert's Travel Notes & Letters*, translated from French, edited by Francis Steegmuller. London: Bodley Head, 1972.

Fleischmann, Ellen L. "Our Moslem Sisters: Women of Greater Syria in the Eyes of American Protestant Missionary Women." *Islam and Christian-Muslim Relations* 9, no. 3 (1998): 307–324.

Freas, Erik. "Muslim Women in the Missionary World." *The Muslim World* (April 1998): 141–164.

Hill, Patricia. *The World: Their Household*. Ann Arbor: University of Michigan Press, 1935.

Kahf, Mohja. "The Image of the Muslim Women in American Cinema: Two Orientalist Fantasy Films." *Cinefocus* 3 (1995): 19–25.

————. *Western Representations of the Muslim Woman: From Tergamant to Odalisque.* Austin: University of Texas Press, 1999.

Keen, Sam. *Faces of the Enemy.* Cambridge, Mass.: Harper and Row, 1986.

Lane, Edward. *A Thousand and One Nights: Commonly Called, in England, the Arabian Nights' Entertainments.* London: Chatto and Windus, 1889.

Leno, Mavis. Testimony to Joint Hearing of the Subcommittee on International Organizations and Terrorism and the Subcommittee on Near Eastern and South Asia Affairs of the Committee on Foreign Relations of U.S. Senate, October 10, 2001.

Love, Fran, and Jeleta Eckheart, eds. *Ministry to Muslim Women: Longing to Call Them Sisters.* Pasadena, Calif.: William Carey Library Publishers, 2004.

Mahmoody, Betty. *Not without My Daughter: A True Story.* New York: St. Martin's Press, 1987.

Moll, Yasmin. "Islamic Media for Muslim-American Children and the Politics of Identity Construction." *Mentis Vita* 3, no. 2 (spring 2003): 7–27.

Sa'dawi, Nawal. *Hidden Face of Eve: Women in the Arab World.* New York: St Martin's Press, 1997.

Said, Edward. *Orientalism.* New York: Pantheon Books, 1978.

Salem, Lori A. "Far-off and Fascinating Things: Waheeda Atiyeh and the Images of Arabs in the American Popular Theater, 1930–1950." In *Arabs in America: Building a New Future*, edited by Michael W. Suleiman, 272–283. Philadelphia: Temple University Press, 1999.

Shaheen, Jack. *The TV Arab.* Bowling Green, Ohio: The Popular Press, 1984.

————. "Hollywood's Muslim Arabs." *The Muslim World* 90 (spring 2000): 22–42.

————. *Reel Bad Arabs: How Hollywood Vilifies People.* New York: Olive Branch Press, 2001.

Steet, Linda. *Veils and Daggers: A Century of National Geographic's Representation of the Arab World.* Philadelphia: Temple University Press, 2000.

Strawson, John. "Islamic Law and English Texts." *Law and Critique* 4, no. 1: 21–38.

Von Summer, Annie, and Samuel M. Zwemer. *Our Moslem Sisters: A Cry in Need from Lands of Darkness Interpreted by Those Who Heard It.* New York: F. H. Revell; 1907.

Wadud, Amina. "Woman and Islam: Beyond the Stereotypes." *Pakistan Journal of Women's Studies: Alam-e-Niswan* 4, no. 2 (1997): 1–14.

Wilkins, Karin Gwinn. "Middle Eastern Women in Western Eyes: A Study of U.S. Press Photographs of Middle Eastern Women." In *The U.S. Media and the Middle East: Image and Perception*, edited by Yahya R. Kamalipour, 50–61. Westport, Conn.: Greenwood Press, 1995.

Yegenoglu, Meyda. *Colonial Fantasies: Towards a Feminist Reading of Orientalism.* Cambridge: Cambridge University Press, 1998.

Muslim Periodicals

Al-Jumuah: www.al-jumuah.com/home.html

Islamic Horizons: www.isna.net/services/horizons/

KAMILAT, *The Muslim Magazine:* www.kamilat.org

Muslim Organizations

Council on American-Islamic Relations (CAIR): www.cair-net.org/
KARAMAH: Muslim Women Lawyers for Human Rights: www.karamah.org/
Muslim Women's League: www.mwlusa.org/

Newspaper and Magazine Articles

Gardiner, Beth. "Cherie Blair Condemns Taliban Mistreatment of Women During Rule of Afghanistan." Associated Press, November 11, 2001.

Lacayo, Richard. "About Face for Afghan Women." *Time*, December 3, 2001: 34–49.

Malik, Nadia. "Beyond the Veil Arlington Heights, Illinois, *Daily Herald* Reporter Nadia Malic Shares how the Islamic Head Covering Liberated Her. Her Mom Was Initially Opposed." *Daily Herald*, February 27, 2005.

Internet Web Sites

Bush, Laura. "Radio Address, Crawford, Texas," November 17, 2001. Available www.whitehouse.gov/news/releases/2001/11/20011117.html.

Native Deen. "M-U-S-L-I-M," *For the Cause of Allah* (music album), 2002. Available www.nativedeen.com.

"Pictures of Muslim Women Around the World." *National Geographic*, with Special thanks to Shakir Muhammad. Found online at www.ece2.engr.ucf.edu/~kba/world.html.

CHAPTER 3 EMBRACING ISLAM

Anway, Carol. *Daughters of Another Path: Experiences of American Women Choosing Islam.* Lee's Summit, Mo.: Yawna Publications, 1996.

———. "American Women Choosing Islam." In *Muslims on the Americanization Path?* edited by Yvonne Yazbeck Haddad and John L. Esposito, 145–162. Oxford: Oxford University Press, 2000.

Bawany, Ebrahim Ahmed. *Islam—Our Choice.* Karachi, Pakistan: Begum Aisha Bawany Waqf, 1977.

Brooks, Geraldine. *Nine Parts of Desire.* New York: Anchor Books, 1995.

Dannin, Robert. "The Greatest Migration?" In *Muslim Minorities in the West*, edited by Yvonne Haddad and Jane Smith, 59–76. Walnut Creek, Calif.: AltaMira Press, 2002.

García-Arenal, M. "Jewish Converts to Islam in the Muslim West." *Israel Oriental Studies* 17 (1997): 227–248.

Goodwin, Jan. *Price of Honor.* New York: Plume, 1995.

Haddad, Yvonne Yazbeck. "The Quest for Peace in Submission: Reflections on the Journey of American Women Converts to Islam." In *Women Embracing Islam: Gender and Conversion in the West*, edited by Karin van Nieuwkerk. Austin: Texas University Press, forthcoming.

Haleem, Muzaffar, and Betty Batul Bowman. *The Sun Is Rising in the West*. Beltsville, Md.: Amana Publications, 1999.

Hasan, Asma. *American Muslims: The New Generation*. New York: Continuum, 2002.

Hermansen, Marcia. "Keeping the Faith: Convert Mothers and the Transmission of Female Muslim Identity in the West." In *Women Embracing Islam: Gender and Conversion in the West*, edited by Karin van Nieuwkerk. Austin: Texas University Press, forthcoming.

Hill, Jennifer Lynn. "Women in the Nation of Islam." Typescript, September 29, 2002.

———. Themes in Conversion Accounts of Caucasian Women. Typescript, January 14, 2003.

Jameelah, Maryam. *Quest for the Truth: Memoirs of a Childhood and Youth in America, 1945–1962*. Delhi, India: Aakif Book Depot, 1989.

Jones, J. Lynn. *Believing as Ourselves*. Beltsville, Md.: Amana Publishing, 2002.

Köse, Ali. "Post-Conversion Experiences of Native British Converts to Islam." *Islam and Christian-Muslim Relations* 5, no. 2 (1994): 195–206.

———. *Conversion to Islam*. London: Kegan Paul International, 1996.

———. "Journey from the Secular to the Sacred." *Social Compass* 46, no. 3 (September 1999): 301–312.

Kysia, Alison. The Role of Race and Gender in My Conversion to Islam. Typescript, May 1, 2003.

Love, Fran, and Jeleta Eckheart, eds. *Ministry to Muslim Women: Longing to Call Them Sisters*. Pasadena, Calif.: William Carey Library, 2000.

Månsson, Anna. *Becoming Muslim: Meanings of Conversion to Islam*. Lund, Sweden: Lund University, 2002.

McCloud, Aminah. *African American Islam*. New York: Routledge, 1995.

Poston, Larry. *Islamic Da'wah in the West*. New York: Oxford University Press, 1992.

———. *The Changing Face of Islam in America*. Camp Hill, Pa.: Horizon Books, 2000.

Rambo, Lewis R. "Theories of Conversion: Understanding and Interpreting Religious Change." *Social Compass* 46, no. 3 (September 1999): 259–271.

Rouse, Carolyn Moxley. *Engaged Surrender: African American Women and Islam*. Berkeley: University of California Press, 2004.

Shatzmiller, M. "Marriage, Family, and the Faith: Women's Conversion to Islam." *Journal of Family History* 21, no. 3 (1996): 235–266.

Stern, G. H. "The First Women Converts in Early Islam." *Islamic Culture* 13 (1939): 290–305.

Sultan, Madeleine. "Choosing Islam: A Study of Swedish Converts." *Social Compass* 46 (September 3, 1999): 325–335.

Van Nieuwkerk, Karin, ed. *Women Embracing Islam: Gender and Conversion in the West*. Austin: Texas University Press, forthcoming.

Vanzan, A. "In Search of Another Identity: Female Muslim-Christian Conversions in the Mediterranean World." *Islam and Christian-Muslim Relations* 7, no. 3 (1996): 327–333.

Why Did They Become Muslims? Istanbul, Turkey: Waqf Ikhlas Publications, 1995.

Wolfe, Michael, ed. *One Thousand Roads to Mecca*. New York: Grove Press, 1997.

Zohara-Simmons, Gwendolyn. "Are We up to the Challenge? The Need for a Radical Reordering of the Islamic Discourse on Women." In *Progressive Muslims*, edited by Omid Safi, 235–248. Oxford: One World, 2003.

———. "African American Islam as an Expression of Converts' Religious Faith and Nationalist Dreams and Ambitions." In *Women Embracing Islam: Gender and Conversion in the West*, edited by Karin van Nieuwkerk. Austin: Texas University Press, forthcoming.

Newspaper and Magazine Articles

Berrington, Lucky. "Why British Women are Turning to Islam." *The Times* (UK), November 9, 1993.

Chu, Jeff. "The Convert." *Time Atlantic*, December 16, 2002.

Compton, Nick. "The New Face of Islam." *The Evening Standard*, London, March 15, 2002.

Dooley, Tara. "From Christianity to Islam." *Chicago Tribune*, September 8, 1999.

Ganeshram, Ramin. "Steadfast in Their New Faith." *New York Times*, December 9, 2001.

Hashim, N. "Iman Finds Islam." *Islamic Voice*, January 1997.

Hauser, Christian. "From Bathing Suit to Hijab." *Islamic Voice*, September 1997.

Jardine, Kay. "Mum, I've Decided I Want to Follow Allah." *The Herald*, Glasgow, March 8, 2002. www.theherald.co.uk

Jimenez, Marina. "New Muslims." Victoria, Canada, *National Post*, January 19, 2002.

Khan, Muqtedar. "The Manifest Destiny of American Muslims." *Washington Report on the Middle East* 19 (December 2000): 168.

Malhotra, Priya. "Islam's Female Converts." February 16, 2002. Available at www.newsday.com.

McBride, Sarah. "Converts in Kuwait." *Kuwait Times*, January 3, 1996.

Pipes, Daniel. "In Muslim America." *National Review*, February 21, 2000.

Tu, Janet I. "Muslim Converts Try to Dispel Myths." *Seattle Times*, November 21, 2002.

Virk, Sobia. "Concordia Students Tell of Their Conversion to Islam." *The Link*, February 5, 2002.

Whittell, Gilles. "Allah Came Knocking at My Heart." *The Times* (UK), January 7, 2002.

Wiener, Jocelyn. "Young, Female and Muslim." *St. Petersburg Times*, October 7, 2002.

Wilgoren, Jodi. "Islam Attracts Converts by the Thousands." *New York Times*, October 22, 2001.

Zuckerman, Julia. "Muslim Converts Discuss Pros, Cons at Awareness Week Convocation." *Brown Daily Herald*, Providence, RI, November 12, 2002.

Internet Web Sites

www.convertstoislam.org (aimed at new converts, some bad links)
www.geocities.com/embracing_islam
www.thetruereligion.org (archive of articles and testimonials)
www.usc.edu/dept/MSA/newmuslims (archive of testimonials)

CHAPTER 4 PRACTICES OF THE FAITH

Abdel-Nabi, Shereen. *Duroos*: Religious Lessons and Muslim Women. Typescript, April 28, 2004.

Abul-Fadl, Mona. *Introducing Islam from Within: Alternative Perspectives*. Markfield, Leicester, UK: Islamic Foundation, 1991.

Ali, Kecia. "Acting on a Frontier of Religious Ceremony: With Questions and Quiet Resolve, a Woman Officiates at a Muslim Wedding." *Harvard Divinity Bulletin* (fall/winter 2004): 8–9.

Bakhtiar, Laleh. *Sufi Women of America: Angels in the Making*. Chicago: KAZI Publications, 1996.

Giorgio-Poole, Marilyn. "The Religious Lives and Ritual Practices of Arab Muslim Women in the United States," PhD diss., University of Pittsburgh, 1999.

Haddad, Yvonne Yazbeck, and Jane I. Smith. *Mission to America: Five Islamic Sectarian Movements in the United States*. Gainesville: The University Presses of Florida, 1993.

Hermansen, Marcia. *Mystifying Identities in Muslim America: The Case of American Sufi Movements*, forthcoming.

McCloud, Aminah. "African-American Muslim Women." In *The Muslims of America*, edited by Yvonne Y. Haddad, 177–187. Oxford: Oxford University Press, 1991.

Nomani, Asra. *Standing Alone in Mecca: An American Woman's Struggle for the Soul of Islam*. SanFrancisco: HarperSanFrancisco, 2005.

Qureshi, Regula. "Transcending Space. Recitation and Community among South Asian Muslims in Canada." In *Making Muslim Space in North America and Europe*, edited by Barbara Daly Metcalf, 46–64. Berkeley: University of California Press, 1996.

Schmidt, Garbi. *Islam in Urban America: Sunni Muslims in Chicago*. Philadelphia: Temple University Press, 2004.

Siddiqi, Muzammil, George B. Grose, and Benjamin J. Hubbard, eds. *The Abraham Connection: A Jew, Christian and Muslim in Dialogue*. Notre Dame, Ind.: Cross Cultural Publications and Cross Roads Books, 1994.

Smith, Jane I. "Women's Issues in American Islam." In *Encyclopedia of Women and Religion in North America*. Bloomington: Indiana University Press, 2006; Reprinted in Union Seminary Quarterly Review *Festschrift* for Rosemary Skinner Keller 57, no. 3 (2003): 197–216.

Wadud, Amina. "Alternative Qur'anic Interpretation and the Status of Muslim Women." In *Windows of Faith: Muslim Women Scholar-Activists in North America*, edited by Gisela Webb, 3–21. Syracuse, N.Y.: Syracuse University Press, 2000.

Wadud-Muhsin, Amina. "On Belonging as a Muslim Woman." In *My Soul is a Witness: African-American Women's Spirituality*, edited by Gloria Wade-Gayles, 253–265. Boston: Beacon Press, 1995.

Yousef, Hoda Ahmed. *Hafizat al-Ghayb*: Qur'anic Science of *Tajwid*. Typescript, May 26, 2004.

Newspaper and Magazine Articles

Goodstein, Laurie. "Muslim Women Seeking a Place in the Mosque." *New York Times*, July 22, 2004.

Scrivener, Leslie. "Woman's Sermon Breaks Tradition at Local Mosque." *Toronto Star*, November 13, 2004.

El-Tablawi, Tarek. "Celebration Honors Young Muslim Girls Donning the Veil." *Detroit Free Press*, May 21, 2004.

Internet Web Sites

The Council on American-Islamic Relations (CAIR): http://www.cair-net.org/

Islamic Society of North America (ISNA): www.isna.net/

Jamal, Amany. "The Role of Mosques in the Civic and Political Incorporation of Muslim Americans," Muslims in New York City Project: Middle East Institute, Columbia University. Available at www.sipa.columbia.edu/muslim/nyc/research/projects/role%20of%20muslims.html#

Safi, Louay. "Toward Women Friendly Mosques," ISNA Leadership Development Center at www.ildc.net/articles/2005/6/26/toward-women-friendly-mosques .html.

CHAPTER 5 GENDER AND FAMILY

Ammar, Nawal H. "Simplistic Stereotyping and Complex Reality of Arab-American Immigrant Identity: Consequences and Future Strategies in Policing Wife Battery." *Islam and Christian-Muslim Relations* 11, no. 1 (2000): 51–68.

Ayyub, Ruksana. "Domestic Violence in the South Asian Muslim Immigrant Population in the United States." *Journal of Social Distress and the Homeless* 9, no. 3 (2000): 237–248.

Azmi, Shaheen Hussain. "Perceptions of the Welfare Response to Wife Abuse in the Muslim Community of Metropolitan Toronto." Unpublished PhD diss., Faculty of Social Work, University of Toronto, 1996.

Campo, Juan. *The Other Sides of Paradise: Explorations into the Religious Meanings of Domestic Space in Islam*. Columbia: University of South Carolina Press, 1991.

Al-Faruqi, Ismail, and Lamya (Lois) al-Faruqi. *Cultural Atlas of Islam*. New York: Macmillan, 1968.

Haddad, Yvonne Y., and Adair T. Lummis. *Islamic Values in the United States: A Comparative Study*. New York: Oxford University Press, 1987.

Haddad, Yvonne Yazbeck, and Jane I. Smith. "Muslim Women in Inter-Cultural Perspective." In *Gender among American Muslims: Issues Facing Middle Eastern Immigrants and Their Descendants*, edited by Barbara Aswad and Barbara Bilge, 19–40. Philadelphia: Temple University Press, 1996.

——. "Adjusting the Ties that Bind: Challenges Facing Muslim Women in America." In *Muslim Women in the United Kingdom and Beyond*, edited by Haifaa Jawad and Tansin Benn, 39–64. Leiden: Brill, 2003.

Islamic Society of North America. "The Final Stages: Living and Dying with Dignity." *Islamic Horizons* (January 2004): 16–37.

Kobeisy, Ahmed N. *Counseling American Muslims: Understanding the Faith and Helping the People.* Westport, Conn.: Praeger, 2004.

Manji, Irshad. *The Trouble with Islam: A Muslim's Call for Reform in Her Faith.* New York: St. Martin's Press, 2003.

McCloud, Aminah. *African American Islam.* New York: Routledge, 1995.

Orgocka, Aida. "Communication and Education about Sexuality among Muslim Immigrant Girls." *Muslim Immigrant Women in the U.S. Brief No. 1 and 2,* University of Illinois PhD diss., Urbana Champaign, 2003.

Peek, Lori. "Women, Gender and Marriage Practices in the United States." In *Encyclopedia of Women and Islamic Cultures.* EWIC, Vol. 3. Leiden: Brill, 2005, forthcoming.

Rouse, Carolyn Moxley. *Engaged Surrender: African American Women and Islam.* Berkeley: University of California Press, 2004.

Siddiqui, Shahina. "Muslim Women: Gender and Mental Health." In *Encyclopedia of Women and Islamic Cultures.* vol. 3. Leiden: Brill, 2005, forthcoming.

Smith, Jane I. "Islam and the Family in North America." In *American Religions and the Family,* edited by Don Browning, University of Chicago Press/Columbia University Press, 2004.

Newspaper and Magazine Articles

Badawi, Jamal. "Touched by a Feather." *Islamic Horizons* (March/April 2001): 28.

Horan, Deborah. "Abuse Counselors Reach out to Arab Women." *Chicago Tribune,* April 6, 2004.

Khan, Sheema. "Don't Misread the Koran." *Globe and Mail,* February 14, 2001.

Dating Web Sites

www.matrimony.org
www.muslimgatherings.com
www.muslimweddings.com
www.naseeb.com
www.shiamatch.com
www.soundvision.com
www.zawaj.com

Internet Web Sites

Islamic Society of North America (ISNA): www.isna.net/

CHAPTER 6 MUSLIM WOMEN IN THE CRUCIBLE

Bartkowski, John P., and Jen'nan Ghazal Read. "Veil Submission: Gender, Power and Identity Among Evangelical and Muslim Women in the United States." *Qualitative Sociology* 26, no. 1 (spring 2003): 71–92.

Al-Hibri, Azizah. "Islamic Law and Muslim Women in America." In *One Nation Under God? Religion and American Culture*, edited by Marjorie Garber and Rebecca Walkowitz, 128–144. N.Y.: Routledge, 1999.

———. "An Introduction to Muslim Women's Rights." In *Windows of Faith: Muslim Women Scholar-Activists in North America*, edited by Gisela Webb, 51–71. Syracuse, N.Y.: Syracuse University Press, 2000.

———. "Muslim Women's Rights in the Global Village: Challenges and Opportunities." In *Journal of Law and Religion* 15, nos. 1–2 (2000–01): 37–66.

Moore, Kathleen M. "The *Hijab* and Religious Liberty: U.S. Anti-Discrimination Law and Muslim Women in the United States." In *Muslims on the Americanization Path?* edited by Yvonne Y. Haddad and John L. Esposito, 129–158. New York: Oxford University Press, 2000.

Quraishi, Asifa, and Najeeba Syeed-Miller. "No Altars: A Survey of Islamic Family Law in the United States." Available at the Web site of the Emory School of Law, Islamic Family Law: www.law.edu/IFL/cases/USA.htm

Internet Web Sites

KARAMAH: Muslim Women Lawyers for Human Rights: www.karamah.org
U.S. Equal Employment Opportunity Commission: www.eeoc.gov

Court Cases

Akileh v. Elchahal (666 So.2d. 246 [Fla.2d. Dist. Ct. App. 1996]).

Chaudry v. Chaudry (388 A.2d 1000 [N.J. Super. Ct. App. Div. 1978]).

Habibi-Fahnrich v. Fahnrich (1995 WL 507388 [N. Y. Sup. Ct. 1995]).

In Re Marriage of Dajani (251 Cal. Rptr. 871 [Ct. App. 1988]).

In Re Marriage of Shaban (105 Cal. Rptr. 2d 863 [Ct. App. 2001]).

Odatalla v. Odatalla (355 N. J. Super. Ct. 305, 810 A.2d 93 [Ch. Div. 2002]).

Sheveka Gibson v. The Finish Line, Inc., of Delaware (261 F. Supp. 2d 785, W. D. Kentucky, April 25, 2003).

Sultaana Lakiana Myke Freeman v. State of Florida, Department of Highway Safety and Motor Vehicles (9th Cir. For Orange County, Fl., Case no. 2002-CA-2828, decided on June 6, 2003).

Venters v. City of Delphi (No. 96-1355, U.S. Court of Appeals for Seventh Circuit, 123 F.3d 956; 1997 U.S. App. LEXIS 22360).

CHAPTER 7 CLAIMING PUBLIC SPACE

Afkhami, Mahnaz, and Haleh Vaziri. *Claiming Our Rights: A Manual for Women's Human Rights Education in Muslim Societies*. Bethesda, Md.: Sisterhood is Global Institute, 1998.

Ahmed, Leila. *Women and Gender in Islam: Historical Roots of a Modern Debate*. New Haven, Conn.: Yale University Press, 1992.

———. *A Border Passage: From Cairo to America—A Woman's Journey*. New York: Farrar, Straus and Giroux, 1999.

Anwar, Ghazala. African American Muslim Women in Prison: Some Theoretical and Practical Issues. Typescript.

Bakhtiar, Laleh. *Sufi Women of America: Angels in the Making.* Chicago: Kazi Publications, 1997.

Douglass, Susan, ed. *Strategies and Structures for Presenting World History: With Islam and Muslim History As a Case Study.* 1st ed. Beltsville, Md.: Amana Publications, 1994.

al-Faruqi, Ismail, and Lamya (Lois) Faruqi *Cultural Atlas of Islam.* New York: Macmillan, 1986.

Handal, Nathalie. *The Poetry of Arab Women: A Contemporary Anthology.* New York: Interlink Books, 2001.

Hasan, Asma Gull. *American Muslims: The New Generation.* New York: Continuum, 2000.

————. *Why I Am a Muslim: An American Odyssey.* London: Element, 2004.

Hilal, Dima. "Ar-Rahman Road." In *The Poetry of Arab Women: A Contemporary Anthology,* edited by Nathalie Handal, 119. New York: Interlink Books, 2001.

ISNA. *Leadership Development Center Program Report.* Summer Leadership Institute SLI 2004, August 11, 2004.

Kahf, Mohja. *Western Representations of the Muslim Woman from Termagant to Odalisque.* Austin: University of Texas Press, 1999.

Mattson, Ingrid. "Debating Form and Function in Muslim Women's Leadership." In *Women and Religious Leadership,* edited by Scott Alexander. New York: Sheed and Ward, forthcoming.

"Old Paradigms and New Possibilities: Muslim Women Taking Charge of their Future," *Listening: Journal of Religion and Culture* 31, no. 3 (fall 1996): 206–218.

Qadri, Yasmeen. "Leadership in the 21st Century: New Challenges for Islamic School Principals." Presented at the ISNA Education Forum: Chicago, Ill., March 29–31, 2002.

Schmidt, Garbi. *Islam in Urban America: Sunni Muslims in Chicago.* Philadelphia: Temple University Press, 2004.

Serageldin, Samia. *The Cairo House.* Syracuse, N.Y.: Syracuse University Press, 2000.

Shakir, Evelyn. *Bint Arab: Arab and Arab American Women in the United States.* Westport, Conn.: Praeger, 1997.

Smith, Jane I. "Joining the Debate. Muslim Women Participate in Building a Vital Islamic Society for the Next Century." *The World and I* (September 1997): 60–67.

Webb, Gisela, ed. *Windows of Faith: Muslim Women Scholar-Activists in North America.* Syracuse, N.Y.: Syracuse University Press, 2000.

Muslim Organizations

The Council on American-Islamic Relations (CAIR): www.cair-net.org/
The International League of Muslim Women, Inc.
Islamic Society of North America (ISNA): www.isna.net/
Muslim Education Resource Council, Inc.
Muslim Educational Council
Muslim Home School Network and Resource

Muslim Student Association (MSA): www.msa-natl.org

Muslim Wake Up: www.muslimwakeup.com

Muslim Youth of North America (MYNA): http://www.myna.i-p.com/

North American Council of Muslim Women

Rahima Foundation: http://rahima.org/

Sisters in Islam: www.sistersinislam.org/

Sisters United in Human Service, Inc.

Women's Learning Partnership for Rights, Development and Peace

Newspaper and Magazine Articles

Fattouh, Alia. "An Arab Liberal's Anguish." *Christian Science Monitor*, December 15, 2003.

al-Marayati, Laila. "The Biases of Elliot Abrams." *Counterpunch*, December 16, 2002. Available at www.counterpunch.org/laila1216.html.

Serageldin, Samia. "I live in Interesting Times." *NC Writers' Newsletter*, September/ October 2000.

Internet Web Sites

Amri, Judi. "Unraveling the Case Against School Choice." Islamic Schools' League of America. Available at www.4islamicschools.org/student_papers.htm.

Keyworth, Karen. "Trial by Fire: Islamic Schools after 9–11." Islamic Schools League of America. Available at www.4islamicschools.org.

Ulen, Eisa N. "Muslims in the Mosaic." *Essence*, January 2002. Available at www.findarticles.com/p/articles/mi_m1264/is_9_32/ai_81470492

CHAPTER 8 COMPETING DISCOURSES

Abd al-Ati, Hammudah. *The Family Structure in Islam*. Indianapolis, Ind.: American Trust Publications, 1977.

———. *Islam in Focus*. Indianapolis, Ind.: Amana Publications, 1998.

Abdul-Rauf, Muhammad. *The Islamic View of Women and the Family*. New York: R. Speller, 1979.

———. *Marriage in Islam: A Manual*. Alexandria, Va.: Al-Saadawi Publications, 1995.

Abugideiri, Hibba. "Egyptian Women and the Science Question: Gender in the Making of Colonized Medicine, 1893–1929." PhD diss., Georgetown University, 2001.

Abu-Lughod, Lila. "Feminist Longings and Postcolonial Conditions." In *Remaking Women: Feminism and Modernity in the Middle East*, edited by Lila Abu-Lughod, 3–31. Princeton, N.J.: Princeton University Press, 1998.

———. "Orientalism and Middle East Feminist Studies." *Feminist Studies* 27, no. 1 (spring 2001): 101–115.

———. "Do Muslim Women Really Need Saving? Anthropological Reflections on Cultural Relativism and Its Others." *American Anthropologist* 104, no. 3 (September 2002): 783–790.

———. "Hagar: A Historical Model for 'Gender Jihad.'" In *Daughters of Abraham: Feminist Thought in Judaism, Christianity and Islam*, edited by Yvonne Y. Haddad and John L. Esposito, 81–107. Gainesville: University Press of Florida, 2001.

Afary, Janet. "Feminism and the Challenge of Muslim Fundamentalism." In *Spoils of War: Women of Color, Cultures and Revolutions*, edited by T. Denean Sharpley-Whiting and Renée T. White, 83–100. Lanham, Md.: Rowman and Littlefield, 1997.

———. "The War against Feminism in the Name of the Almighty: Making Sense of Gender and Muslim Fundamentalism." *Women Living under Muslim Laws: Dossier* 21 (February 1999): 7–31.

———. "The Human Rights of Middle Eastern and Muslim Women: A Project for the 21st Century." *Human Rights Quarterly* 26, no. 1 (February 2004): 106–126.

Afkhami, Mahnaz. *Faith and Freedom: Women's Human Rights in the Middle East.* Syracuse, N.Y.: Syracuse University Press, 1995.

Afshar, Haleh. *Islam and Feminisms: An Iranian Case-Study.* London: Macmillan Press Ltd., 1998.

Ahmad, Kurshid. *Family Life in Islam.* Leicester, UK: Islamic Foundation, 1974.

Ahmed, Leila. *Women and Gender in Islam: Historical Roots of a Modern Debate.* New Haven, Conn.: Yale University Press, 1992.

Ali, Kecia. "Rethinking Women's Issues in Muslim Communities." In *Taking back Islam: American Muslims Reclaim their Faith*, edited by Michael Wolfe, 91–98. Emmaus, Pa.: Rodale Inc., St. Martin's Press, 2002.

———. "Progressive Muslims and Islamic Jurisprudence: The Necessity for Critical Engagement with Marriage and Divorce Law." In *Progressive Muslims: On Justice, Gender, and Pluralism*, edited by Omid Safi, 163–189. Oxford: One World, 2003.

Anwar, Ghazala. "Muslim Feminist Discourses." In *Feminist Theology in Different Contexts*, edited by Elisabeth S. Fiorenza and Shawn Copeland, 55–61. London: SCM Press, 1996.

———. "Reclaiming the Religious Center from a Muslim Perspective: Theological Alternatives to Religious Fundamentalism." In *Religious Fundamentalisms and the Human Rights of Women*, edited by Courtney W. Howland, 303–314. New York: St. Martin's Press, 1999.

Badawi, Jamal A. "The Status of Women in Islam," *al-Ittihad* 8, 2 (Sept. 1971): 8–9.

———. *Gender Equality in Islam: Basic Principles.* Indianapolis, Ind.: American Trust Publications, 1995.

Badran, Margot. *Feminists, Islam, and Nation: Gender and the Making of Modern Egypt.* Princeton, N.J.: Princeton University Press, 1995.

Bakhtiar, Laleh. *Sufi Women of America: Angels in the Making.* Chicago, Ill.: Institute for Traditional Psychoethics and Guidance, Distributed by KAZI Publications, 1996.

Barlas, Asma. *"Believing Women" in Islam: Unreading Patriarchal Interpretations of the Quran.* Austin: University of Texas Press, 2002.

Barzanji, Nimat. "Muslim Women's Islamic Higher Learning as a Human Right: Theory and Practice." In *Windows of Faith: Muslim Women Scholar-Activists in North America*, edited by Gisela Webb, 22–50. Syracuse, N.Y.: Syracuse University Press, 2000.

el Guindi, Fadwa. *Veil: Modesty, Privacy and Resistance*. New York: Berg Publishers, 1999.

al-Faruqi Lamya Lois. "Islamic Traditions and the Feminist Movement: Confrontation or Cooperation." Jannah.or/sisters/feminism.html-21k

al-Faruqi, Lois. *Women, Society, and Islam*. Indianapolis, Ind.: American Trust Publications, 1988.

Gole, Nilufer. *The Forbidden Modern: Civilization and Veiling*. Ann Arbor: University of Michigan Press, 1996.

Haddad, Yvonne. "The Study of Muslim Women in Islam and the West: A Select Bibliography." *Hawwa* 3, no. 1 (2005): 111–157.

Haddad, Yvonne, and John Esposito, eds. *Muslims on the Americanization Path?* Atlanta: Scholars Press, 1998.

Haeri, Shahla. *Law of Desire: Temporary Marriage in Shi'i Iran*. Syracuse, N.Y.: Syracuse University Press, 1989.

———. *No Shame for the Sun: Lives of Professional Pakistani Women*. Syracuse, N.Y.: Syracuse University Press, 2001.

Hasan, Asma Gull. *American Muslims: The New Generation*. New York: Continuum, 2000.

———. *Why I Am a Muslim: An American Odyssey*. London: Element, 2004.

Hassan, Riffat. "The Role and Responsibilities of a Muslim Woman in the Universe." *Al-Ittehad* (Indianapolis) 13, no. 3 (October/November 1976): 1–4.

———. "Equal before Allah? Woman-Man Equality in the Islamic Tradition." *Harvard Divinity Bulletin* 17, no. 2 (1987): 2–14.

———. "Muslim Women and Post-Patriarchal Islam." In *After Patriarchy: Feminist Transformations of the World Religions*, edited by Paula M. Cooey, William R. Eakin, and Jay B. McDaniel, 39–69. Maryknoll, N.Y.: Orbis Books, 1991.

———, ed. *Women's and Men's Liberation: Testimonies of Spirit*. New York: Greenwood Press, 1991.

———. "Muslim Feminist Hermeneutics." In *In Our Own Voices: Four Centuries of American Women's Religious Writing*, edited by Rosemary S. Keller and Rosemary R. Ruether, 455–459. SanFrancisco: Harper SanFrancisco: 1995.

———. "Feminist Theology: The Challenges for Muslim Women." *Critique: Journal for Critical Studies of the Middle East* 9 (1996): 53–65.

———. "Feminism in Islam." In *Feminism and World Religions*, edited by Katherine Young and Arvind Sharma. Albany: State University of New York Press, 1999.

———. "Human Rights in the Qur'anic Perspective." In *Windows of Faith, Muslim Women Scholar-Activists in North America*, edited by Gisela Webb, 241–248. Syracuse, N.Y.: Syracuse University Press, 2000.

———. "Is Family Planning Permitted by Islam: The Issue of a Woman's Right to Contraception." In *Windows of Faith, Muslim Women Scholar-Activists in North America*, edited by Gisela Webb, 226–237. Syracuse, N.Y.: Syracuse University Press, 2000.

———. "Women in Islam: Feminist Theology as an Agent of Social Change." In *Annals of the International Institute of Sociology*. New Series. 2000 Vol. 5: 221–233.

———. "Challenging the Stereotypes of Fundamentalism: An Islamic Feminist Perspective." *The Muslim World* 91, nos. 1/2 (spring 2001): 55–70.

Hermansen, Marcia (translator). *The Conclusive Argument of God.* Leiden, New York: E. J. Brill, 1996.

al-Hibri, Azizah. "Capitalism is an Advanced Stage of Patriarchy." In *Women and Revolution: A Discussion of the Unhappy Marriage of Marxism and Feminism,* edited by Lydia Sargent, 166–167, 190. Boston: South End Press, 1981.

———. "Tear Off Your Western Veil." In *Food for Our Grandmothers,* edited by Joanna Kadi, 160–164. Boston: South End Press, 1994.

———. "An Introduction to Muslim Women's Rights." In *Windows of Faith: Muslim Women Scholars Activists in North America,* edited by Gisela Webb, 51–71. Syracuse, N.Y.: Syracuse University Press, 2000.

Hijab, Nadia. *Womanpower: The Arab Debate on Women at Work.* New York: Cambridge University Press, 1988.

Hussain, Freda. *Muslim Women.* Worcester, UK: Croom Helms, 1984.

Kandiyoti, Deniz. "Reflections on the Politics of Gender in Muslim Societies: From Nairobi to Beijing." In *Faith and Freedom: Women's Human Rights in the Muslim World,* edited by Mahnaz Afkhami, 19–32. London: Tauris, 1995.

———. "Contemporary Feminist Scholarship and Middle East Studies." In *Gendering the Middle East: Emerging Perspectives,* edited by Deniz Kandiyoti, 1–27. London: Tauris, 1996.

———, ed. *Gendering the Middle East: Emerging Perspectives.* London: Tauris, 1996.

———. "Islam and Feminism: A Misplaced Polarity." *WAF Journal* 8 (1996): 10–13.

———. "Beyond Beijing: Obstacles and Prospects for the Middle East." In *Muslim Women and the Politics of Participation: Implementing the Beijing Platform,* edited by Mahnaz Afkhami and Erika Friedl, 3–10. Syracuse, N.Y.: Syracuse University Press, 1997.

———. "The Politics of Gender and the Conundrums of Citizenship." In *Women and Power in the Middle East,* edited by Suad Joseph and Susan Slyomovics, 52–58, 208–209. Philadelphia: University of Pennsylvania Press, 2001.

Karam, Azza M. "Women, Islamisms, and State: Dynamics of Power and Contemporary Feminisms in Egypt." In *Muslim Women and the Politics of Participation: Implementing the Beijing Platform,* edited by Mahnaz Afkhami and Erika Friedl, 18–28. Syracuse, N.Y.: Syracuse University Press, 1997.

———. *Women, Islamisms and the State: Contemporary Feminisms in Egypt.* New York: St. Martin's Press, 1998.

———. "Muslim Feminists in Western Academia: Questions of Power, Matters of Necessity." In *Islam in the Era of Globalization: Muslim Attitudes towards Modernity and Identity,* edited by Johan H. Meuleman, 171–187. London: Routledge/Curzon, 2002.

Kassam, Tazim R. "On Being a Scholar of Islam: Risks and Responsibilities." In *Progressive Muslims: On Justice, Gender, and Pluralism,* edited by Omid Safi, 128–144. Oxford: One World, 2003.

Khan, Shahnaz. *Muslim Women: Crafting a North American Identity.* Gainesville: University Press of Florida, 2000.

Manji, Irshad. *The Trouble with Islam: A Muslim's Call for Reform in Her Faith.* New York: St. Martin's Press, 2003.

Marsot, Afaf Lutfi al-Sayyid. *Women in Egypt: Gender Relations and Political Liberalization*. Los Angeles: G. E. von Grunebaum Center for Near Eastern Studies, University of California–Los Angeles, 1992.

McCloud, Aminah. *African American Islam*. New York: Routledge, 1995.

Mernissi, Fatima. *Beyond the Veil: Male and Female Dynamics in Modern Muslim Society*. Bloomington: Indiana University Press, 1987.

————. *The Forgotten Queens of Islam*. Oxford: Polity Press, 1993.

Moghissi, Haideh. *Feminism and Islamic Fundamentalism: The Limits of Postmodern Analysis*. London: Zed, 1999.

Murata, Sachiko. *The Tao of Islam: A Sourcebook on Gender Relationships in Islamic Thought*. Albany: State University of New York Press, 1992.

Najmabadi, Afsaneh. *The Story of the Daughters of the Quchan: Gender and National Memory in Iranian History*. Syracuse, N.Y.: Syracuse University Press, 1998.

Nashat, Guity, ed. *Women and Revolution in Iran*. Boulder, Col.: Westview Press, 1983.

Ramazani, Nesta. "Women in Iran: The Revolutionary Ebb and Flow." *Middle East Journal* 47, no. 3 (summer 1993): 409.

————. *The Dance of the Rose and the Nightingale*. Syracuse, N.Y.: Syracuse University Press, 2002.

Rouse, Carolyn Moxley. *Engaged Surrender: African American Women and Islam*. Berkeley: University of California Press, 2004.

Sa'dawi, Nawal. *The Hidden Face of Eve: Women in the Arab World*, translated and edited by Sherif Hetata. Boston, Mass.: Beacon Press, 1982.

Safi, Omid, ed. *Progressive Muslims: On Justice, Gender and Pluralism*. Oxford: One World, 2003.

Schimmel, Annemarie. *My Soul is a Woman: The Feminine in Islam*. New York: Continuum, 1997.

Sonbol, Amira al-Azhari. *Women, the Family and Divorce Laws in Islamic History*. Syracuse, N.Y.: Syracuse University Press, 1996.

Tohidi, Nayereh. " 'Islamic Feminism': Perils and Promises." *Middle East Women's Studies Review* 16, nos. 3/4 (fall 2001/winter 2002): 13.

Wadud, Amina. "Alternative Qur'anic Interpretation and the Status of Muslim Women." In *Windows of Faith: Muslim Women Scholar-Activists in North America*, edited by Gisela Webb, 3–21. Syracuse, N.Y.: Syracuse University Press, 2000.

Wadud-Muhsin Amina. *Qur'an and Woman*. Kuala Lumpur: Fajar Bakti, 1992 (1993 printing).

Webb, Gisela. "Tradition and Innovation in Contemporary American Islamic Spirituality: The Bawa Muhaiyaddeen Fellowship." In *Muslim Communities in North America*, edited by Yvonne Haddad and Jane Smith. Albany: Syracuse University Press, 1994.

Women's Committee. *Parents' Manual: A Guide for Muslim Parents Living in North America*. Indianapolis, Ind.: American Trust Publications, 1976.

Yamani, Mai, ed. *Feminism and Islam: Legal and Literary Perspectives*. New York: New York University Press, 1996.

Zohara-Simmons, Gwendolyn. "African American Islam as an Expression of Converts' Faith and Nationalist Dreams and Ambitions." In *Gender and*

Conversion to Islam in the West, edited by Karin van Nieuwkerk. Austin: Texas University Press, forthcoming.

Newspaper and Magazine Articles

Mojab, Sharzad. "Islamic Feminism: Alternative or Contradiction." *Fireweed* 47 (winter 1995): 18–25.

Internet Web Sites

Manji, Irshad. "Muslims Need Critical Thinking." Interview with Dirk Verhofstadt, staff member of *Liberales*, August 18, 2004. Available http://www.secularislam .org/articles/manji.htm

Index